Under the editorship of **Leonard Carmichael**

HOUGHTON MIFFLIN COMPANY   BOSTON
New York   Atlanta   Geneva, Illinois   Dallas   Palo Alto

NORMAN L. MUNN

The University of Adelaide

The Evolution
of the Human Mind

TO BARBARA

Library of Congress Catalog Card Number:
75-146722

ISBN: 0-395-11149-8

EDITOR'S FOREWORD

No one can doubt that there was a long time in the geologic history of our globe when there were no human minds. Dr. Munn considers in a clear, orderly, interesting and yet not over-technical way the great topic of how such minds first began and how they evolved from simpler, non-human mammalian minds. This long racial development is compared with the growth of mental capacity in each individual from infancy to adult life. Also discussed are the mechanisms that make possible the passing on to each member of every new generation the skills, technical knowledge, human wisdom, and esthetic understanding that cultural, as distinct from biological, evolution has gradually and sometimes painfully produced since *Homo sapiens* first began freely to roam the earth.

This book makes clear how mutations occurred that have been basic in the evolution of both body structures and body functions. We learn how behavior has been all-important in fitting organisms for life in the specialized and ordinarily isolated environmental niches in which they arose and in which they as a population have survived. We see how each species has perpetuated itself or become extinct because its behavior either did not adapt to new predators or other changing conditions in its old niche or did not allow it to occupy a previously "empty" environmental area. Dr. Munn shows that knowledge of behavioral evolution is basic to a modern scientific understanding of the origin and development of many important human psychological capacities.

The specialized findings of many modern scientific fields together elucidate human evolution: In this book facts are painstakingly marshalled from research findings in genetics, anatomy, physiology, embryology, ecology, biogeography, paleontology, archaeology, and sociology, as well as psychology. The author has skillfully sifted and organized these findings in such a way that a cumulative understanding of the book's central theme grows as we read, chapter by chapter.

If I were asked "Who should read or study this book?" I would be tempted to say: "Every literate man or woman who

PREFACE

This book is intended for the general reader and for the student who would like to know how recent advances in the fields of psychology, zoology, genetics, paleontology, archaeology, and anthropology have contributed to our understanding of how the human mind evolved. It may also be of interest to psychologists who have been too preoccupied with their respective specialized fields to keep in touch with information bearing upon the general problem of mental evolution. I was in that position myself, yet I could find no satisfactory synthesis of the relevant information. This information existed only piecemeal, in specialized books and articles which, if they dealt with mental evolution at all, did so in a more or less cursory fashion. The specialized information was also highly detailed, containing much that had little or no direct bearing on the mental aspects of what was being considered. There was often much more than one wishes or needs to know in order to obtain an understanding of the general trend of mental evolution. I recall, in this connection, a story that I once heard, of a boy who asked his mother some question about the heavens. She said, "Your father is an astronomer. Why not ask him?" To which the boy replied, "Yes, but I don't need to know that much!"

What I have attempted here is to provide a meaningful, yet not too detailed, synthesis of what can be told today about the evolution of mind from lower animals to man and, in man, from his beginnings until he reached his so-called "civilized" status. This account embraces cultural as well as biological evolution, and it deals, among other things, with the shaping of modern minds. It begins with a consideration of the nature of mind and the dependence of psychological functions upon the brain, and it ends with some current speculations about the future of man.

Norman L. Munn
Adelaide, South Australia

Dr. Leonard Carmichael read the entire manuscript and made many helpful suggestions. Chapters 5 and 6 were read and criticized by Dr. John R. Napier, with the result that some questionable statements were revised and various references to human origins were updated. Although they must not be held responsible for any of the ideas presented in this book, the reactions of these scientists to the original manuscript have greatly improved the presentation and their contributions are appreciated by the writer. Robert C. Rooney and Diane Faissler of the Houghton Mifflin editorial staff and Pamela McClellan, who arranged the illustrations, have also made important contributions. My wife has contributed in many ways, not the least through her keen critical evaluation of many ideas discussed with her while the book was being written. Appreciation is also due to Heather Logan, who typed the final manuscript, and to the staffs of the Barr Smith and Medical Libraries of the University of Adelaide.

CONTENTS

CHAPTER ONE

EVOLUTION AND THE CONCEPT OF MIND

The idea that human beings evolved from lower forms of life has had a tremendous impact on modern concepts of the nature and origins of the human mind. Evolutionists at first centered their attention upon body structure and related behavioral adaptations. It soon became apparent, however, that mental processes also have evolved and have adaptive significance. Their evolution was seen to parallel that of the nervous system—more specifically, the increasing size and complexity of the brain.

Our main concern in this preliminary chapter is the nature of mind, as at present conceived, and its dependence upon the structures and functions of the brain, insofar as this dependence is evident today. But to place our discussion in its proper setting we must first provide a brief sketch of the main features of the theory of evolution.

The idea of evolution goes back to ancient times, and by the eighteenth and early nineteenth centuries several philosophers held that man's structures and his behavioral adaptations are foreshadowed in the structure and behavior of prehuman organisms. Thus, the concept of evolution, often credited to Charles Darwin, did not originate with him, although he did more than any other individual to give this concept its present scientific standing.

Darwin's *Origin of Species* was published in 1859. Until then, the prevailing opinion, even among naturalists and philosophers, had been that man and each of the other species were independently created and unchangeable. Evidence to the contrary had existed for ages—in geological formations and in the structural and functional similarities of the different species—but little of this had been revealed, and even the significance of that was not recognized. Although a few philosophers had presented on theoretical grounds the view that simpler forms of life give rise to higher forms, they failed to dislodge the belief in separate creation and the immutability of species, which found support in the biblical story of creation. Theories unsupported by factual evidence had no hope of dislodging such beliefs.

Darwin himself had not questioned the prevailing belief when, at the age of 22, he set out for a five-year voyage around the world on H.M.S. Beagle. His appointment as naturalist on this ship gave him an unprecedented opportunity to observe the diversity of animal life and to note similarities and differences among species living under a variety of geographical conditions. Darwin's observations on this voyage led him to the conclusion that often one species had been ancestral to many others which differed from it because they had become adapted to the peculiar conditions of their particular habitats.

For example, Darwin observed sparrow-like finches in the Galapagos Islands, a group of islands lying on the equator some 600 miles west of the South American coast. Each island had its own species of finch, with a beak especially adapted to the available food supply, yet all of these birds bore a close resemblance to the finches of the South American mainland. It seemed incredible that each of the thirteen species which inhabited the Galapagos Islands could have been created independently, some to eat insects, some seeds, some cactus, and so on. Darwin thought it more reasonable to suppose that all of these finches were derived from a common ancestor and that the ancestral birds had been somehow modified in time by the conditions in which they found themselves. Many other examples of this nature, involving various plants and animals, were observed in the Galapagos Islands and other places.

Darwin became increasingly aware of other evidences for evolution. Living animals came to be viewed as modified versions of those whose remains are found embedded in ancient rock formations. It could be observed, moreover, that the living species most resembled the fossils in the upper geological strata.

After returning to England, Darwin spent several years organizing his own observations and searching for additional information in the fields of comparative anatomy, embryology, and geology. He was evaluating the evidence, pro and con, and at the same time seeking an explanation of how evolution might have occurred. A draft of his views was written in 1844, but not published. Work continued on the manuscript, which was to become the *Origin of Species*. In 1858, about a year before that book was published, Darwin discovered that another naturalist, completely unaware of his work, had come to similar conclusions. This was Alfred Russel Wallace. He and Darwin presented their views before the Linnaean Society at the same time, on July 1, 1858. But it was Darwin's marshalling of the evidence in his book which did most to establish the theory of evolution. His presentation was so convincing that it eventually overthrew the ideas of independent creation and immutability of species.

Darwin's *Origin of Species* did not specifically include human beings, but man was included by implication, as those who read the book could plainly see. This implication aroused criticism of Darwin's views, for men found it even more difficult then than they do now to picture themselves as animals. In 1871, however, Darwin published *The Descent of Man,* in which he clearly presented the evidence showing that man evolved from lower forms of life. The human mind, including man's ability to reason, was now regarded by Darwin and others as a product of evolution.

Darwin's books revolutionized man's concept of himself, and also of zoology and other fields of science. The accumulated evidence has now assumed such proportions that evolution is generally regarded by scientists and others acquainted with the relevant information as fact rather than theory. On the other hand, there is still much to be learned about its mode of operation.

Darwin and Wallace concluded quite independently that evolution occurs through a process referred to as *natural selection.* They asserted that variations in structure (and the behavior which depends upon it) will naturally occur and that, in the struggle for existence, only those having the most adaptive variations will survive, or at least they will survive in greater numbers and have more offspring than those not so equipped. Darwin's version was that:

. . . if variations useful to any organic being ever do occur, assuredly individuals thus characterized will have the best chance of being preserved in the struggle for life; and from the strong principle of inheritance, these will tend to produce offspring similarly characterized. This principle of preservation, or the survival of the fittest, I have called natural selection. It leads to the improvement of each creature in relation to its organic and inorganic conditions of life; and consequently, in most cases, to what must be regarded as an advance in organization.[1]

Although Darwin referred to inheritance as the basis of variations and their transmission to the offspring of those who survive in the struggle for existence, the hereditary mechanisms were not yet known. It was assumed that parental traits were somehow blended in offspring, and one widespread belief had it that the blood was blended. However, Darwin and others realized that a blending type of in-

---

[1] Charles Darwin, *The Origin of Species* (6th London edition), Murray, 1859, pp. 122–123.

heritance would soon eliminate variations. These would have to be retained from generation to generation if evolution were to occur.

In 1856, three years before the publication of Darwin's *Origin of Species,* an Austrian monk named Gregor Mendel began a series of cross-breeding experiments which demonstrated that hereditary traits result from the transmission of discrete "particles" which do not blend but retain their characteristics from generation to generation. This was the sort of information the evolutionists needed, but it did not come to scientific attention until 1900, after both Mendel and Darwin were dead.

Mendel had discovered how the carriers of hereditary traits are assorted, and he could predict the outcome of crosses between pure-bred plants, but he did not know the cellular basis of transmission. This was discovered in the present century, following a suggestion that the nucleus of each cell might carry the hereditary determiners, or "genes," as they came to be called.

Mendel's work and subsequent investigations gave rise to genetics, a science concerned with all aspects of inheritance and its role in evolution—of the mind as well as body structure. We return to genetics in later discussions, but let us now examine the meaning of the term "mind." Anyone about to study the evolution of the human mind should have a clear concept of what is meant by mind, or mental processes.

THE CONCEPT OF MIND

Many aspects of our world are clearly evident to us. We see, hear, feel, taste, or smell them. And so, also, may other people. For these reasons we say that rocks, animals, and people, along with countless other things, are directly observable. But we also recognize the existence of phenomena which, in themselves, are beyond direct observation. Electricity is one; mind is another. The existence of electricity is inferred from magnetic, thermal, and other phenomena said to be manifestations of it. Mind is inferred from conscious experience and behavior.

Conscious experience is, of course, private and personal. One can observe it only in himself. But we can describe our experience, and others acquainted with the language used may obtain a certain degree of information from it, even to the point of recognizing that they also have similar experiences under comparable circumstances. The inference of mind thus obtains support from verbal behavior. Nonverbal behavior also supports it. In observing the behavior of other people, we may notice expressions indicative of surprise or other emotion; we may see persistence in pursuit of a goal, which warrants the inference that strong motivation is present; or we may witness the abrupt solution of a problem with which the individual has been struggling, the suddenness of the solution suggesting the emergence of insight, or understanding. Our inference about emotion, motivation, insight, or other mental processes can be verified by asking the individual to tell us what emotion he was experiencing, why his behavior was so persistent, what ideas preceded solution of the problem, and so on.

IMMEDIATE EXPERIENCE AND PAST EXPERIENCE

Immediate experience is conscious experience. It involves an awareness of our world and also of internal processes which we experience as feelings, emotions, images, memories, and ideas. This is the conscious aspect of the human mind. But there is an aspect of which we are not aware at any particular moment, and this "unconscious" aspect is based on accumulated earlier experience.

From birth onward, our brain stores information about aspects of the world which enter the range of our senses and our attention, and also information about us as a person. This information influences all subsequent mental processes.

How the brain stores information is not fully known. Quite obviously, it somehow stores coded representations of what has happened to us, perhaps analogous to the magnetically coded signals of a tape-recorded message which under appropriate conditions can be recreated. In modern computers functioning as "electronic brains" or "thinking machines," there are various ways of feeding in and storing coded information. There are also provisions for retrieving and decoding the information as it is needed.

We continually draw upon information based on past experience—as when we recognize a friend not seen in years; recall the words needed to express what is "on our mind"; focus "what we know" upon some problem in an effort to solve it; or engage in creative imagination, putting together in novel ways the things we have already experienced. We experience a passing parade of memories, images, and ideas which originated in direct experience, in what we have been told, and in what we have read. In his *Psychology*, William James spoke of the continuity of mental life provided by this "stream of consciousness." Continuity of mental life is supported by our accumulating information. All habits depend upon this, and so does our ability to "think our way through" the problems of everyday life. If this store of information were somehow obliterated, we would be as "simpleminded" as infants, even though biologically mature.

Little of our stored information is evident at any given moment. We know that it exists only because it "comes to mind" as appropriate circumstances arise—such as the need to recall it for some purpose. It is also called forth adventitiously, as when a voice, an odor, or the sound of footsteps bring memories of a relevant past experience. In reverie we think of one thing after another. This process enables us to "relive" much of what has happened to us.

Sigmund Freud placed great emphasis upon the unconscious aspects of mental life. He called attention to the fact that very little of the potentially conscious mind is brought to the level of awareness. The iceberg, with a very small portion of its bulk above the ocean surface, provided him with a useful analogy. Some information below the threshold of consciousness is easily recalled when needed. Some is difficult to recall. And some is ordinarily beyond recall. This is so for various reasons. An event may not have made a sufficient impression to enter the permanent memory storage. Stored records of an event may have been weakened or destroyed by subsequent happenings. Quite often, too, something interferes with recall—such as not wanting to remember a highly unpleasant event. Memories that would have appeared irretrievable are sometimes brought to consciousness through brain stimulation, drugs, hypnosis, and psychoanalytic procedures such as free association of ideas and analysis of dreams.

Each of us is influenced in varied and subtle ways by information that is below the level of awareness at the time. We perceive many features of our world without realizing how we do so. Perception of depth, for example, is immediate, yet much "judgment" based on physiological cues and past experience is involved. This process is carried on below the level of awareness. Helmholtz, the great German physiologist, referred to it as "unconscious inference."

We often wonder why we feel as we do about people and situations, particularly when there seems to be no good reason for it. William Brown was impressed with this aspect of mental life when he wrote:

> I do not love thee, Dr. Fell
> The reason why I cannot tell.

There are also mental undercurrents which go unrecognized, yet lead our thoughts astray. These are present in an exaggerated way in the delusions of the mentally ill.

In attempting to solve a problem we may reach a solution without full awareness of how we did so. Sometimes the solution comes in a flash, and it appears that "unconscious cerebration" rather than conscious thought has produced this insight.

MIND AND SELF

We are easily convinced that we have a conscious mind, and not much persuasion is required to convince us that mind means more than consciousness—that it involves a vast repository of information derived from influences going back to the beginning of our life. All that goes into this repository has a very personal reference. It is mediated through *our own* sensory and neural mechanisms, and it is somehow stored in *our* brain. In due course, a concept of *self* emerges: we develop an *ego*. Then the mental functions of which we are aware are conceived of as *personal capacities*. From this time on we say, "*I* see," "*I* remember," "*I* imagine," "*I* feel," and "*I* think."

These and other mental functions are dependent upon and integrated through memory storage. The continuity of mental life is anchored in this storage and involves mechanisms which facilitate retrieval of information from time to time. In terms of individual consciousness, all mental functions are organized around and continuous with *self*, which brings "forward continually the experience of the past to modify present actions and future plans."[2]

BASIC MENTAL FUNCTIONS

The basic mental functions which together comprise mind may be classified in the most general way as cognitive, affective, and conative.

Cognitive Processes

Cognitive processes are concerned with the acquisition of information—knowledge about ourselves and our world. Sensory reception is a cognitive process basic to all other mental processes; basic because, as the philosopher Thomas Hobbes pointed out, "there is no conception in a man's mind which hath not at first, totally or by parts, been begotten upon the organs of sense." Other terms for sensory reception are seeing, hearing, smelling, and so on. These depend upon the sensory receptors, sensory nerves, and specialized sensory areas in the brain.

Activation of a receptor process by stimulation—as of the

[2] The psychiatrist D. Ewen Cameron, as quoted by *Time*, June 24, 1966, p. 34.

visual process by light waves—may result in some action (like dilation of the pupil), or it may lead to awareness of the object from which stimulation emanates. Whenever there is such an awareness we speak of *sensation* or *perception*. Theoretically, sensation is an irreducible sensory experience such as might exist the first time a receptor process occurs— like the experience of light without any meaning attached to it. When meaning is evident—when the light is experienced as sunlight, the light from a bulb, or the illuminated object— we speak of *perception*. Perception begins with sensory processes but involves much more. We perceive objects, situations, relationships. Quite often, more than one sense contributes to the totality of perception, as when we see, hear, and smell aspects of a situation at the same time.

Learning is another basic cognitive process. This also depends upon receptor processes. It involves modifications of the organism which underlie what we perceive, what we know, what we think, what we believe, and what we do. The organization and meaning of perceptual experience are largely learned. Without learning there would be no storage of information, there would be no skills, and there would be no linguistic representations of past experience—hence nothing to think about.

Learning is demonstrated in the form of retention, or memory. We are most aware of our retentive ability when we recall or recognize something experienced earlier. But retention is also evident when, in acquiring some skill, we advance instead of having to start from scratch at every performance. The accumulating information retained as we develop is our "memory storage." We call upon this in perceiving, making judgments, forming concepts, and thinking.

Thinking is also a cognitive process. In thinking, we recall and bring into various relationships what we already know. And when we focus our thought processes on some problem, thinking our way through it until a solution is found, we are reasoning. In finding solutions we are, of course, adding to our store of information.

Cognitive functions are obviously of major importance in

their contribution to experience and in their facilitation of behavioral adjustment. In large measure they account for the increase in our versatility—our intelligence—as we grow from infancy to maturity. Language plays a very significant role in this development. It is an outgrowth of cognitive processes, and it also facilitates their further operation. This facilitation of learning, memory, and thinking comes from the use of words to represent objects, situations, and ideas. Indeed, it has been said that, "in a most important sense, the development of language in the individual is the growth of the human mind in that person."[3]

In tracing the evolution of mind from lower to higher levels of animal life we are also dealing with what is sometimes called *the evolution of animal intelligence.* Major emphasis is given to such cognitive processes as sensitivity, learning, retention, and reasoning. Aristotle called man the reasoning animal, but, as we shall see, the ability to reason emerges long before the human level of evolution is reached.

Affective Processes

Affective processes are feelings and emotions. They find conscious expression in our experiences of pleasantness, excitement, happiness, fear, rage, and love. We see their outward expressions in smiling, laughing, weeping, trembling, persistent seeking (or avoidance) of objects, and various other reactions aroused by emotion-provoking situations. Such feelings are often expressed verbally, as when we say "I love you," "I hate you," or "You annoy me." We have no certain knowledge of the feelings of animals, but their emotional expressions are observable, and, as Charles Darwin pointed out in *The Expression of the Emotions in Man and Animals*, animal and human emotional expressions have much in common.[4]

[3] Leonard Carmichael, *Basic Psychology*, Random House, 1957, p. 193.

[4] A reprint of this classic discussion of emotional expression was published in 1965 by the University of Chicago Press. The original appeared in 1872.

Conative Processes

Whereas cognition refers to *knowing* and affection to *feeling,* conation refers to *striving* or *doing.* It includes motivating influences, particularly our conscious striving to satisfy desires or to achieve goals. We say that a person exerts "will power" when he persists in following some line of activity in spite of barriers or potentially distracting influences. Such persistence against odds is an important aspect of human behavior. Without it, man could not have advanced very far in his struggle with the forces that surround him.

SOME DEFINITIONS

We have said that the mind most directly known to the individual is his own and that the various mental functions are conceived of as *his* capacities, or as functions of his *self.* The mental functions, referred to most generally as cognitive, affective, and conative, together are what we refer to as the *mind.* We do not consider them the functions of something called *mind* but rather as, in themselves, constituting the mind. Thus, we may say that *a person's mind is the integrated totality of the conscious and unconscious processes involved in acquiring, storing, and utilizing information in his interactions with his environment.* Briefer definitions, which mean about the same thing when elaborated, are: Mind is *"the entirety of the intelligent processes which occur in the organism."*[5] *"Mind is a more or less well-integrated set of capacities."*[6] *"Mind is a loose reference to the processes inside the head that control behaviour in its more complex manifestations."*[7]

Modern psychologists often consider that certain kinds of behavior *qua behavior* are mental, or at least manifestations of mental processes. Emotional behavior is a case in point. The behavior called "anger" may be regarded as mental, or

[5] J. R. Angell, *Psychology,* Holt, 1908, p. 2.

[6] C. J. Ducasse, "Minds, Matter and Bodies," in J. R. Smythies (Ed.), *Brain and Mind,* Routledge and Kegan Paul, 1965, p. 81.

[7] D. O. Hebb, *A Textbook of Psychology* (2nd ed.). Philadelphia, 1966, p. 334.

we may say that the person behaves as he does because he is angry. Likewise, behavior may be said to be intelligent (or nonintelligent) or a manifestation of intelligence. Linguistic behavior, sometimes referred to as "oral thought," is another example. Speech is the outcome of mental processes, although not of "ghost words in the head," and it may also be considered a mental process.

The term *intellect* has a more restricted meaning than *mind*. It refers specifically to the thinking aspect of mental processes. *Intelligence* is a related term, often defined as the ability to carry on abstract thinking, but we shall use it to represent general versatility of mental and behavioral adjustment, in which abstract thinking becomes important at the human level of evolution.

Psychologists are naturally concerned with what goes on "inside the head" even when they refer to the brain as a *black box* because they cannot see what transpires between input (stimulation) and output (behavior). They often infer the existence of "intervening variables" which bridge the gap between input and output. The basic intervening variables are neurological, but there are also psychological (mental) intervening variables, such as cognitions, emotional experiences, and the desire to say something. All of these depend, in the last analysis, upon neural functions, and their evolution has been an aspect of the evolution of the nervous system. Mental processes are particularly dependent upon functions of the brain. Indeed, this organ is sometimes referred to as "the matrix of the mind"; even as the "master of destiny."[8]

MIND AND THE NERVOUS SYSTEM

The brain and other structures of the human nervous system warrant some consideration here, not only to show their relation to mental processes but also to provide a reference

[8] See Frederick Wood Jones and Stanley D. Porteus, *The Matrix of the Mind*, University of Hawaii, 1928; and Frederick Tilney, *The Master of Destiny*, Doubleday, Doran, 1930. The referent of each title is the human brain.

for later discussions of mental evolution in animals and man. Our discussion is as brief as a meaningful one can be, and it should be supplemented by reference to the accompanying illustrations (identified by letter on pages 14–19).

ELEMENTARY STRUCTURES AND FUNCTIONS

The elementary neural structure is a *neuron*—a nerve cell and its projections, referred to as *nerve fibers*. A *nerve impulse* travels along the fibers from the point of activation. This impulse is a chemical-electrical disturbance. Some nerve fibers, known as *dendrites,* carry nerve impulses toward the *cell body*. Other fibers, referred to as *axons,* convey the impulses away from the cell body. These impulses may activate muscles or glands. Some are transmitted, across *synapses,* to the dendrites or cell bodies of adjacent neurons. Impulses may be either transmitted or blocked at the synapse. (See A.)

Nerve fibers transmitting impulses from receptors to the brain or spinal cord come together in bundles, each bundle

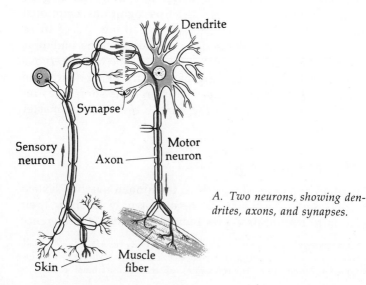

A. *Two neurons, showing dendrites, axons, and synapses.*

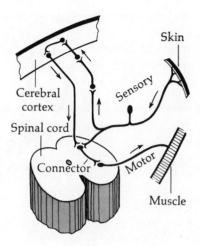

B. Schematic representation of circuits in spinal cord and brain.

C. Some interconnecting circuits in spinal cord, brain stem, and cerebral cortex. A, a feedback loop.

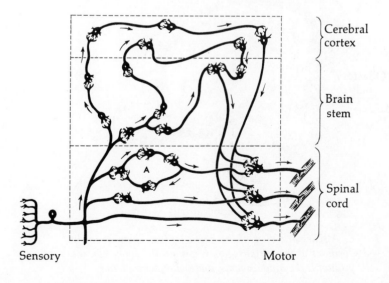

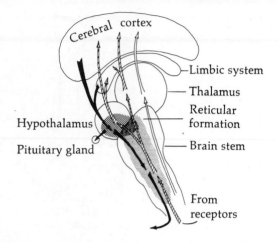

D. Locations of reticular formation, thalamus, hypothalamus, and limbic system, together with schematic representation of the directions followed by ascending and descending nerve impulses.

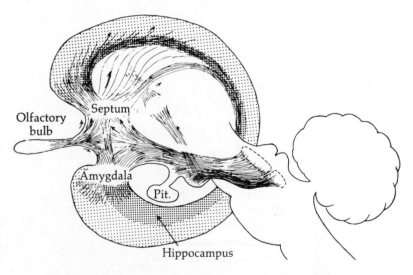

E. A schematic view of the limbic system, showing relative positions of the septal region (septum), the amygdala, the pituitary, the hippocampus, and the olfactory bulbs.

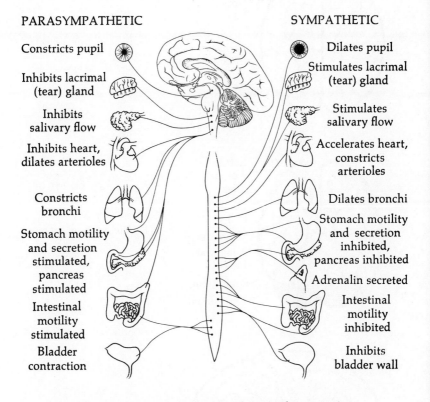

PARASYMPATHETIC

Constricts pupil

Inhibits lacrimal
(tear) gland

Inhibits
salivary flow

Inhibits heart,
dilates arterioles

Constricts
bronchi

Stomach motility
and secretion
stimulated,
pancreas
stimulated

Intestinal
motility
stimulated

Bladder
contraction

SYMPATHETIC

Dilates pupil

Stimulates lacrimal
(tear) gland

Stimulates
salivary flow

Accelerates heart,
constricts
arterioles

Dilates bronchi

Stomach motility
and secretion
inhibited,
pancreas inhibited

Adrenalin secreted

Intestinal
motility
inhibited

Inhibits
bladder wall

*F. The autonomic nervous system, showing the two major
divisions and the general nature of the connections between
these and the various internal organs. From BIOLOGY, Third
Edition, W. H. Johnson, et al., Holt, Rinehart and Winston,
Inc., 1966.*

The human brain from three aspects.

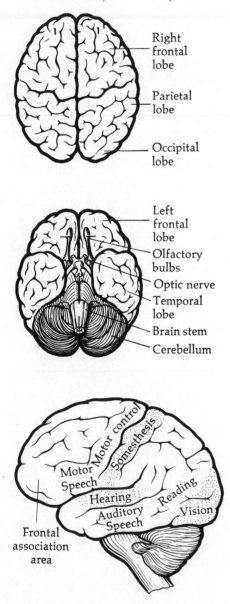

G. Viewed from above.

H. Viewed from below.

I. Left side.

Visual pathways to the brain.

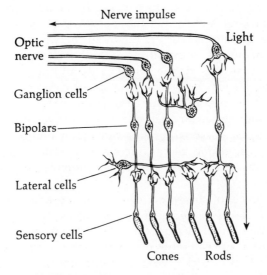

J. From rods and cones to optic nerve.

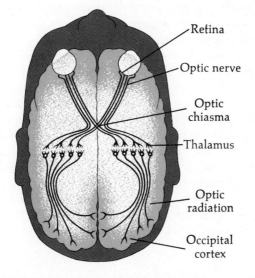

K. From retina to occipital cortex.

like a cable with many insulated wires. These structures are the sensory nerves. One such nerve is the auditory nerve. Axons carrying impulses to the motor organs also come together in bundles. These are the motor nerves. The sensory and motor nerves, transmitting impulses from receptors to motor mechanisms via the spinal cord and brain, constitute the *peripheral nervous system.* The spinal cord and brain together are referred to as the *central nervous system.*

In addition to sensory neurons, which convey information to the central nervous system, and motor neurons, which activate muscles and glands, there are *association,* or *connector,* neurons. All of these are in the central nervous system. (See B, C.)

At all levels of the spinal cord there are neurons whose main function is to mediate reflex activities. They do this by transmitting impulses from the axons of sensory neurons to the dendrites or cell bodies of motor neurons. When we step on a thorn and quickly withdraw our foot, impulses come from the foot to the lower spinal cord. There, connector neurons transmit the impulses to motor neurons running to our leg muscles. When impulses reach the muscles, reflex withdrawal of the foot occurs. This reaction occurs quickly, even before we are aware of what is happening.

Connector neurons also ascend the spinal cord, interconnecting various levels. Many reach the brain itself. Thus, we not only withdraw our foot reflexly from the thorn, but we also soon know that we have been pricked. Other neurons descend from the brain, thus giving it control over bodily activities. These connections are involved when we intentionally lift our foot. In addition to neurons which carry impulses between sensory and motor neurons at lower levels of the central nervous system and those which ascend and descend, there are others which interconnect various regions of the brain, both "vertically" and "horizontally."

THE BRAIN

Just above the spinal cord, and continuous with it, is the brain stem. (See C–E.) This and the attached *cerebellum* are concerned primarily with automatic activities, although, as we shall see, the brain stem also plays an important role in various functions relating to conscious experience.

Next to the brain stem, and partially surrounding its upper end, is the *cerebrum*, or what we usually think of as the brain. This has two segments, the *cerebral hemispheres*, which are joined together through the brain stem and also by a large band of fibers called the *corpus callosum*. This interconnection of the hemispheres makes it possible for one hemisphere to have a "carbon copy" as it were, of the information gained by the other. (See G, H.) The cerebrum has a layer of nerve cells (gray matter) spread over its outer surface like a mantle, or the bark on a tree. This is the *cerebral cortex* (Latin for bark). It is the so-called *new brain*.

At the base of the cerebrum, in a ringlike formation around the upper part of the brain stem, is a series of structures referred to in general as the *limbic system*. This comprises what is often referred to as the *old brain*, a structure involved in the sense of smell, but with additional functions which have been recognized only in recent years. Some of these will receive attention later. (See D–E.)

The brain stem, as we said, is primarily concerned with the automatic functions of the organism. These include breathing, reflex movements of the eyes and head, pupillary contraction and dilation, motor coordination as in walking, and vegetative functions such as eating, drinking, and sleeping. Within the brain stem there are also some structures of special importance for mental functioning. One of these, a mass of nerve cells running through its center, is the *reticular formation*. When the reticular formation is removed in animals, they lapse into a deep lethargy, and nothing will arouse them. The same effect is produced by drugs which inactivate the reticular formation. (See D.)

Nerve fibers carrying sensory information to the cerebral cortex send off collaterals which enter the reticular formation. Ascending impulses activate it on their way through the brain stem. Impulses also descend to the reticular formation from the cerebral cortex. When activated, either from above or from below, this discharges in such a way as to arouse the entire cortex. The organism then becomes wide awake, alert, vigilant, attentive. Thus, the arousal function of the reticular formation prepares the cerebral cortex for information to come.

The uppermost part of the brain stem, sometimes considered a basal aspect of the cerebrum itself, is the *thalamus.* (See D.) One thalamic function is to switch impulses of sensory origin to various areas of the cerebral cortex. But the thalamus also mediates some relatively crude forms of sensitivity without the participation of the cerebral cortex. Cutaneous sensitivity is experienced by human beings deprived of the cortex which normally mediates it. In animals there often is crude brightness vision and sensitivity to sound after the specialized cortical areas for these senses have been removed. Thus, some sensitivity is presumably associated with thalamic activity, over and beyond its switchboard function. Simple habits also may be acquired by animals without a cerebrum, which suggests that the thalamus can function in its own right as a learning mechanism. It is possible, also, that the thalamus controls habits which have become automatic, so that attention need no longer be focused upon them.

Below the thalamus and somewhat toward the front of the cerebrum is the *hypothalamus,* a structure containing nerve centers of great importance in emotion and various aspects of motivation. (See D.) Much of this importance comes from the fact that the hypothalamus triggers the *autonomic nervous system,* a peripheral network connecting inner organs like the stomach and intestines with the central nervous system. (See F.) One division of the autonomic nervous system, the *sympathetic system,* controls the adrenal glands, which during emotion secrete excessive amounts of the hormone *adrenalin,* causing widespread effects throughout the body. The arousal of this system is believed to be brought about by action of the hypothalamus. It is through this system that such emotional reactions as excessive sweating, heart palpitation, and inhibition of digestive activities are initiated. Also of emotional significance is the fact that direct electrical stimulation of a region in the hypothalamus elicits emotional expressions indicative of rage; cats so stimulated may attack the investigator. Various other automatic functions are influenced by hypothalamic stimulation. Some of these involve the *parasympathetic system,* a division of the autonomic nervous system which normally functions in opposition to the sympathetic system. The parasympathetic connections stimulate digestive activities, for example, while the sympathetic connections, when aroused in emotion, inhibit them. Other examples are given in F.

The hypothalamus also has regions which, when stimulated with a weak electric current, arouse responses which suggest that this stimulation is pleasant. Comparable stimulation of other regions elicits responses suggesting the presence of painful experience. The hypothalamus, in association with a neighboring area known as the *septal region,* is thus said to have "pleasure" and "pain" centers. (See E, Septum).

In experiments involving electrical stimulation of these regions, rats were given an opportunity to stimulate their own brains by pressing a lever. Electrodes were chronically implanted in septal and hypothalamic regions. These were connected to the lever by a long overhead cord so that the animal could move around freely within its cage. When the electrodes were placed in certain regions, the rats pressed the stimulating lever repeatedly and at very high rates. This led to the inference that such stimulation was enjoyable, and the regions involved were designated *pleasure centers.* With the electrodes placed in certain other regions of the hypothalamus and septal area, there was a very different outcome. The rat stimulated its brain once or twice and then refrained from doing so again. This suggested a painful effect, and these areas were called *pain centers.* Other regions yielded an indifferent response—the rats stimulated their brain by pressing the lever only once in a while during the experimental period.

Still other regions of the hypothalamus are known to play important roles in the arousal of hunger, thirst, and sexual responses. Electrical stimulation of one region arouses eating in animals so well fed that they would not otherwise eat. Comparable stimulation of another area stops even hungry animals from eating, hence its designation as a satiation center. Drinking in nonthirsty animals is also aroused by hypothalamic stimulation in appropriate regions. Sexual behavior aroused by stimulating the hypothalamus includes mounting, penile erection, and ejaculation. But enough has been said to show that experience and behavior are influenced in part by the functions of the hypothalamus.

The *amygdala*, or *amygdaloid complex*, is another limbic mechanism which participates in emotional behavior, apparently in conjunction with the hypothalamus. (See E.) Destruction of a particular hypothalamic region produces reactions in cats which simulate those associated with rage and aggression. These animals are calmed, however, by destruction of a region within the amygdala. This suggests that part of the amygdala may have a modulating effect on rage and aggression. But the amygdala is complex, with many interacting centers, and stimulating some of these electrically has produced such reactions as flight and defensive behavior. Research is continuing, and some of these apparently contradictory results may be explained. All that can be said with any degree of assurance at the present time is that amygdaloid reactions are involved in emotional behavior related to anger and aggression.

Still another limbic structure requires attention here. This is the *hippocampus,* which begins near the amygdala. (See E.) The hippocampus is sometimes removed in human epileptics, with a resulting alleviation of seizures. What is of particular interest in the present connection, however, is the fact that such removal has a marked influence on memory storage. Memories established before the operation are not disturbed, nor are short-term memories, involving things just experienced. The memory defect produced by the operation is an inability, under normal circumstances, to *store* recent experiences for more than a limited time; they are remembered for a few minutes, then completely forgotten. This defect can be offset, in some patients, by repetition of the new material. It is said that "Without repetitious practice, these patients are able to remember something new only as long as they 'keep their mind on it.' Once their attention turns to a subsequent event, the memory of the preceding one is apt to vanish."[9] Apparently a setting process of some kind is necessary for permanent storage, and the hippocampus normally contributes to such a process.

Even this brief discussion of subcortical mechanisms shows that they make important contributions to mental life, which once was thought to depend entirely upon the cerebral cortex. The cortex is, as we have seen, aroused, or alerted, by the reticular formation of the brain stem. Various aspects of emotional behavior, and possibly emotional awareness as well, involve subcortical mechanisms. Among these are the hypothalamus, the septal region, and the amygdaloid complex. The hypothalamus also makes important contributions to appetitive processes like hunger, thirst, and sex. Even the process of memory storage, once thought to be a purely cortical function, is influenced by such subcortical structures as the thalamus and the hippocampus.

The Cerebral Hemispheres
Each cerebral hemisphere has four more or less distinct lobes —frontal, temporal, parietal, and occipital. (See G–I.) The lobes are not really separate, for each is intricately interconnected with the others.

Each frontal lobe has a motor area which mediates voluntary movements on the opposite side of the body. It also contains large areas with purely associative functions— information storage, retrieval of information, and association of ideas. The left frontal lobe (see I, Motor speech) normally plays a dominant role in speech functions. Our frontal lobes are important, also, for such processes as recall, reasoning, projecting ourselves into the future, and self-consciousness. But these processes also depend upon other parts of the

[9] Robert A. McCleary and Robert Y. Moore, *Subcortical Mechanisms of Behavior*, Basic Books, 1965, pp. 131–132.

brain. They cannot correctly be regarded as "located" within the frontal lobe. We say this because popular discussion of brain functions often labels the frontal lobes as centers for thought, a process which actually involves various association areas and also the speech mechanism.

The other lobes of the cerebrum contain specialized areas for reception of sensory information, and also association areas. Sensory information is projected to the cerebrum from the thalamus. The *parietal* lobe receives impulses originating in the skin, the muscles, and the tendons and joints. These impulses go to the *somesthetic* or body feeling area. The *temporal* lobe receives information originating in the structures of the ear that are specialized for the sense of hearing. The *occipital* lobe receives information from the retinas of the eyes.

The association areas of these lobes are concerned primarily with storage and retrieval of information. Parts of the temporal lobe, probably in relation to the nearby hippocampus, have also been shown to have a rather general mnemonic function. When stimulated by an electrode during brain operations for removal of tumors, they elicit memories, often of childhood experiences apparently long forgotten. Wilder Penfield, the surgeon who reported these results, has pointed out that they do not mean that the engram (or neurogram, which stores the memory) is located under his electrode, but only that the local brain stimulation sets up impulses which, being carried to other regions and becoming involved in other neural circuits, serve to revive the memories that the patient reports.[10]

FOUNDATIONS OF SENSORY EXPERIENCE

As an example of the cortical contribution to conscious experience let us delve a little more deeply into the nature of visual experience. Visual receptors are activated by light, which initiates chemical reactions. These reactions, in turn,

[10] Wilder Penfield, *The Excitable Cortex in Conscious Man*, Charles C Thomas, 1958.

set off nerve impulses which travel along the optic nerve to the thalamus. The thalamus switches them to the visual cortex, where the visual experience is aroused. (See J–K.) The visual message is encoded in terms of its origin, the nature of the nerve impulses involved in its transmission, and the cortical termination of these impulses.

The receptor in which a message originates is important in two respects. In the first place, this receptor is one especially attuned to a certain kind of stimulation. Some retinal structures (the *cones*) are specialized to respond to the wavelength of electromagnetic waves. Others (the *rods*) are responsive only to the energy or intensity aspect of these waves. (See J.) Moreover, a certain type of cone is most sensitive to long wavelengths, another to short wavelengths, and still another to intermediate wavelengths. Second, the receptors are gateways, as it were, to particular regions of the cerebral cortex. The visual receptors, as we have seen, have access to the visual area of the occipital cortex. Impulses originating in them go to a specialized area of the thalamus (the *optic thalamus*) which projects them to the visual cortex. (See K.)

The nerve impulses originating in different receptors are similar. There are not different kinds of impulses, such as visual, auditory, or cutaneous. Moreover, different impulses passing over a particular nerve fiber are also alike in that they have the same electrical potential. Thus, an intense stimulus does not arouse a stronger impulse than a weak stimulus, which can also activate the nerve fiber. How, then, is the message coded after it leaves the receptor? We have already said that nerve fibers which originate in different sense organs form bundles (nerves) which transmit their impulses to different loci within the central nervous system. Fibers originating in the retinas of the eyes make up the optic nerve; those originating in the inner ears, the auditory nerve; and so on. Impulses of retinal origin terminate in their specialized thalamic center (the optic thalamus), and fibers from the inner ear terminate in a corresponding specialized auditory center of the thalamus. The thalamus then relays (projects) these impulses to the cerebrum—again to their respective specialized loci.

Impulses originating in the retina find their ultimate locus in the occipital lobe; those originating in the inner ear, in the temporal lobe. These different loci determine the visual or auditory character of the resulting experiences. In the case of vision, then, the termination of impulses in a particular region of the occipital lobe determines whether we see black or white or red or blue or some visual complexity involving many visual qualities. Likewise, the ultimate locus of impulses from the inner ear alone determines the nature of the auditory experience of pitch or the complexities involved in a symphony. Coding of the sensory message after it leaves the receptor is therefore in terms of the ultimate termination of the impulses. In short, there are not different kinds of impulses underlying the different senses but different origins (receptors) and different loci (cortical projection areas).

The intensive aspect of experience, such as the brightness of what is seen or the loudness of what is heard, has a somewhat different basis. Whereas vision, or some particular quality such as a color, depends upon the place in which nerve impulses terminate, the brightness of the experience is coded in terms of impulse frequency. This kind of coding is observed in the responses of nerve fibers to variations in stimulus intensity.

The stimulus sets off an impulse, after which the fiber must recover sensitivity before it can respond again. This cycle continues, so that there is a succession of impulses. However, the more intense the stimulus, up to a certain maximum, the closer the nerve impulses follow one another. Thus, the stronger the stimulus, within these limits, the greater the frequency of nerve impulses. A more intense stimulus not only increases the frequency of response in a given fiber, but it also increases the number of fibers responding. For both of these reasons, the intensity of stimulation is coded in terms of the number of impulses per second. In the case of vision, the cortex decodes a higher rate of impulses as an increase in brightness.

As we have already seen, the qualitative aspects of vision are dependent upon termination of impulses in the region of the occipital lobe specialized for vision. Thus, the cortex decodes the impulses as visual when they reach this area, as auditory when they reach the temporal lobe, and so on. Likewise, impulses are decoded as colors in terms of their termination within the visual cortex (if they come from different retinal structures, they terminate at different loci) and possibly also in terms of their patterned aspects, both spatial and temporal. Perceiving a visual pattern, such as a face, involves a cortical pattern correlated with the pattern on the retinas, including its color aspects. In addition to decoding visual messages in terms of their destination, the cortex, as we have seen, also decodes them in terms of their frequency aspects. Thus, we perceive a color in terms of where the impulses terminate, and we perceive it as having a particular brightness because of the frequency of these impulses.

What has been said about the qualitative and intensive aspects of visual experience applies, in principle, to the other modalities of sensory experience, such as hearing, touch, taste, and smell.

CEREBRAL CONTROL OF ACTION

Motor areas within the frontal lobes are of special importance for the so-called *conative* aspects of mind, those involving purposive behavior. (See I, Motor control.) When the motor areas are stimulated electrically in a person undergoing a brain operation, various movements are elicited. Stimulation of one region moves the hand; of another, the lips; of still another, the tongue; and so on. The stimulated patient finds that he cannot help making these movements. On the other hand, as Wilder Penfield points out, the patient "knows he did not will the action. He knows there is a difference between automatic action and voluntary action."[11]

[11] Wilder Penfield, "The Cerebral Cortex and the Mind of Man" in P. Laslett (Ed.), *The Physical Basis of Mind,* Macmillan, 1950, p. 64.

Under normal circumstances each voluntary act is preceded by a conscious intention to act. Underlying this intention there are no doubt very complicated neural activities which come to a focus, as it were, in the motor cortex, where they give rise to impulses which terminate in the structures to be moved. Quite frequently it is as though we said to ourselves, "Do so and so." The neural activities involved in such a verbalization could trigger the motor impulses which, as they descend to lower regions of the nervous system, produce the intended movements. Indeed, language may be of crucial importance in voluntary activity. The psychologists Walters S. Hunter and Clarence V. Hudgins say that:

The particular stimuli most significantly involved in the control of voluntary movement are those generated by the behavior of the organism itself. The kinesthetic, tactual, and auditory stimuli involved in language are the most important self-induced stimuli in man. By the aid of such receptor processes the organism becomes relatively independent of its external environment and can regulate its own behavior to an extent impossible in infrahuman animals. Behavior controlled by the organism's own language responses is voluntary to the highest degree.[12]

COMPLEX FOUNDATIONS OF MIND

Although we have mentioned centers which control particular mental functions, it should be recognized that the central nervous system operates in complex intermingling circuits in which the so-called centers play a crucial role. Many of these circuits, once activated, are self-exciting. The feedback loop shown in our illustration of neural circuits at various levels of the central nervous system (see Figure C, p. 15) is one such self-exciting system. Many automatic activities are controlled by feedback from the muscles. Muscle movements, by stimulating receptors within the muscles themselves, set up impulses which go to the spinal cord and brain. These inform the motor control centers of what is

[12] Walter S. Hunter and Clarence V. Hudgins, "Voluntary Activity from the Standpoint of Behaviorism," *Acta Psychologica*, 1935, Vol. 1, p. 114.

happening in the muscles. Impulses based on this information are relayed back to the muscles, to regulate further activity in terms of what has gone before.[13]

In the cerebral cortex there are innumerable circuits of great complexity. No illustration could possibly portray this complexity. However, some suggestion of it is contained in the following quotation[14] from a book by the eminent neurologist, Sir Charles Sherrington:

Imagine a scheme of lines and nodal points, gathered together at one end into a great ravelled knot, the brain, and at the other trailing off to a sort of stalk, the spinal cord. Imagine activity in this shown by little points of light. Of these some [that are] stationary flash rhythmically, faster or slower. Others are travelling points streaming in serial trains at various speeds. The rhythmic stationary lights lie at the nodes. The nodes are both goals whither converge, and junctions whence diverge, the lines of travelling light. . . .

Suppose we choose the hour of deep sleep. Then only in some sparse and out-of-the-way places are nodes flashing and trains of light points running. . . . The great knotted headpiece of the whole sleeping system lies for the most part dark. . . . Occasionally at places in it lighted points flash or move but soon subside. . . .

Should we continue to watch the scheme we should observe after a time an impressive change which suddenly accrues. In the great head end which had been mostly darkness spring up myriads of twinkling stationary lights. . . . It is as though activity from one of those local places which continued restless in the darkened main-mass suddenly spread far and wide and invaded all. The great topmost sheet of the mass . . . where hardly a light had twinkled or moved, becomes now a sparkling field of rhythmic flashing points with trains of travelling sparks hurrying hither and thither. The brain is waking and with it the mind is returning. It is as if the milky way entered upon some cosmic dance. Swiftly the head mass becomes an enchanted loom where millions of flashing shuttles weave a dissolving pattern, always a meaningful pattern though never an abiding one.

[13] The scientific study of such regulatory or control mechanisms—whether in automatic steering devices, in the nervous system, or in behavior—is known as *cybernetics*, derived from the Greek word for *steersman*.

[14] Charles S. Sherrington, *Man: On His Nature*, Cambridge University Press, 1941, pp. 223–224.

MECHANICAL SIMULATION OF BRAIN AND MIND

A great deal of insight into the basic functions of the brain and the mental processes which depend upon them has come from attempts to design machines which act like animals and men. These are computer-controlled robots. Robots have been designed so that they "seek goals," explore their environment, find their way through a labyrinth by capitalizing on successes and failures in earlier attempts, "recognize" and respond appropriately to visual patterns, play chess, simulate speech, translate languages, and even plan strategies and carry on incompletely specified tasks.[15]

The computers which perform such functions have a multiplicity of simple interconnected units somewhat analogous to neurons. Digital computers simulate a number of brain functions. They contain "neurons" which are, in effect, two-way switches, each responding or not responding in accordance with the message received. The computer is designed to receive information, store it in an appropriate location, retrieve what is needed to satisfy certain instructions, collate the recovered information, and yield a solution to the problem that it has been programmed to solve. Information fed into the computer is coded. For example, when cards are used, each contains a particular pattern of punched holes. This pattern is a message. Messages are carefully programmed so that the machine gets precise information about each step in a series leading to the final output. Having completed one step, the computer carries out the next, and so on.

Every basic mental process, with the possible exception of

[15] W. Ross Ashby, *Design for a Brain* (2nd ed.), Chapman and Hall, 1960; and "An Imitation of Life," *Scientific American*, May 1950, pp. 42–45. Also, C. E. Shannon, "Presentation of a Maze-Solving Machine," *Transactions of the Eighth Cybernetics Conference*, Josiah Macy Junior Foundation, 1951, pp. 173–180; and, all in a special issue of *Science Journal* (Illiffe Industrial Publications, London), *Machines Like Men*, October, 1968: N. S. Sutherland, "Machines Like Men; J. A. Weaver, "Machines that Read"; J. N. Holmes, Machines that Talk"; D. Michie, "Machines that Play and Plan"; J. C. Loehlin, "Machines with Personality"; W. K. Taylor, "Machines that Learn"; and C. A. Rosen, "Machines that Act Intelligently."

consciousness, has to some degree been simulated mechanically. We say "with the possible exception" of consciousness because claims have been made that even this is simulated in some of the latest computers. In fact it might be maintained that, if consciousness has not been simulated, it is because we have not defined it behaviorally, or with sufficient exactness. To quote Dr. Donald M. MacKay, a professor of communications, "any attempt to 'maintain the dignity of man' by searching for limits to the information-processing powers of artifacts is misguided and foredoomed. This is no prophecy, but a deduction from the demonstrable fact that to specify exactly a behavioral test of information-processing capability amounts in principle to specifying a mechanism that can meet it.[16] Other people in the communications field have taken the same position, and there is apparently little reason for disputing such claims.[17] With respect to consciousness, however, one must point out that there would be no more access to this in a machine than in animals or in human beings who are unable to communicate their experiences verbally.

While he accepts the claim that machines can simulate mental processes, Professor Ulric Neisser has called attention to several basic differences between the mental processes of human beings and the most "intelligent" robots.[18] The human being and the robot often accomplish the same result, but they do it very differently. The robot, when purposive, is too much so. It has a single-track mind, continuing its programmed sequence to the end. People, on the other hand, "get bored; they drop one task and pick up another, or they may just quit work for awhile." Moreover, "the computer is

---

[16] Donald M. MacKay, "From Mechanism to Mind," in J. R. Smythies (Ed.), *Brain and Mind: Modern Conceptions of the Nature of Mind*, Routledge and Kegan Paul, 1965, p. 190.

[17] See the chapters on thinking, perception, cognitive processes, the brain, and the nerve net theory in Harold Borko (Ed.), *Computer Application in the Behavioral Sciences*, Prentice-Hall, 1962.

[18] Ulric Neisser, "The Imitation of Man by Machine," *Science*, 1963, Vol. 139, pp. 194–195.

very likely to waste its time on trivialities and to solve problems which are of no importance. Its outlook is a narrow one ... it lets the rest of the world go hang while it plays chess or translates Russian relentlessly." Of course the computer is not self-motivated. It is designed by others, it is fed information which others impose upon it, it carries on only the processes which others have programmed for it, and the culmination of a sequence of behavior ends when the program says it must.

Another difference stressed by Professor Neisser is that "Computers are more docile than men. They erase easily: an instruction or two can wipe out anything ever learned." On the other hand, "a man rarely has single-minded control over what he will learn and forget; often he has no control at all. Thus he lives willy-nilly in an accumulating context of experience which he cannot limit if he would." In writing about the complexity of human thought processes as compared with those simulated in computers, Professor Neisser makes the following highly pertinent comment: "Human mental activity is more complex than existing computer programs by many orders of magnitude. The 'intelligence' that has been achieved artificially is either extremely specialized or almost trivial. Moreover, The Human Mind may—indeed probably does—have resources and methods that are unimaginable in machines such as those in existence today."[19]

Other differences between computer "intelligence" and the intelligent activity of human beings have been discussed by Professor Hubert L. Dreyfus of M.I.T. As reported in *Science News*, he points out that there are three processes in human thinking which no machine has yet duplicated. One of these, referred to as the "fringe of consciousness" or "global awareness" is involved in scanning a situation for relevant or familiar material, as when one looks for a familiar face in a crowd. Insight is another of these processes. The human mind "grasps essentials" and does not, like a ma-

[19] Ulric Neisser, "The Multiplicity of Thought," *British Journal of Psychology*, 1963, Vol. 54, p. 5.

chine, have to follow elaborate rules. Human beings are able to "see similarities between various problems and objects. They move to the essence, ignoring the non-essential." Still another process not duplicated by machines is "ambiguity tolerance." "Before understanding language, humans do not have to reduce it to absolutely precise, unambiguous rules. But the machine does."[20] In comparing human mental functions with those simulated by computers, and in noting some limitations of the latter, we have added to our understanding of what is involved in human mental activity.

The contrast between human mental processes and those built into computers probably holds also for animals and computers. About all a computer can do is compute, even though this may simulate a number of mental processes. Animals and human beings do many other things besides. They engage in a wide range of activities. Human beings dream and create, and they even invent robots which imitate some of their own mental functions. Animals and human beings play, carry on courtships, and engage in many interpersonal activities. By contrast, the "mental life" of an electronic robot must be dull indeed.

THE ANIMAL MIND

Since animals cannot talk, we have no direct evidence of conscious processes in them. Inferences about the mind of an animal can therefore be based only on intuition, comparative anatomy of the nervous system, and observations of what the animal does in various natural or experimentally contrived situations. This problem has long been recognized. Some observers of animal behavior have tried to solve it intuitively, by attempting to "feel their way" into the animal mind. Since they can imagine no mental processes different from their own, this results in attribution of human mental traits to animals, called *anthropomorphism*. Here is a well-known Chinese example:

[20] Hubert L. Dreyfus, "Alchemy and Artificial Intelligence," written for the Rand Corporation, and summarized in *Science News*, July 2, 1966, p. 6.

Chuang Tzu and Hui Tzu were standing on the bridge across the Hao River. Chuang Tzu said, "Look how the minnows are shooting to and fro! How joyful they are!"

"You are not a fish," said Hui Tzu. "How can you know that the fishes are joyful?"

"You are not I," answered Chuang Tzu. "How can you know I do not know about the joy of the fishes? . . . I know it from my own joy of the water."[21]

Animal psychologists have also made inferences about consciousness in animals; inferences based on sensory, neural, and motor structures and observations of adaptive behavior. Professor Robert M. Yerkes[22] pointed out, for example, that the sea anemone has visual receptors and appears to use these in discriminating between various visual aspects of its environment. On such grounds he concluded that this animal "probably possesses consciousness of the sensory discriminative grade." The simplicity of its nervous system and the elementary nature of its behavioral adaptations, on the other hand, give "no signs of either intelligent or rational consciousness." Doctor Margaret Washburn reasoned along somewhat similar lines when she said: "We know not where consciousness begins in the animal world. We know where it surely resides—in ourselves; we know where it exists beyond a reasonable doubt—in those animals of structure resembling ourselves which rapidly adapt themselves to the lessons of experience. Beyond this point, for all we know, it may reside in simpler and simpler forms until we reach the lowest of living beings."[23]

Since we have no access to conscious experience in animals, inferences about animal consciousness may be re-

[21] From *The Old Chinese Tschuang-Tse*, abbreviated from the version which appears in Bierens de Haan's *Animal Psychology*, Hutchinson's University Library, 1946.

[22] Robert M. Yerkes, "Animal Psychology and the Criteria of the Psychic," *Journal of Philosophy*, 1905, Vol. 2, p. 145.

[23] Margaret F. Washburn, *The Animal Mind* (3rd ed.), Macmillan, 1926, p. 33.

garded as purely speculative. We are on surer ground if we focus our attention on particular processes revealed by behavior—for example, discrimination, learning, and reasoning. Such basic mental processes may be studied without reference to conscious experience.

SENSORY DISCRIMINATION

All animals have some degree of sensitivity to their surroundings. Indeed they could not survive unless this were so. But sensitivity in the lower animals is limited to the grosser aspects of stimulation. There is response to light, for example, but only to such aspects as light and dark, direction, and movement. Color vision is absent and so are depth perception and perception of visual patterns. There is response to mechanical contact, and perhaps to mechanical vibration, but no sense of hearing. Other aspects of sensitivity are similarly limited in scope. We shall see that the evolution of specialized sensory receptors and associated neural mechanisms brought with it a widening of sensory horizons. This not only allowed a more discriminating interaction with the environment, it also facilitated development and application of every other mental process. One of the most important of these is learning.

LEARNING

It appears that some of the simplest animals may be incapable of learning. Nobody has been able to teach an amoeba anything. The paramecium's behavior is modifiable to a slight degree, but some have attributed this to temporary physiochemical changes produced by the stimulating conditions. Moreover, defects in the experimental procedures are evident in some of the experiments purporting to demonstrate learning at this level of animal life.[24] One thing clearly indicated by an examination of the experimental evidence on

[24] N. L. Munn, *The Evolution and Growth of Human Behavior* (2nd ed.), Houghton Mifflin, 1965, pp. 131–137.

learning in unicellular, as well as in some of the simpler multicellular organisms is that unequivocal indications of learning ability are difficult if not impossible to achieve at these levels of animal life. At successively higher levels of evolution, however, there is increasing evidence that animals learn—and that they learn more rapidly, remember better, and acquire information and skills of greater complexity.

We would hardly infer mind from animal behavior unless learning played a part in it. This is because, when speaking of mind, we usually have reference to inner control based on information acquired by the individual. Thus, we speak of a person as "absent-minded" when he acts automatically—that is, without thinking about what he does. Likewise, when acquired controls break down, we say that the individual has "lost his mind."

Nevertheless, many of the reactions of men as well as animals are inborn and automatic. Our reflex actions are of this nature. In each reflex, a part of the body responds automatically to a stimulus, as the pupil responds to light, the salivary glands to food in the mouth, and the hand and arm to painful stimulation of a finger. These reactions are automatic because they depend upon inherited "wired-in" connections which carry nerve impulses from the point of stimulation to the reacting organ. This sort of reaction is so automatic that one does not usually think of including any reflex, or other unlearned response, among mental processes. Nevertheless, a word of caution is in order. There are those who hold that even though learned responses play a predominant role in mental life, especially as the higher levels of evolution are reached, some unlearned responses (passed on through the genetic code) must also be considered mental. Thus, "when a hungry kitten raised on bread and milk and nothing else is offered both *bread and milk* and *salmon* which it has never seen or smelled before and neglects the bread and milk to eat the salmon ravenously . . . we have a 'mental' act but not a learned one."[25] The attractiveness of sweet sub-

---

[25] Leonard Carmichael, personal correspondence.

stances and rejection of bitter ones prior to learning illustrate the same point. Even in man there are such innate aspects of mind. The optical illusions with which almost everyone is familiar do not have to be learned, yet they are aspects of human mental life. According to Immanuel Kant, the noted German philosopher of the eighteenth century, and more recently the Gestalt psychologists, our mind (or brain) possesses certain inborn organizing tendencies which do much to shape whatever information comes to the senses. Both cognitive processes and behavior are dependent to a degree upon innate organizing properties of the nervous system. The dependence of vision, hearing, and other senses upon the structure of the respective receptors and their connections with the brain are illustrations of this point. The ability to learn is similarly dependent upon inborn structures even though *what is learned* by an organism with the capacity to learn depends upon experience or stimulating circumstances.

Behavior that is naturally dependent, entirely or almost so, upon innate organization of the responding mechanisms is exemplified not only by reflexes but also by tropisms and instincts. Tropisms are orienting movements toward or away from sources of stimulation, such as a moth flying into a flame or a cockroach avoiding the light. The moth has a positive phototropism; the cockroach, a negative one. Tropistic responses are prevalent among insects, but they are seen less frequently as we go up the evolutionary scale to fishes, birds, and mammals. Tropisms do not preclude the possibility of learning. It may well be that cockroaches, for example, are normally well adapted without the need to learn anything. Nevertheless, they are capable of learning, as shown by the fact that if we give them an electric shock whenever they run to the dark, this reverses their inborn reaction: they learn to avoid the dark.

Many animals exhibit unlearned patterns of reflexes called *instincts.* Some examples are: web-spinning by spiders, nest-building by birds, flying, mating, and maternal behavior. Such behaviors follow patterns which are characteristic for the species. They are, to a considerable extent, "biologically programmed." Each act takes place more or less automatically as the appropriate situation arises, and the instinct typically runs its course in serial fashion, each response providing the stimulus for the next in the chain, until the sequence is completed.

Instinctive behavior is particularly evident in insects, where learning appears to play a minor role in adaptation. Here it appears that the animal acts essentially as an automaton. A good example is provided by a wasp which goes through the following instinctive routine: It finds a caterpillar, gives it a paralyzing sting, drags it to a tunnel, lays an egg upon it, then covers it with dirt. This behavior insures that the egg will be kept warm and that the grub will have food. It appears that the wasp is showing intelligence, but insofar as any intelligence exists, it is built-in rather than individually acquired. That the wasp is not in fact acting intelligently is shown by a simple experiment.

Hingston[26] made the first two steps in the instinctive chain unnecessary by providing, from a wasp's nest, a caterpillar that had already been captured and paralyzed. All the wasp had to do was drag the caterpillar away. But the wasp, provided with this short-cut, did not capitalize on it. To quote the investigator, "She seized hold of the helpless caterpillar, pierced it with her sting in the orthodox manner eight successive times. Then she proceeded according to routine to crush her victim's head." This was followed by the remaining steps in the chain.

Not all instinctive behavior is as routine as this. Indeed, as one goes from insects to higher organisms, instinctive behavior patterns become more variable and more adaptable to altered conditions. Moreover, instinctive behavior becomes less and less evident, until at the human level instincts are either absent or so modified and overshadowed by learned behavior that one fails to recognize their existence.

As we said earlier, certain aspects of mind are inborn, and reflexes, tropisms, and instincts could be regarded as illus-

[26] R. W. G. Hingston, *Problems of Instinct and Intelligence*, Macmillan, 1929, pp. 41–42.

trations of this fact. But when behavior departs from innately programmed routines such as these, and shows evidence that new controls are acquired, we must credit the organism with having achieved a degree of intelligence and mind that is not inborn.

The simplest learning is that in which some inborn reaction is modified, as when a dog comes to salivate in response to a bell that has been associated with the feeding situation or when a cockroach avoids the dark that originally initiated approach. At a somewhat higher level, we observe that an animal learns such skills as finding its way to food by traversing the shortest pathway in a maze, escaping from a box by lifting a latch or pulling a string, and making a differential response to such stimuli as horizontal versus vertical stripes. We shall see that while even ants and worms learn a simple maze, higher animals can learn complicated ones. We shall also see that animals at higher stages of evolution learn to solve problems which are too difficult for animals lower in the scale. This applies to discrimination problems and other tasks in which the animal is required to extricate itself from a frustrating situation.

SYMBOLIC PROCESSES

The clearest evidence for mental processes in animals comes from experiments requiring them to respond in terms of information acquired previously. In some of these tests, to be considered in a later discussion, the animal cannot respond correctly unless it *recalls an absent clue*. This means that some internal process must represent what is no longer present. Since anything which represents something else is a symbol, we speak, in this connection, of *symbolic processes*. Another ability, based on the animal's repertoire of symbolic processes, is the solution of problems by reasoning. We shall see that animals ranging from rats to human beings solve problems of varying degrees of complexity by reasoning, or "putting two and two together." How do we know that the animal is reasoning? We know because it solves problems so devised as to be impossible to solve without reasoning.

Thus, although we know nothing about conscious experience in animals and have no verbal evidence of mental processes, the existence of the latter may be inferred from the results of suitably arranged experiments. We can observe from these experiments whether or not an animal discriminates certain stimuli, whether or not it learns, the degree to which it remembers what it has learned, whether or not it can be induced to acquire and use symbolic processes, and whether or not it shows evidence of reasoning. Beyond the sheer presence of such processes we can also detect something of their upper limits of complexity. We know, for example, that the chimpanzee's color discrimination is almost as good as our own, that the chimpanzee not only learns simple mazes but also acquires highly complex skills such as riding a bicycle and improvising and using tools, that it retains what it has learned for long periods, that it uses symbolic processes of considerable complexity, and that its reasoning ability is about as good as that of a three-year-old child.

Some of the most important procedures for investigating mental processes in animals are discussed in Chapter Four, which also presents the major findings about the evolution of mind in organisms below man.

CHAPTER TWO

THE RACIAL DEVELOPMENT
OF ORGANISMS

That man is an animal which evolved from simpler forms of life now goes without question among those who have carefully examined Darwin's evidence and that accumulated by later investigators. But even though the reality of evolution has been clearly established, there are still questions as to how this incredibly complex process takes place. Darwin's view, as we pointed out earlier, was that large variations occur within each species; that these have an hereditary basis; that under diverse conditions of life some variations are more advantageous than others; and, therefore, that those which possess such variations survive the "struggle for existence" and perpetuate their kind in greater numbers than those not so fortunately endowed. This, in essence, is the theory of natural selection.

Natural selection must, however, have inheritable variations present on which to work. It does not account for the occurrence of such variations. Darwin recognized the existence of what he called "sports" and what DeVries (1909) and

43

later investigators have referred to as "mutations." But these suddenly appearing inheritable variants, as well as their mode of transmission, were not understood until the development of the modern science of genetics. As we said earlier, Mendel's discovery of basic hereditary mechanisms as early as 1856, three years before the *Origin of Species* was published, did not receive scientific recognition until 1900. His findings were subsequently seen to have great significance for our understanding of the evolutionary process as well as the development of individuals. They provided the foundation for the science of genetics. ◆

In this chapter we begin by sketching the main features of genetics which have specific importance for an understanding of the origin and hereditary transmission of such variations as "nature selects" in the "struggle for existence." We then provide a brief background for later chapters by referring to the geologic time scale and general trends in the racial development of organisms ranging from the simplest known animals to modern man.

THE GENETIC BASIS OF EVOLUTION

In the nucleus of every cell, as revealed microscopically, there are threadlike bodies which, because they color when stained, are called *chromosomes* (see illustrations, p. 45). Cells not involved in reproduction contain matched pairs of chromosomes. Human beings have 46 pairs. In the formation of reproductive cells, the pairs of chromosomes separate, each member of a pair going to a different cell. Thus, when a sperm and an ovum unite, each contributes one half of the chromosomes characteristic of the species.

Our parents had 92 chromosomes between them, 23 from each of our grandparents. Our 46 chromosomes were randomly drawn, as it were, from the 92 potentially available to us. The 23 received from our father represents a random assortment of his maternal and paternal chromosomes. Our mother's contribution was similarly derived from her maternal and paternal chromosomes. Thus, at fertilization, there

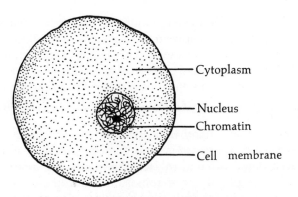

Schematic representation of a typical cell.

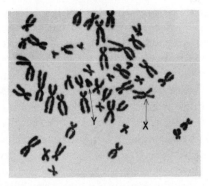

Human chromosomes. There are 46 shown, 22 pairs plus an X and a Y, the sex chromosomes.

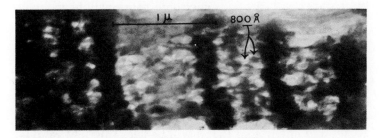

A small portion of a chromosome, enlarged 26,000 times. This is from the giant salivary gland of the fruit fly.

is a random selection from among the variously constituted ova and sperms. As a specific example, take the sex chromosomes and their assortment. The female combination is XX; the male, XY. Every ovum has an X chromosome. Fifty per cent of the sperms have an X and 50 per cent a Y chromosome. There is thus a fifty-fifty chance that the offspring will be male.

Since there are many inherited traits, each chromosome carries a large number of genetic determiners called *genes*. It has been demonstrated, in fact, that genes are distributed along the length of the chromosome. Chromosome maps have been made for fruit flies showing their locations. In view of this arrangement, genes are often referred to as analogous to beads strung on a thread.

Chromosomes of a pair separate when reproductive cells (ova and sperms) are formed. Each goes to a different ovum or sperm. At fertilization there is a "random" assortment of chromosomes to form new pairs, as described above.

In focusing upon a particular heritable trait, as Mendel did in his experiments, it is possible to predict the outcome of particular crosses. Take, for example, a cross between pure-breeding black Andalusian fowls and pure-breeding white ones. The genes for this trait (color) may be represented by letters—*bb* for the pair of genes determining black and *ww* for the pair of genes determining white. When the fowl with the *bb* genes produces ova and sperms, each of these will have the *b* gene. Likewise, each ovum and sperm produced by the fowl with the *ww* gene combination will have the *w* gene. Thus, all offspring of such a cross must be *bw*. These fowls have a grayish appearance.

Reproductive cells (ova and sperms) of the gray fowls contain either the *b* or the *w* gene and, in cross-breeding, the gene combinations shown at the top of p. 47 will occur. Observe that the chances are one in four that the gene combination *bb* will result, two in four that the combination will be *bw*, and one in four that it will be *ww*. This 1:2:1 ratio is approximated when a large number of crosses are involved. The resulting fowls are, respectively, black, gray, and white.

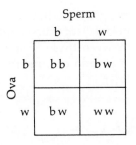

Dominant and Recessive Genes

In the example given, neither gene of the pair is dominant and the *bw* combination produces something resembling a blend between black and white characteristics. To take another example of this, white (*w*) and red (*r*) sweet peas produce pink flowers when the gene combination is *rw*.

Quite often one gene of a pair is *dominant*, the other *recessive*. In guinea pigs for example, black coat is dominant and white coat recessive. In such inheritance the dominant gene is represented by a capital letter (*B*) and the recessive by a lower-case letter (*b*). Thus, a pure-breeding black animal has the combination *BB* and a pure-breeding white one the combination *bb*. In a cross between these, the resulting combination will, of course, be *Bb*. Since *B* is dominant, all offspring from such a cross will be black. However, if black animals with the *Bb* gene combination are crossed, the resulting combinations will be *BB*, *Bb*, and *bb*, with two *Bb*s to every *BB* or *bb*. Since *B* is dominant, the outcome will be a ratio of three black guinea pigs to one white.

As another example, take running and waltzing in mice.[1] The normal (running) mouse may have the gene combination *RR* or *Rr*. *R* is dominant. On the other hand, the waltzing

[1] These and other mutant forms of locomotion in mice are discussed in Earl L. Green (Ed.), *Biology of the Laboratory Mouse* (2nd ed.), McGraw-Hill, 1966. We have already observed that mutations are suddenly appearing inheritable variations. In this instance the mutation is an inheritable defect in the labyrinthine structure of the ear, which, in turn, produces this deviant form of locomotion.

mouse always has the gene combination *rr*. A cross between an *RR* and an *rr* mouse will, of course, produce running mice. However, crosses between these *Rr* mice will produce runners and waltzers in a ratio of three runners to one waltzer (see illustration below).

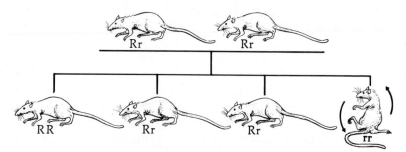

Inheritance of waltzing locomotion in mice. The presence of the dominant gene (RR or Rr) results in normal running locomotion. The absence of the dominant gene (rr) results in a defect in locomotion, called waltzing.

Although particular genes play a crucial role in the determination of specific hereditary traits such as those mentioned, other genes may be involved. Thus, one's heredity is said to be determined by his *gene complex,* defined as "the sum total of the genetic factors . . . interacting to produce an internal environment in which all of the genes must operate."[2]

Polygenic Inheritance

Gene pairs, operating according to Mendelian principles, produce discrete classes of individuals—such as one white fowl to two gray to one black; or three running mice to one waltzer. Certain discretely occurring traits (such as eye color, hair texture, and shape of nose) are transmitted in this way. But there are many inherited characteristics which do not fall into such definite groupings. Skin color in human beings

[2] W. H. Dowdeswell, *The Mechanism of Evolution,* London: Heinemann, 1963, p. 117.

is one of these. It covers a wide range from light to dark, which suggests the contribution of multiple genes. The inherited aspects of intelligence, based on differences in brain structure and possibly brain chemistry, must depend upon many genes, for there is an unbroken range from idiot to genius, if all have had equal opportunities to develop their intelligence. When a characteristic that is expressed over such a range is hereditary, it must depend upon the cumulative action of many genes, and inheritance is then said to be *polygenic*. The genes are paired, they separate during development of reproductive cells, and they recombine at fertilization just as any other genes do. The only difference between polygenic inheritance and the examples given earlier is the number of genes whose effects are combined to produce the inherited characteristic in question.

Phenotype and Genotype

It is important, in evaluating theories of evolution, to recognize that individuals may be alike with reference to an externally evident trait, yet have different genes. Thus, two black guinea pigs may have the same appearance but different gene combinations, either *BB* or *Bb*. In this event their similarity is *phenotypic*. But all *BB*s (or all *Bb*s), since they have the same genes, are also *genotypically* similar. Whether or not a particular visible or detectable trait is transmitted from one generation to another depends upon the genotype involved. All *BB* animals mating with other *BB*s will have black offspring which also have the *BB* combination. The *Bb*s, however, will have some black offspring and some white, unless they should mate only with *BB*s, in which case all of their progeny would be black; thus the offspring would have the phenotype of both parents but some would carry the recessive gene. The same principle applies to all inherited traits, whether or not dominance is involved. Thus, all the *bw* hens of our earlier example are the same genotype, but their offspring are gray like themselves only when they receive the *bw* gene combination. (In this case, all the gray hens and offspring are both genotypically and phenotypically similar.)

THE GENETIC CODE

Genes, as pointed out earlier, have been referred to as determiners of hereditary traits. Geneticists have often referred to them as "packets of chemicals" within the chromosomes. We now know that chromosomes are composed largely of nucleic acid, more specifically, deoxyribonucleic acid, or DNA. This has been pinpointed as the "hereditary chemical." There is evidence that its structure contains coded information which controls construction of the body in all of its details. Thus, the gene, beyond being referred to generally as an hereditary determiner is now considered to be some aspect of DNA structure, or a "unit" of DNA.

The DNA molecule is found in the cell nuclei of all plants and animals above the level of viruses and may be regarded as "remarkable evidence of the unity of all living things."[3] The DNA molecule consists, primarily, of four nucleotide bases (adenine, thymine, cytosine, and guanine). These are strung together in sugar-phosphate chains. According to the model posited by Watson and Crick, the structure of DNA is, as illustrated (p. 51), somewhat analogous to a rope ladder twisted to form a chain of helixes, a structure which is formed if the upper rung is held while the lower rung is twisted spirally. The rungs represent pairs of nucleotides, but with adenine (A) and thymine (T) always linked together and cytosine (C) and guanine (G) similarly linked. There is a succession of such A-T and C-G rungs, in varying sequence, held together by a sugar chain on one side and a phosphate chain on the other. Although A and T, and C and G are always linked, with the amount of A equaling the amount of T, and the amount of C equaling the amount of G, different proportions of A-T and C-G have been found in different organisms.

Since the chromosomes are duplicated in cell division, with each subsequent cell obtaining a complete set of chromosomes, the DNA molecule must somehow reproduce itself. According to the Watson-Crick model, the A and T,

[3] John Beuttner-Janusch, *Origins of Man*, Wiley, 1966, p. 430.

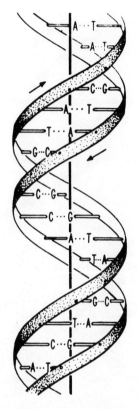

"A schematic illustration of the double helix. The two sugar-phosphate backbones twist about on the outside with the flat hydrogen-bonded base pairs forming the core. Seen this way, the structure resembles a spiral staircase with the base pairs forming the steps."

and C and G nucleotides separate as cell division approaches (see illustration, p. 52). Then A attracts a new T, T a new A, C a new G, and G a new C, but with the original sequence of these "rungs" being retained. Thus, the original cell gives rise to millions of cells, each with the same genes. In time, of course, some of these cells become sperms or ova, with

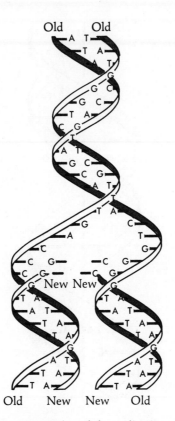

Old   Old

New New

Old   New   New   Old

Schematic representation of the replication of DNA.

only one half of the full complement of chromosomes (and genes). Then, as already described, one complete chromosome of every pair goes to a different cell.

The genetic code through which DNA specifies what sort of organism will develop, how one member of a species shall differ from another of the same species, and, in the last analysis, what any particular cell will become, is believed to have as its "alphabet" the nucleotides A, T, C, and G. How could these four nucleotides convey the extremely wide range of information required for development of an organism? In the Watson-Crick model, the "message" is written in terms of the sequence of the A-T and C-G linkages in the DNA molecule. In any one of the paired strands, the nucleotides A, T, C, and G may appear in all possible permutations, but the position of one automatically determines the position of the partner in the other strand, A always linked with T, and C always with G. The Morse code, with only three letters (dot, dash, and gap), is capable of transmitting every possible message in the English language. The genetic code contains only four "letters," but their permutations on the genetic ladder can convey many more messages than the conceivable number of effective genes. Thus, as Professor Dobzhansky says:

Suppose that a gene is a section of the double helix of the polynucleotide chains containing ten base pairs. The number of possible permutations of four letters is then 4^{10}, or 1,048,576. If the action of the gene depends upon the sequence of base pairs, more than a million genes are possible. It is of course improbable that any kind of sequence of the bases will always make a functional gene, just as many letter combinations are nonsense combinations and not meaningful words. However, even if a majority of the theoretically possible sequences are nonsense combinations, practically an infinity of gene structures may arise if the gene is a section of the helix containing hundreds or thousands of nucleotides.[4]

Even though their DNA carries the same code, cells differentiate to become muscle, bone, nervous tissue, and so on. The process involved is extremely complicated and not completely understood. However, the genes must change the cell structure by modifying the cytoplasm which surrounds them. In this process DNA apparently produces ribonucleic acid (RNA), which has a similar structure, and this "messenger RNA" translates the genetic code into action by assembling the amino acids which determine the protein structure

[4] Theodosius Dobzhansky, *Mankind Evolving,* Yale University Press, 1962, p. 38.

of the cell. It has been said, therefore, that DNA is like the architect's master plan for a structure and RNA is analogous to the blueprint which, in particular places, controls relevant details of the overall plan.

DEVELOPMENT

The genes do not, of course, act in a unitary fashion. As we said earlier, it is the gene complex (rather than individual genes) which controls the development of hereditary characteristics. However, the development of a cell into some specialized structure such as muscle or nerve tissue does not depend upon its gene complex alone. The cytoplasm is a substrate upon which the genes work, but as it changes under their influence it also limits their further action. Some genes, as they work on this substrate, put themselves out of action but at the same time prepare the substrate so that other genes can come into play. In this interaction between genes (or messenger RNA) and cytoplasm the cell is gradually changed in a specific direction. It becomes increasingly specialized.

But cellular development also depends upon interaction between cells. Because of their identical genes, the cells are, at the outset, capable of developing into any specialized cell structure characteristic of the organism. However, as cell division continues, the location of a particular cell has a great deal to do with its further development. Thus, two cells, although they have identical genes, may become quite different if one is located near the developing brain and the other near what is becoming skin. The former will become a brain cell and the latter perhaps a cutaneous cell, even part of a touch receptor. Thus, cellular differentiation is dependent upon the nature of the cytoplasm and interaction between cells as well as the gene complex as such. However, the nature of the cytoplasm and the timing of cell division and interaction is as characteristic of the organism as its gene complex, and development normally proceeds in accordance with an overall plan. If this were not so, there would be much less similarity than there is between different members of the same species.

The influence of the genes, in a normal internal environment, may be seen in identical twins, which develop independently but within the same uterus and at the same time, and obviously are built on the same pattern. Likewise, all human beings, because of their heredity, are built on the same overall pattern, although individuals are not identical in all details.

THE EVOLUTIONARY PROCESS

Although it is now evident that the higher organisms evolved out of simpler forms of life, there are various theories as to how this happened. One of the pre-Darwinian evolutionists, Jean-Baptiste Lamarck (1744–1829), presented the theory that acquired characteristics are inherited, a theory sometimes referred to as *Lamarckianism*. According to Lamarck, "It is not the organs—that is to say, the form and character of the animal's bodily parts—that have given rise to its habits and peculiar properties, but, on the contrary, it is its habits and manner of life and the conditions in which its ancestors lived that has in the course of time fashioned its bodily form, its organs, and its qualities."[5] It is thus assumed that the use or disuse of organs already present, as well as general environmental conditions (such as temperature, the availability of food, and conditions of illumination), produce structural changes which are subsequently transmitted, through inheritance, to the progeny of the affected organisms. Lamarck referred to moles that lost their sight by living underground, animals that acquired long legs and necks through stretching to reach food, and birds whose feet in time became webbed because they stretched their toes apart. Lamarckians have also claimed that the instincts which adapt animals to their

[5] Quoted by Erik Nordenskiöld in *The History of Biology*, Alfred A. Knopf, 1928, p. 322, as translated from Lamarck's *Recherches sur l'organisation des corps vivants*, Paris, 1802.

environment without training were originally learned, then transmitted through inheritance. Lamarck believed that in the "limitless time" available to evolution, all of the existing organisms could have arisen by inheriting the traits acquired by their ancestors.

This intriguing theory dies hard, even though it runs counter to everything now known about genetics. Experimental studies have yielded no scientifically acceptable evidence that acquired characteristics are inheritable. Geneticists have shown, in many experiments involving plants and animals, that the genes are impervious to the kinds of influences stressed by this theory. Animals do undergo structural changes during their lifetimes as the result of various environmental conditions and modes of behavior, but their offspring are in these respects like *they* were in the beginning. If the offspring are to become as their parents are, they must also experience the same kinds of environmental influence and acquire the same forms of behavior. Thus, mice, deprived of their tails for many generations still have offspring with tails, and as long as ever. The Jews have circumcised their boys for many generations without any evidence of structural changes which would make the operation unnecessary. And rats have been taught simple habits for as long as fifty generations without their progeny showing any evidence that they had inherited these habits. To those who argue, "Yes, but nature has had limitless time to transform acquired traits into inherited ones," it can only be said that geneticists have no evidence that this takes place and they cannot see how anything that happens to body cells during life can influence the germ cells in any way.[6]

Darwin accepted the idea that acquired characters may be inherited, but he emphasized the individual differences

[6] More detail on this problem and the research relating to it will be found in the following references: John Maynard Smith, *The Theory of Evolution*, Penguin Books, 1966, Chapter 4; and, for behavioral studies, Norman L. Munn, *The Evolution and Growth of Human Behavior* (2nd ed.), Houghton Mifflin, 1965, pp. 70–77.

which are so evident in plants and animals and also the sudden emergence of new structures, referred to as "sports." "Organic beings," he said, "present individual differences in almost every part of their structure." The theory of natural selection, as we have seen, supposes that some of these structural variations are more adaptive than others, giving their possessor an advantage in the struggle for existence. Some of the suddenly appearing "sports" might also be advantageous under certain circumstances.

Darwin differed from Lamarck in assuming that individual differences and "sports" have a *hereditary* origin at the outset. The giraffe illustration can serve to clarify this difference. Lamarck supposed that necks became longer from use and that their acquired length was somehow transmitted to the next generation. Darwin, on the other hand, assumed that some giraffes would have *inherently* longer necks than others, that longer necks would have survival value where foliage was high, that more long-necked than short-necked giraffes would survive and pass this trait to their offspring, and that the neck length would thus increase in successive generations.

Darwin did not invoke the inheritance of acquired characters, but his theory about the transmission of advantageous hereditary variations was defective in that it failed to take into account what is now known about phenotypic as compared with genotypic traits. Many traits are phenotypic only, such as black coat in guinea pigs with the *Bb* gene combination and running locomotion in *Rr* mice. To return to the giraffe illustration: if long necks were only phenotypic, the offspring of long-necked giraffes might or might not inherit long necks. Even more important than these considerations is the fact that naturally occurring variations like those referred to by Darwin are too small to account for the appearance of new species. We may get giraffes with longer and longer necks, up to a certain point, but nothing really new has been added to the animal's structure. Professor Thomas Hunt Morgan pointed out, in this connection, that:

Darwin's contemporaries seem to have understood that by selection of extreme individuals in any population the next generation will be moved in the direction of the selection. This is true, however, only when different genetic factors are present, and even there the process comes to an end as soon as these factors are sorted out. Nothing really new is accomplished, except that there are more of given kinds of individuals; but the limits of the original population are not transcended.[7]

MUTATIONS

Since acquired characteristics are not inherited and selection in terms of naturally appearing individual differences produces nothing essentially new, geneticists have come to the conclusion that the "sports" referred to by Darwin, now called "mutations," are the variations upon which evolution depends. Mutations are changes which appear suddenly and are then transmitted through inheritance. Among the well-known mutations in man are extra digits, albinism, and hemophilia. Thus, a child may be born with extra fingers and toes (see illustration, p. 59), something not previously evident in its ancestry. The heritability of the change is evidenced by the fact that some of this individual's offspring have the same trait. Many mutations are much less obvious than these, and some may not be evident at all until, after many generations, their cumulative effect changes the genic balance sufficiently.

When mutations occur, there is obviously some change in the chromosomes as a whole or in the genes. Chromosome mutations involve changes in the number of chromosomes. A type of feeblemindedness called mongolism, for example, is associated with the presence of an extra chromosome. Sometimes the number of chromosomes in plants and animals is doubled or tripled. Sometimes a chromosome is missing, as in females with one instead of two X chromosomes, who suffer resulting sexual abnormalities. Chromo-

[7] Thomas Hunt Morgan, *The Scientific Basis of Evolution*, W. W. Norton, 1932, p. 96.

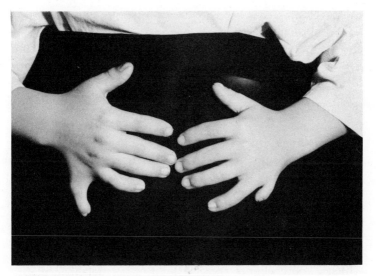

Polydactyly. The inheritance of six fingers and six toes runs in certain families. Sometimes the extra finger is removed surgically.

some mutations result from some sort of irregularity in cell division, possibly during the development of reproductive cells. Since they add nothing essentially new to the genetic variations already present in the population, these mutations are not credited with much importance in the process of evolution.

The most significant mutations for evolution occur in genes. Gene mutations produce essentially new structures. In the fruit fly, in which mutations have been studied in great detail, many inheritable changes can be observed, such as altered wing structure, bristle formation, and eye or body color. These alterations are known to involve particular points within a chromosome. Beyond this, nothing definite is known about the nature of gene, or "point," mutations. In terms of the Watson-Crick model, it is believed that they involve some sort of change in the nucleotide bases, or the sequence of these along the ladder-like DNA molecule. What results, in any event, is a change in the genetic code, so that the developing cells become something other than what they would normally become.

One important outcome of research with fruit flies was the discovery of conditions which influence the mutation process. Although mutations occur with apparent spontaneity, their frequency may be increased greatly by exposing animals to X-rays, cosmic rays, high-energy radiation (as from nuclear explosions), ultraviolet rays, and certain chemicals, including mustard gas.

Most of the mutations known to geneticists may be considered undesirable from an adaptive standpoint. Under changed environmental circumstances, however, some seemingly undesirable mutations may aid in survival. Take, for instance, the emergence among normally pale moths of a melanic form, in which the pigment melanin produces a blackened appearance. Where trees and other objects on which a moth alights are of a light color, melanism places the moth at a decided disadvantage (see illustration, p. 61). It can be readily seen and pounced on by birds and other animals. One is not surprised, therefore, to find that this moth is extremely rare under such circumstances. But in an industrial area which has accumulated soot for a century, the situation is reversed. The paler moths are rare, and the melanic form predominates. This is because the mutation is more advantageous than the normal state in these areas, since it enables more of the melanic moths than the paler ones to survive and reproduce.

It is interesting to observe, in this connection, that melanism is a dominant trait. Many mutations are recessive, which means, of course, that they do not influence the phenotype unless both parents possess the altered gene. This is most likely to happen if there is close inbreeding. However, both dominant and recessive mutations of a given kind occur repeatedly. A form of dwarfism in man (achondroplasia) is estimated to have a mutation rate of 42–70 in a million sex cells. Albinism, another well-known mutation, occurs an estimated 28 times in a million sex cells. Hemo-

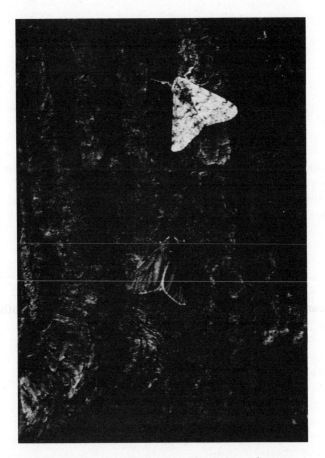

Melanism, an adaptive variation in industrial areas.

philia has a rate estimated to be 32 per million sex cells. In discussing these estimates, Professor Dobzhansky points out that the mutants referred to are sharp and clear. He says, "It is relatively easy to recognize an albino, an hemophiliac, or an achondroplastic dwarf. But not all mutations are so distinctive and many cause slight and not easily detectable alterations. Moreover, the evidence from organisms other than man . . . shows that these small mutations are actually the most frequent type of mutational changes."[8]

DEVELOPMENTAL TRENDS

If we think of mutations as changes in the gene complex which alter the organism's genic balance, we can appreciate that even the slight changes may start developmental trends which culminate in the appearance of a new structure. Such effects may be cumulative, so that generations may elapse before they become manifest. It has often been pointed out, in this connection, that we may not be as much aware of beneficial mutations as we are of deleterious ones, because the former have already been incorporated into our gene structure to make us what we are.

In studying the different forms of animal life it is often possible to arrange a sequence which shows the more or less gradual appearance of a particular characteristic, such as transition from a three-toed to a one-toed horse, from a small to a large reptile, from a simple to a complex brain, and so on. This implies what has often been referred to as "oriented evolution," "straight-line evolution," or "orthogenesis." The last term is often used to represent a broad overall plan in evolution, as if the earlier forms of life carried the germ for all future developments, a pre-established design to culminate in the emergence of man.[9]

After marshalling the evidence for oriented evolution, George Gaylord Simpson concludes that there are recognizable trends but that these are decidedly limited in extent, with many exceptions even where a trend is indicated. To the

[8] Theodosius Dobzhansky, *Mankind Evolving*, Yale University Press, 1962, pp. 49–50.

[9] Pierre Teilhard de Chardin has given an extensive exposition of this concept in *The Phenomenon of Man* (London: Collins, 1955). He sees all evolution as leading toward the rise of consciousness and, even beyond that, to a universal sphere of thought which he calls the *noosphere*. See Chapter Eight for a further discussion of Teilhard de Chardin and his views on the future of man.

lected birds capable of burrowing into wood for insects: those which could not do this perished. The arctic regions selected animals with heavy fur. In some regions the only surviving animals are those capable of burrowing, or of capitalizing on the shelter provided by small holes in the ground or in rocks or tree trunks. Isolation is also important in this connection. For example, the egg-laying and marsupial mammals became isolated when the land bridge between Australia and South East Asia was broken. Australia had no placentals to prey upon the relatively weak and timid egg-layers and marsupials. These circumstances, together with the nature of the Australian physical environment, led to survival of the world's only two egg-laying mammals, the duck-billed platypus and the echidna (spiny ant eater), and over two hundred species of marsupials, including the kangaroo, wallaby, wombat, and koala bear. Only one marsupial has survived elsewhere, and that is the American opossum. The process of evolution is facilitated when populations become isolated from the parent stock. For one thing, there is closer inbreeding, especially when the isolated groups are relatively small, and this increases the probability that recessive mutations will be perpetuated.

Another aspect that contributes to evolution of new species is the separation of gene pools. The gene pool of a species is the totality of genes from which the individual derives his special allotment. When isolation occurs, the gene pool of the isolated population gradually changes from that of the parent stock. This is because mutations which occur within one pool are not available to the other and because each is subjected to different selective influences. It is believed likely, moreover, that one type of environment may *produce* more and different mutations from those produced in another environment. This would be an additional differentiating factor, over and beyond the influence of the environment in *selecting* mutations. For these and possibly other reasons, the gene pools of the derived and the parent stock may eventually become so different that even when barriers are removed inbreeding no longer occurs. This is the main basis for saying that the isolated animals have become a different species.[12]

The foregoing is only the barest outline of what is known about the evolutionary process, but it is sufficient to provide a background for later discussions of mental evolution. Its aim has been to show that the only well-founded theory of evolution stresses the combined roles of gene mutations and natural selection—gene mutations as the sources of novel variations and natural selection as the process that determines which variations shall survive and be transmitted. In this process, the mutations most likely to endure are those which best fit the organism to its environment, but no characteristic, however adaptive, is of significance for evolution unless it is inheritable. This rules out acquired characteristics, which have no representation in the genes.

THE HISTORY OF LIFE

We do not know how life began, but biochemists, who have already synthesized some basic constituents of living matter, may yet find a clue to its origins. We do know that inorganic elements did at some time give rise to living substance and thus started the process of organic evolution.

It appears that life may have originated as long ago as 2000 million years, when the originally molten earth had sufficiently cooled so that land, sea, and a suitable atmosphere could come into existence, but there is no doubt on one point: that life originated in the sea, for the earliest plants and animals of which we have fossilized remains were marine organisms. These existed for an estimated 1000 million years before plants and animals appeared on land.

There is no evidence that life is being created out of inorganic elements today. The conditions necessary for its

[12] The entire problem of "speciation" is dealt with in considerable detail by Professor Ernst Mayr in *Animal Species and Evolution,* Harvard University Press, 1966. The preceding discussion has dealt with what Mayr calls "the genetic reconstruction of a population during a period of geographic (spatial) isolation" (p. 556).

origin apparently existed in primeval times, then disappeared, possibly as the earth and its atmosphere underwent further change.

The first living organisms were no doubt much simpler than any existing today. Even the one-celled animals such as amoeba and paramecia are probably very complex in contrast with their most ancient predecessors, of which, unfortunately, there are no known remains. The entire Precambrian era (see the Geologic Time Scale), stretching back beyond 600 million years ago, yields little clear evidence of living things. From the Cambrian period until the present, however, there is a continuous record of ever-increasing forms of life.

One of the most ancient animals in the fossil record is the trilobite, an extinct marine crustacean which lived during the Cambrian period and whose mineralized form is found embedded in rock derived from sedimentary deposits in which it was buried some 500 million years ago.[13] There were various forms of marine life (sponges, trilobites, mollusks, and many others) before anything like a fish evolved. The

[13] The dating of fossils is based on the succession of geological strata in which their remains are found and by various methods of "absolute dating" based on the known rate of decomposition, or loss of irradiation, in mineral deposits. Potassium-argon, for example, has a half-life of 1,330,000,000 years. This means that half of its atoms would be transformed in this time. How far this transformation has progressed in a particular geological deposit provides an estimate of how long ago it began.

Eras refer to the succession of rock layers on the earth's crust. Each era is subdivided into geologic periods, and each of these into epochs. For example, the most recent period of the Cenozoic is the Quaternary, and the epoch of the Quaternary in which man evolved is the Pleistocene, which is estimated to have begun some two million years ago. The Pleistocene (pleisto, for most) gets its name because more fossils represent this epoch than any other. (From American Heritage Dictionary, *Houghton Mifflin, 1969, p. 551)*

GEOLOGIC TIME SCALE

ERA	PERIOD		EPOCH	YEARS BEFORE THE PRESENT
Cenozoic	Quarternary		Holocene (Recent)	11,000
			Pleistocene (Glacial)	500,000 to 2,000,000
	Tertiary		Pliocene	13,000,000
			Miocene	25,000,000
			Oligocene	36,000,000
			Eocene	58,000,000
			Paleocene	63,000,000
Mesozoic	Cretaceous			135,000,000
	Jurassic			180,000,000
	Triassic			230,000,000
Paleozoic	Permian			280,000,000
	Carboniferous	Pennsylvanian (Upper Carboniferous)		310,000,000
		Mississippian (Lower Carboniferous)		345,000,000
	Devonian			405,000,000
	Silurian			425,000,000
	Ordovician			500,000,000
	Cambrian			600,000,000
Precambrian				

most ancient fossil of a fish takes us back more than 400 million years, to the Silurian period. During the Carboniferous period and later, both fish and amphibians are plentiful in the fossil record. Reptiles became abundant during the Permian period, and the best known of these are the dinosaurs. These were followed by primitive birdlike creatures and early mammals.

Modern mammalian types came much later. The horse, for example, was represented during the Eocene (58 million years ago) by *Eohippus*. Various "horses" appeared and were succeeded, some 12 million years ago (later Cenozoic era, Pliocene epoch), by *Equus*, the genus which includes horses of the present day as well as the ass and zebra. Human evolution can be traced most directly from the appearance, some 60 to 75 million years ago, of such insect-eating tree dwellers as shrews. These preprimates and such early primates as the lemurs and tarsiers preceded modern monkeys and apes by some 30 millions of years. The precursors of modern anthropoid apes were living 28 million years ago, Cenozoic era, Tertiary period, Oligocene epoch (as shown in the Geologic Time Scale). Man himself did not come upon the scene until the Pleistocene epoch, the beginning of which goes back two million years, according to the geologic time scale reproduced here.

The evolution of animal life, from its earliest recorded beginnings through the various forms which culminated in the emergence of man, is represented by a many-branched tree, the branches of which portray not only the evolutionary succession of animal types but also relationships, insofar as these are evident from the fossil record and other sources of information. Fossils, as we have seen, tell a great deal about the order in which various forms of life evolved. They also reveal the gross structural characteristics of earlier forms of life and thus make it possible to compare these with modern forms and with each other.

Comparative anatomy, whether based on fossils or living animals, reveals structural similarities in different animals— such as the serial arrangement of similar bones in the wing of a bird, the leg of a frog and a cat, the arm of a man, the wing of a bat, and the flipper of a whale. Similarly homologous organs are found in many animals, and they give abundant evidence of "genetic relationship, through the principle of evolution."[14]

Interrelationships of widely different forms of animal life are also found in embryology, where vestigial organs are commonly observed. The human embryo, for example, goes through a process of development in which gill arches are transformed into ears, very much like those of an ape initially, and then increasingly human, and in which a tail appears and, except in rare instances, is gradually superseded by a more human posterior.[15] Here we have evidence of man's ancestral relationship with fishes and apes.

Each major branch of the evolutionary tree represents one of the chief animal groups, or phyla. At the bottom of the tree are viruses, bacteria, algae, and other primitive organisms. The first distinct phylum represented is that of the *protozoa,* unicellular organisms which include the amoeba and paramecium. Some other phyla, in approximate order of appearance are *porifera* (sponges), *coelenterates* (including sea anemones and jellyfish), *platyhelminthes* (flatworms such as the planaria), *nemathelminthes* (round worms), *annelida* (segmented worms), *mollusca* (including snails and octopuses), *arthropoda* (the various insects), *echinodermata* (including starfishes), and *chordata* (fish, amphibians, reptiles, birds, and mammals). The phylum *chordata* is so named because at some stage in the animal's development there is a flexible rodlike structure running from the head to the tail end. In higher forms this becomes the spinal column. Animals with vertebrae along the spinal axis form a subphylum of the phylum *chordata* known, in general, as *vertebrates.*

The branch of the evolutionary tree which represents the vertebrates has subsidiary branches for the various classes of vertebrates. These are the fishes, amphibians, reptiles,

[14] Wolfgang F. Pauli, *The World of Life,* Houghton Mifflin, 1949, p. 115.

[15] Some children are born with a tail.

birds, and mammals. They are believed to have evolved in that order, although not each directly out of the other, as we shall see presently.

The class *mammalia* (which includes egg-laying mammals and marsupials as well as placental mammals) is further sub-divided to include, as one of its divisions, the primate order, which includes tree-shrews, tarsiers, lemurs, monkeys, apes, and man. A suborder, *anthropoidea,* includes only the monkeys, apes, and man. The superfamily *hominoidea* is restricted to the great apes and man. A further restriction is represented by the family *hominidae,* which includes only the tool-making primates, from early manlike creatures to modern man. The genus *homo,* within this family, includes all living and extinct human beings. Of this genus, modern man (*homo sapiens sapiens*) is the only living species. Thus, each of us (of whatever race) is an animal, a vertebrate, a mammal, a primate, an anthropoid, a hominid, and a member of the genus *homo* and the species *sapiens.*

A prevalent misconception about man's evolution is that there was a ladder-like progression from, say, fish to man, with fishes giving rise to amphibians, amphibians to reptiles, reptiles to birds, birds to mammals, and, within this class, monkeys to apes and apes to man. According to the best evidence now available, the arborial insectivores existing 75 million years ago began a primate line with various branches, each culminating in such existing preprimates as arboreal shrews and the tarsiers, lemurs, and so on, as illustrated in the family tree of the primates. According to this conception, the ancestors of man and the great apes, after diverging from a common preprimate stock, developed in their separate ways. The existing primates, including man, are the end-products of these divergent developments.

Many of the predecessors of monkeys, apes, and men are unknown to us because no remains have been found. This is not surprising, for the primates were tree dwellers, as most of them are today, and they moved with great facility in trees and on the ground. They were thus less likely to be buried and fossilized than the more slow-moving and less intelligent ground dwellers.

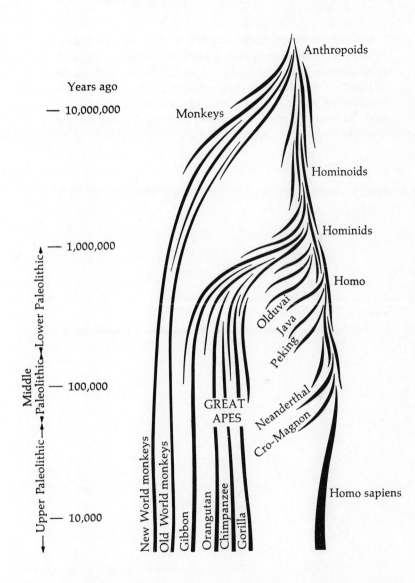

The family tree of the primates. The time scale is exponential.
From "Tools and Human Evolution," Sherman L. Washburn.

Having sketched major trends in human evolution, we now focus more specifically upon the evolution of reaction mechanisms, thus providing a background for consideration of mental evolution in animals and men. We return, in a later chapter, to the transition from apelike men to modern men and the emergence of the human mind as it is known today.

CHAPTER THREE

EVOLUTION OF
REACTION MECHANISMS

The behavior of animals depends upon sensitivity to environmental changes—to stimulation. In all but the lowest organisms, this function is mediated by receptors grouped together as sense organs such as the eye and ear. If sensitivity is to be followed by reaction, there must also be reacting mechanisms (such as the muscles of the mouth, limbs, and hands) and also some way of carrying messages to them from the receptors. These messages are conducted from receptors to muscles by the nervous system. The functions of sensitivity, conduction, and reaction underlie all aspects of mental life.

In discussing the role of these functions in mental life (p. 37), we called attention to their presence, in rudimentary form, in unicellular animals like the amoeba, an organism without specialized receptor, conductor, and motor structures (see illustration, p. 74). The amoeba's entire body is sensitive in a generalized way. It responds to light, but only to its intensity, direction, and movement. Specialized visual

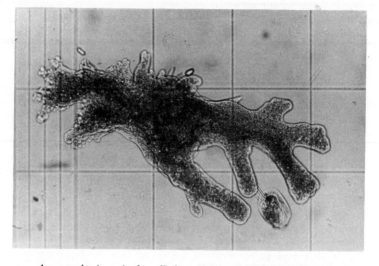

An amoeba is a single-celled organism which combines within itself, insofar as the properties are shown at all, the capacity to serve as a receptor, an effector, and a conductor of the results of stimulation. This photomicrograph shows the amoeba extending long pseudopods toward another microscopic organism. Each of the large ruled squares in this picture is one-hundredth of an inch on a side. From R. Buchsbaum, Animals without Backbones, *University of Chicago Press, 1948; photo by Ralph Buchsbaum.*

receptors are necessary for color, shape, and space discrimination. Other forms of sensitivity are similarly limited. Thus, organisms like the amoeba respond only to the grossest aspects of their world. As specialized sense organs evolve, the sensory environment is perceived with increasing appreciation of its details, and reactions become increasingly attuned to the subtler aspects of the environment—colors, tones, scents, as well as smaller and smaller differences in these.

In a similar way, reactions become more versatile as specialized motor mechanisms evolve. The amoeba moves by putting out finger-like projections (pseudopods) from any part of its body. Its movements are slow and clumsy in comparison with those of organisms having specialized motor organs, like cilia, fins, wings, or legs. Hands appear relatively late in evolution. They represent the highest level of motor specialization, and they serve manipulatory as well as locomotor functions.

Conductivity, the third basic function, is also present in the amoeba, again in rudimentary form. Stimulation at one locus is followed by the appearance of a pseudopod at another, indicating that the effects of stimulation are transmitted through the protoplasm. In higher organisms, transmission is mediated by specialized conductors, the neurons, and becomes more precise.

The evolution of the nervous system culminated in the emergence of a brain, simple at first, then increasingly complex. The brain made possible the retention of the effects of stimulation. When it had become sufficiently complex, the brain gave rise to such higher mental functions as learning, memory, and reasoning.

RECEPTOR PROCESSES

We have two major sources of information on receptor functions in animals—structure and behavior. In tracing the evolution of visual reception, for example, we may observe the eye structure in a succession of animals such as fishes, reptiles, birds, rats, monkeys, apes, and man, or we can arrange experiments which test the ability of these organisms to discriminate visual details such as brightness, color, shape, and depth. Information is actually obtained from both sources and correlated: we discover, for example, that the only vertebrates capable of discriminating colors are those with structures called *cones* in the retinas of their eyes.

Comparative anatomy provides structural information, but what about behavioral evidence of sensitivity? How do we know, for example, that rats are color blind and that chimpanzees have color vision as good as ours? This information comes from experiments on sensory discrimination. There are many methods of studying discrimination in animals, and these vary with the sense being tested and the motor versatility of the animal. Here we shall sketch only four methods of investigating visual sensitivity. The study of other senses involves similar principles, although the methods of presenting stimuli to be discriminated are different for different senses.[1]

There are three commonly used methods of studying sensory discrimination. The *direct* method—so designated because no special training of the animal is required—makes use of a natural response to moving stimuli to study visual discrimination, for example. The animal's body is held in a fixed position at the center of a moving cylinder, the walls of which are covered with black and white stripes. As the stripes move in front of the animal's eyes, the eyes follow them momentarily, then jerk back to the original position, and they continue this movement until the cylinder is stopped. In some animals the head moves in response to the moving stripes. If there are no stripes, i.e., only a uniform surface, the optokinetic reflex (head movement) does not occur. If the stripes are gradually reduced in width, a point occurs at which the animal ceases to respond. This indicates the limit of its ability to differentiate the stripes, or its visual acuity. Suppose, now, that the stripes are red and gray of equal brightness. If the optokinetic response occurs under these conditions, the animal is discriminating red from an equally bright gray. In this way, using other colors matched with gray, we can test the range of its color vision. We could also use pairs of colors (say, red and green stripes of equal brightness), and an optokinetic response to a pair of colors would show that the animal discriminates those colors.

Another relatively simple method of testing an animal's sensory capacity, one which requires training, is the *conditioned-response method*. One widely used conditioning

[1] More detail concerning these methods will be found in the author's book, *The Evolution and Growth of Human Behavior* (2nd ed.), Houghton Mifflin, 1965, pp. 88–105.

Operant conditioning box for pigeons. The operant here is pecking the disc. Reinforcement comes from a piece of food which becomes accessible in the aperture below.

procedure requires the animal to perform a simple task in order to get a reward. Mammals may be required to press a lever or push against a panel, while pigeons usually peck a disc, as illustrated above. The bird first learns that pecking the disc releases a piece of grain, which falls into the food tray below the disc. After the pigeon has been trained to peck the disc, a procedure that need not be described here, the situation is altered so that instead of presenting the same disc every time, the experimenter presents now a white disc and now a black one, or now a red one and now a green one, or now a vertically striped one and now a horizontally striped one. The animal is rewarded for responding to one disc and not to the other—for example, pecking red releases the reward whereas pecking green does not. The red and green discs would, of course, be presented in random order. If the bird comes to peck red and refrain from pecking green, as the pigeon does, we know that it discriminates these colors. The range of its color vision may be tested by using other color combinations. It is important, however, that the colors be

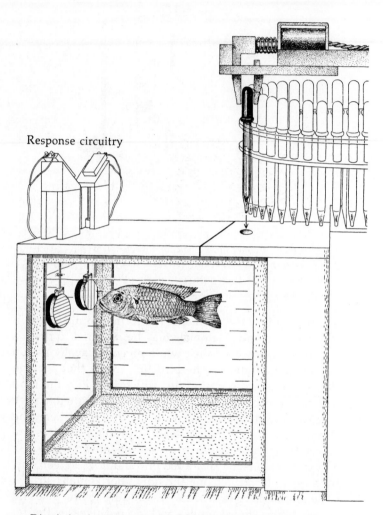

Response circuitry

Discrimination apparatus for fish. When the fish presses its head against the correct disc, the pincers close on the eye dropper, thus releasing a Tubifex worm into the tank.
From "The Evolution of Intelligence," M. E. Bitterman.

of equal brightness; otherwise the animal might be discriminating on the basis of brightness, a much more primitive discrimination than color vision, as we shall observe in more detail presently.

The discrimination method, of which there are again many varieties, requires the animal to choose between two or more simultaneously presented stimuli. A hungry fish, for example, swims toward a vertically striped and a horizontally striped disc at the end of an aquarium (see illustration, p. 78). When the fish presses one of these with its snout, a mechanism makes a piece of worm accessible. Pressing the other has no effect, unless the experimenter has arranged to punish incorrect responses, in which case the fish gets an electric shock. The discs are changed from side to side in a random order, and the other conditions are controlled so that the fish cannot get its reward unless it discriminates one direction of stripe from the other. Figures, colors, or shades of gray can similarly be used to measure aspects of the animal's visual sensitivity. In such experiments, there are a given number of trials per day (usually 10 to 20), and the animal is not considered to be discriminating unless it reacts correctly in, say, 18 out of 20 successive trials.

Small mammals such as rats may be required to jump toward a platform containing the stimuli to be discriminated. An incorrect response is followed by a fall into a net below and a correct one by a bite of food.

In an experiment performed by the writer, kangaroos hopped through a boxlike apparatus toward two doors containing visual stimuli (see illustration, p. 80). They pushed the door with nose or paw. If the correct door was pushed, they could continue until food was reached. The incorrect door was locked from behind, so that pushing it was frustrating. Moreover, this error delayed food-getting because the kangaroo could enter only by the correct door.

In some experiments, touching the incorrect door automatically locks the other door, so that the animal is forced to wait until it has made a correct response before it receives a

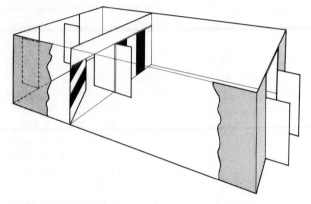

*A discrimination box. The animal enters at the right
and, upon proceeding, is confronted by two closed doors
covered with, respectively, horizontal or vertical black
and white stripes. One is locked from behind but the
other can be opened if the animal pushes it. Beyond
the doors, at a point equidistant from them, is food.
This is an adaptation for kangaroos of an apparatus
first described by the writer in 1931, in the* JOURNAL
OF GENETIC PSYCHOLOGY.

reward. The apparatus can also be arranged so that the animal gets an electric shock if it touches the incorrect door.

The primary motivation in discrimination experiments is
usually hunger. The animal is kept well below normal weight
and is given no food for up to 48 hours prior to the tests.
Then it is given its daily ration immediately after the day's
tests have been completed.

A widely used method of studying sensory discrimination
in primates makes use of the *Wisconsin General Test Apparatus,* a device designed by Dr. Harry Harlow, director of
the University of Wisconsin primate laboratories. In the
illustration (p. 81) a monkey is being tested with two stimulus objects. These differ in color, but they could have differed in size, shape, or some other characteristic. Below each
stimulus object is a small well; the well under the correct
object contains a raisin, a grape, or a small piece of banana.

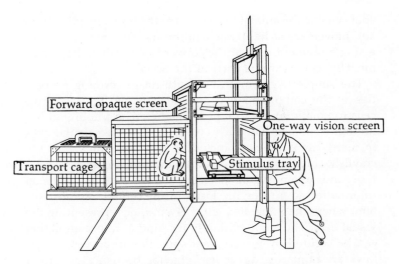

The Wisconsin Test Apparatus used with monkeys.

An opaque screen between the monkey and the stimulus tray prevents the animal from seeing the stimulus objects being arranged and the correct one baited. When the screen is raised, the experimenter moves the test tray within the animal's reach. Selection of the correct object, by lifting it or pushing it aside, gives access to the reward beneath. But if the incorrect object is touched, the tray is withdrawn immediately, and the animal must wait until the next trial for another opportunity to get the reward. As in other discrimination tests, the position of the correct object follows a predetermined chance order of left-right presentation. Other possible cues are also controlled; for example, a difference in odor, due to the presence of the reward under one stimulus object, may be controlled by making both food wells smell of raisin, grape, banana, or whatever the reward may be.

EVOLUTION OF VISION

The simplest visual receptor is a pigment spot, a spot more sensitive to light than any other part of the body. Pigment spots enable the animal to respond to the intensity, direction, and movement of light. Some of the simpler organisms have a single pigment spot at the forward end; others have pigment spots on various parts of the body.

The simplest type of an eye with image-forming properties is the compound eye, in which many light-sensitive cells (ommatidia) are grouped together. The trilobite of 500 million years ago had such an eye, and we see similar eyes in many living animals, including crustaceans (such as the crayfish) and insects. The compound eyes of insects have thousands of ommatidia. Each one sends a fragment of visual information to a receiving locus in the central nervous system, where the integrated effect is a mosaic representing the visual field. Thus, in addition to the kind of information that can be secured by the pigment spot, this improved eye allows an animal to direct its behavior by using patterned visual stimulation. The bee's compound eye also mediates color vision, as shown by the experiments of Karl von Frisch.[2]

Evolution has given rise to many kinds of visual mechanisms, and often these evolved quite independently. The bee's vision is mediated by mechanisms very different from those of vertebrates, and there is no evidence to suggest that vertebrate eyes evolved from compound eyes. Nevertheless, vertebrate eyes also have many separate light-sensitive cells which work together to give an overall representation of what is in the visual field.

The vertebrate eye is foreshadowed in eyes such as those of the planarian, a flatworm. As shown in the illustration (p. 83), a number of light-sensitive cells are grouped together in a depression. An eye more closely resembling vertebrate eyes is found in the nautilus, one of the mollusks. This eye, too, has a cuplike depression; light can enter it only through a small opening. This is one of the earliest "camera" eyes to evolve. Light entering through the hole can, as in a pinhole camera, form an image of what is in front of the eye. In some of the invertebrates, a lens replaces the

[2] See Karl von Frisch, *Bees: Their Vision, Chemical Senses, and Language,* Cornell University Press, 1950.

Eyes of planarian, nautilus, squid, and man.

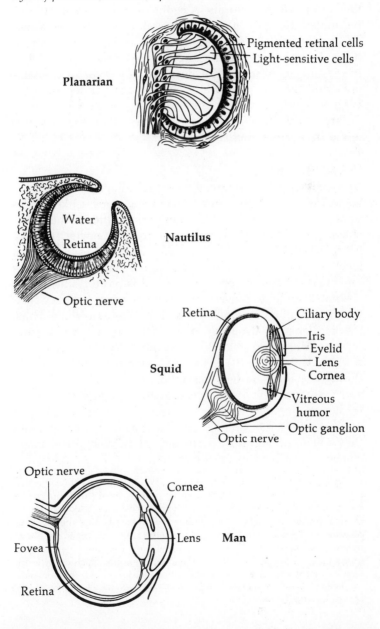

hole. One such lens is that of the cephalopods, for example, the squid and the octopus. A cephalopod eye, as illustrated, resembles the eyes of vertebrates, all of which have a lens and a photosensitive surface (retina) on which images produced by light rays coming through the lens are focused. It is interesting to observe, however, that the eyes of cephalopods and those of vertebrates evolved quite independently. We know this because their embryological development is different, resulting in retinal structures that are very different in origin and characteristics.[3]

Accessory Structures

Vertebrates eyes differ greatly, yet they all have an optic cup, some kind of a retina, and a lens to focus camera-like images upon the retina. From fish to man, lenses differ in their size, shape, and focusing mechanisms. Some characteristics are shown in the illustration on p. 83. The trend as the human level is approached is toward a more flattened lens, one which fills less of the optic cavity and is more resilient.

Some vertebrate lenses cannot change curvature. A clear focus is obtained by movements of the lens as a whole. Thus, the fish lens moves closer to the retina in accommodating for more distant objects. Birds accommodate by moving the cornea instead of the lens. All mammals accommodate through changes in lens curvature. The lens is suspended and maintained in its flattened shape by ligaments. When tension in the ligaments is lessened, the natural elasticity of the lens causes it to bulge. Such actions occur reflexly, and they adjust the curvature of the lens so that the optical image comes to a clear focus on the retina.

[3] As Wolfgang F. Pauli has pointed out: "Whereas in vertebrates the eye cup, including the retina, arises from an outgrowth of the brain, in the cephalopods these structures all have their origin in the ectoderm. Hence in the cephalopod a separate optic ganglion, located behind the eye, concentrates in it the complex ganglionic connections found in the vertebrate retina. Nevertheless, the cephalopod eye and the vertebrate eye present one of the most striking cases of convergent evolution, in which entirely different original structures and totally different courses of evolution have resulted in organs strikingly similar in design." (From *The World of Life*, Houghton Mifflin, 1947, p. 332.)

The cavity between the lens and the retina is filled with a jelly-like substance (the vitreous humor), which in man has the consistency of raw egg white. Its pressure on the lens helps to keep the latter in position.

From the standpoint of visual reception the structures so far considered are merely accessory. They produce a retinal image, but this is without visual effect unless the retina itself is stimulated, sending appropriate nerve impulses to the optic thalamus, which relays them to the part of the cerebrum that has become specialized for visual reception.

The Vertebrate Retina

The retina, embryologically an extension of the brain, is an extremely complex structure which, in man, contains many millions of photosensitive cells called *rods* and *cones*. As shown in our greatly simplified illustration in Chapter One (p. 19), these are connected synaptically with bipolar cells, which pass nerve impulses from the rods and cones to the ganglion cells of the optic nerve. Cross-connections within the retina are also prevalent, leading to interaction at this level as well as in the thalamus and cerebral cortex.

The retinas of some vertebrates, especially the nocturnal species, possess rods exclusively, or almost so. Rods are especially adapted for sensitivity to low intensities of light, for night vision. Cones do not function under low illumination, but they are necessary for color vision. An animal without cones is color blind, but some mammals having both rods and cones also appear to be color blind. Cones respond differentially to the wavelengths of light. In primates the three types of cones are especially sensitive to the short, intermediate, and long wavelengths of the visible spectrum.[4]

The primate retina has a depression known as the *fovea*, within which light rays are most clearly focused. This, then, is the point of clearest vision. Its receptors are exclusively cones. From the fovea outward there are fewer and fewer

[4] See, for example, W. B. Marks, W. H. Dobelle, and E. F. MacNichol, Jr., "Visual Pigments of Single Primate Cones," *Science,* 1964, Vol. 143, pp. 1181–1183; and P. K. Brown and G. Wald, "Visual Pigments in Single Rods and Cones of the Human Retina," *Science,* 1964, Vol. 144, pp. 45–52.

cones, until, on the extreme periphery, rods alone appear. This outer part of the retina is color blind and relatively insensitive to small details, including the shapes of objects. Foveas are not found exclusively in primates, however. Some birds have both a central and a lateral fovea, an arrangement believed to aid their distance discrimination.[5]

Binocular Vision

The position of the eyes is of great importance in the evolution of vision. Many animals have one eye on each side of the head; each eye gets a separate picture. In animals that evolved later the eyes have moved toward the front. In some animals they are at such a distance apart that their visual fields just come together so that the field of both eyes is continuous. Ultimately, however, the eyes are sufficiently close together for their fields to overlap. This trend from separate visual fields to joined fields to overlapping fields is correlated with changes in the visual pathways, as illustrated (p. 87). In animals with separate visual fields, the optic nerves cross over (decussate) completely in the optic chiasma. When the visual fields are joined, there is a partial crossing over, some fibers going to the right side of the brain and some to the left. The final development is hemidecussation, one half of the fibers from each eye going to the right side of the brain and the other half to the left. With this development comes the ability to converge the eyes in fixating an object and to move them conjointly in scanning the visual environment.

When the eyes are sufficiently close together to produce overlapping views, when they can converge and scan, and when hemidecussation of the optic pathways provides the brain with integrated information from the two eyes, we have the foundations of visual perception of depth and distance. The eyes receive overlapping, yet somewhat different retinal images because of the slight difference in their positions. This retinal disparity gives rise to a difference in the

[5] Katherine Tansley discusses this in *Vision in Vertebrates* (pp. 42–43), published as a Science Paperback by Associated Book Publishers, London, 1965.

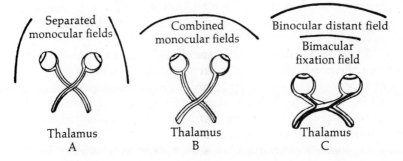

Evolution of the binocular fixation field. Diagrams of the eyes and optic tracts. A. At the stage in which there are separate monocular visual fields, absence of conjugate movements of the eyes, with total decussation of the fibers of the optic nerves. B. At the stage in which there are combined monocular fields and some conjugate movements of the eyes, with subtotal decussation of the fibers of the optic nerves. C. At the stage in which there are developed a binocular distant field, a bimacular (bifoveal) fixation field, conjugate movements of the eyes, and hemidecussation of general retinal and macular fibers of the optic nerves.

patterns of nerve impulses from the two retinas, a difference somehow integrated in the visual cortex to provide the perception of depth. Stereoscopic vision, besides adding a depth dimension to visual experience, greatly facilitates the primate's ability to judge the distance of nearby objects.

Behavioral Comparisons

Comparing the visual mechanisms of animals at various levels of evolution gives us a basis for making inferences about the evolution of vision. However, such inferences need support from behavioral studies. The white rat, for example, has both rods and cone-like structures, yet most of the evidence from discrimination experiments suggests that the rat is color blind. Experiments on vision in birds reveal that their visual acuity and distance perception are better than our own. Such facts could not be known, with any degree of certainty, except from the results of discrimination experiments.

Brightness vision exists to some degree in all animals except those without functional eyes, such as some dwellers of caves and the ocean depths.[6] Brightness sensitivity ranges all the way from differential response to light and shadow, as in unicellular organisms, to man's ability to discriminate minute differences in brightness.

Response to movement is also evident in all seeing animals. Visual sensitivity to movement is especially keen in some animals, like the frog, whose prey is relatively safe until it moves.

The presence of color vision in an animal is difficult to assess because colors normally vary in brightness as well as hue. Many investigators make the mistake of testing animals for color vision without equating the test colors for brightness. Behavioral differentiation under such conditions could well be based on the more primitive brightness discrimination rather than on color vision. Color-blind human beings often can distinguish red and green, for example, except when the colors have the same brightness value for the human eye.

When brightness differences are controlled, there is no evidence of color vision in animals below the level of the arthropods; the color vision of the bee, an arthropod, has already been mentioned. Some fish apparently respond to differences in wavelength, but it is possible that the brightness aspect was not adequately controlled. The evidence for color vision in amphibians and reptiles is also poor, again because it is probably contaminated by brightness differences. Birds have exceptionally good color vision, perhaps as good as our own. They discriminate a wide range of hues, even when these are equated for brightness.

Mammals below the primate level show little or no evidence of color vision when the brightness factor is adequately controlled. We have already said that rats appear

[6] See Tansley, *Vision in Vertebrates*, pp. 48ff.

to lack color vision. The most carefully controlled experiments designed to reveal whether cats have color vision have failed to disclose any clear evidence of it. Dogs and horses have also been tested for color vision, but the experiments have not yielded conclusive evidence. Primates unquestionably have good color vision, perhaps as good as our own.

Discrimination of visual details (such as vertical versus horizontal stripes, triangles versus circles, and large versus small figures of the same shape) is evident to some degree in the arthropods and in most vertebrates that have been tested. The chief difference noted as the primate level is approached is in the smallness of detail that animals can distinguish. This is a function of their visual acuity and also, possibly, of their ability to *attend* to small differences.

Responsiveness to depth (stereoscopic vision) is evident only in the primates, although monocular distance discrimination is present in a wide range of vertebrates.[7]

THE EVOLUTION OF HEARING

The stimuli for hearing are vibrations transmitted to auditory receptors through a medium such as water or air. But vibratory stimulation also has tactile effects, for example, on the lateral line organs of fish and some amphibians. These structures, although not actually auditory in nature, may be precursors of auditory organs, for their hairs and nerve cells are similar to those found in mammalian ears.

Some of the lower marine animals, including mollusks, have organs known as *statocysts*, small hair-lined cavities containing one or more solid particles, or *statoliths*. As the animal's body orientation changes, the statoliths press against the hairs, setting up nerve impulses which signal the position of the body. Statocysts have no auditory function;

[7] The evidence on which these conclusions about animal sensitivity are based is summarized, with references, in the writer's *The Evolution and Growth of Human Behavior* (2nd ed.). Other summaries may be found in Tansley's *Vision in Vertebrates,* and in a chapter by Eckhard Hess in Rolland Waters, Dorothy Rethlingshafer, and Willard Caldwell, *Principles of Comparative Psychology,* McGraw-Hill, 1960.

they are simplified versions of the equilibratory receptors of higher organisms, such as those of the semicircular canals, a nonauditory structure found in the ear.

Auditory Mechanisms

Although some insects have eardrums, in other respects their auditory organs are very different from those of vertebrates. Fishes and amphibians also have eardrums which, like our own, respond to pressure variations produced by vibratory stimuli.

In the evolution from fish to man it is possible to trace the gradual emergence of a typically mammalian ear structure. In addition to their lateral line organs, which mediate variations in tactile vibratory stimuli, fishes and amphibians have ears located in the head. Their inner ear, including its equilibratory organs, is basically similar to that of birds and mammals.

The bones of the middle ear, which carry vibrations from the eardrum to the inner ear, are foreshadowed in the bony structure of the fish ear. In fish, as shown in our illustration (p. 91), there is a bone, the *hyomandibular,* in close proximity to the auditory receptors. This bone has no auditory function, yet as the ears of higher vertebrates evolved, it became transformed into the *stapes* of the mammalian ear. The other two bones of the mammalian middle ear, the *malleus* and *incus,* also evolved from nonauditory structures, the *quadrate* and *articular* bones of the upper and lower jaws of amphibia and reptiles. The three auditory ossicles of the mammalian ear thus evolved from structures which originally had different functions.

The *cochlea* of the mammalian ear, to which the auditory ossicles convey vibrations from the eardrum, is clearly an elaboration of the *lagena* of the bird's inner ear. As the mammalian ear evolved, this structure became elongated and formed a snail-like coil with three liquid-filled canals (see illustration, p. 91). The stirrup exerts vibratory pressure against the *oval window* at the end of the *vestibular canal.* This pressure is transmitted through the liquid of the vestibular and then the *tympanic canal* and is compensated for at the

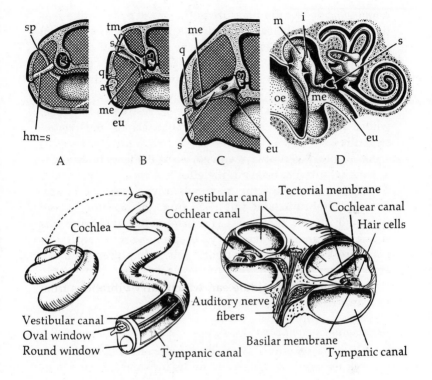

*Stages in the evolution of the ear apparatus. "A. In the fish,
the ear structure consists only of the deep-lying sacs and semicircular canals. B. Amphibian. The hyomandibular bone
(hm) of the fish is now a sound transmitter, the stapes (s);
the first gill slit, the spiracle (sp), becomes the Eustachian tube
(eu) and the middle-ear cavity (me), while the outer end of
the spiracle is closed by the tympanic membrane (tm). C. A
mammal-like reptile. The stapes passes close to two skull
bones (q, quadrate; a, auricular) which form the jaw joint.
D. Man (the ear region only, on a larger scale). The two jaw-
joint bones have been pressed into service as accessory ossicles,
the malleus (m) and the incus (i); oe, tube of outer ear." The
curved structure at the lower right is the cochlea. It is shown
in more detail in the three views below—coiled, partially
extended, and in cross-section.*

round window. As the pressure is transmitted, wavelike motion is set up in the *basilar membrane.* Hair cells coming from a structure on the basilar membrane known as the *organ of Corti* project into the *cochlear canal.* As these hair cells move in the liquid, impulses are triggered in the fibers which come together to form the cochlear branch of the *auditory nerve.* (The vestibular branch of this nerve serves the static sense, whose receptors are in the semicircular canals and related structures.)

As auditory receptors evolved, so did the neural mechanisms required to transmit the effects of sound waves to the brain. Animals below the mammalian level have no clearly defined cerebrum, and impulses from the auditory nerve terminate in the thalamus. The mammalian cerebrum has specialized areas for auditory reception—areas which, in man, are located in the temporal lobes. Impulses from the auditory nerve are conveyed to these areas via the thalamus. Each ear has such connections with each side of the brain— in man, with each cerebral hemisphere.

Behavioral Comparisons

It is difficult to know at what level in the animal world hearing begins, partly because vibrations in water, air, and surfaces of contact may produce tactile as well as auditory stimulation. This makes the study of auditory sensitivity in all water-living animals especially difficult.

There is no doubt about the existence of auditory sensitivity in insects. Many of these, with a wide variety of eardrums and associated structures, both produce and respond to sounds. Some, like the noctuid moth and katydid, are known to have a wider range of sensitivity than man. The katydid's auditory organ responds to frequencies as high as 45,000 cycles per second, whereas 20,000 cycles per second is our upper limit. In the noctuid moth and some grasshoppers the upper range of hearing is estimated to be about 90,000 cycles.[8]

[8] Some interesting experimental studies of the auditory processes in moths appear in Kenneth D. Roeder, *Nerve Cells and Insect Behavior,* Harvard University Press, 1963.

There is no evidence that any invertebrate, other than a few insects, is able to hear. Even some of the vertebrates, with the beginnings of an ear like our own, show no evidence of hearing. Many fish, however, have an air bladder which can both make and respond to vibrations. The vibrations picked up by the air bladder are carried by bone linkages to the inner ear, which, as previously illustrated, has labyrinthine static and auditory mechanisms somewhat similar to our own. Minnows discriminate auditory stimuli. Such discrimination is clearly auditory, for it fails after the auditory mechanisms of the inner ear are removed, while equilibrium is not disturbed by this loss. We now know from many investigations that the oceans are full of sounds produced by their inhabitants. It is possible, although not clearly established, that fish respond to such sounds—that the sounds have communicative significance for them.

Little is known about hearing in amphibians, although the frog has evidenced ability to respond to frequencies ranging from 50 to 10,000 cycles per second. As everybody knows, frogs also make and respond to sounds in chorus.

Some reptiles, including snakes, do not respond to airborne vibrations, although they may respond to vibrations transmitted through the ground. This could be a responsiveness to tactile rather than auditory stimuli. Other reptiles, such as alligators, crocodiles, and some lizards, have an elaborate ear which should enable them to register auditory stimuli. According to data summarized by Eckhard Hess, these have an auditory organ which "has evolved considerably beyond the attainment of the amphibians. The crocodile and alligator have a fold of skin above the ear opening which could be called a rudiment of an external ear. In the alligator, at least, the lagena has undergone a change to form three ducts of the inner ear and the basilar membrane . . . the columella has also changed and is now formed of two bones."[9] Hess also says that the breathing of these animals is influenced by sound and that, in the case of lizards, hearing is undoubtedly present.

[9] In Waters, Rethlingshafer, and Caldwell, *Principles of Comparative Psychology*, pp. 92–93.

The anatomy of the bird's ear, together with naturalistic and experimental findings, give ample evidence of auditory sensitivity. Electrical responses initiated by the pigeon's cochlea suggest that this structure responds to frequencies ranging from 100 to 10,000 cycles per second. It is well known that bird songs cover a wide range of pitch, that one bird can mimic another, and that birds communicate by sound.

All mammals apparently have good hearing, and experiments with rats, dogs, and bats show that the upper limit of their frequency range is far above our own. In rats and dogs this limit is 35,000 to 40,000 cycles. Bats have an upper limit of at least 90,000 cycles, and they make and respond to such high-pitched cries in avoiding obstacles which echo them— a phenomenon known as *echolocation*. This also occurs in dolphins.

Experiments with some lower mammals show that in addition to responding to tonal stimuli, they discriminate tones of different frequency when these are equated for loudness. Rats, for example, have discriminated tones differing by 1000 cycles. Dogs tested in conditioned response experiments have discriminated differences as small as one tone apart on the musical scale. Monkeys have an auditory sensitivity range much like our own, and there is evidence that chimpanzees have even better hearing, with an upper limit above 30,000 cycles. It is doubtful, however, whether any animal discriminates differences in pitch as small as those distinguished by man.

While emphasizing response to auditory frequencies we have made no mention of noise, the type of sound made up of aperiodic vibrations. There is every reason to suppose that response to noise is more primitive than that to tone. It is found in all animals with any hearing at all. The sounds made by fishes, which are believed by some investigators to have communicative significance, are often no more than scraping, clicking, and bumping sounds without the periodicity of tones.

Ability to locate sources of sound is important for various reasons. Sound localization helps many animals to find food and escape from predatory animals. It is quite often helpful in finding the young, or a mate. Animals with high auditory sensitivity, such as the bat and the dolphin, often exhibit quite accurate sound localization. Those with two bilaterally placed ears are aided in their sound localization by the differential stimulation of the ears. Except when sound stimulation comes from objects equidistant from the ears, one ear is stimulated earlier, more intensely, and in a different phase of the sound wave cycle than the other. These differences can be used in perceiving the direction from which the sound comes. Changes in distance are signaled by variations in the loudness and complexity of sounds. Head movements, as well as movements of the ears in some animals, also facilitate sound localization.

EVOLUTION OF THE CHEMICAL SENSES

All animals have a *common chemical sense,* which comes from the irritability of the body surface to certain chemicals, particularly the noxious ones. This aspect of chemoreception is found throughout the animal kingdom, even at the human level. The arthropods and the vertebrates exhibit, in addition, two specialized forms of chemoreception, taste (*gustation*) and smell (*olfaction.*)

Taste

The sense of taste in vertebrates is a specialized response to chemical substances in solution. Fish have taste receptors in other parts of the body as well as the mouth. The barbels of catfish, for example, are taste receptors. To arouse taste sensitivity in the mouth, chemical solutions must come into contact with taste buds, most of which are on the surface of the tongue, where they are grouped together in small elevations, or papillae. Each taste bud has several cells from which nerve fibers go to join a nerve carrying impulses of gustatory origin to the brain.

Smell

Smell is a specialized response to odorous chemicals. In insects and in air-living vertebrates, olfactory stimuli are brought to the receptors in gaseous form, via air currents, and it is relatively easy to study taste and smell independently. However, receptors for taste and smell, and their neural connections with the brain, are so different that it has been possible, even in fish, to differentiate the two senses by observing the effects on behavior of removing the taste or smell receptors, or cutting their nerve fibers.

The olfactory receptors of vertebrates are hair-like processes whose cilia project from the olfactory bulbs of the brain into the epithelium at the top of the nasal cavities. There is thus a direct connection between the olfactory receptors and the brain. In vertebrates from fish to man the olfactory bulbs are clearly defined, and their destruction, in the laboratory or through disease, is followed by anosmia—loss of olfactory sensitivity.

The olfactory bulbs comprise a very large proportion of the brain of lower vertebrates—so large, in fact, that these animals are said to possess predominantly a *smell brain.* This is sometimes also referred to as the *old brain,* upon which the cerebral hemispheres (the *new brain*) evolved. The predominance of olfactory brain mechanisms in lower vertebrates perhaps indicates the importance of smell for these animals—in locating and selecting food, in sensing the presence of other animals, and in courtship and mating. Lower mammals, like the rat, also have a large smell brain. At higher mammalian levels, however, smell and the smell brain decrease in importance relative to the other senses and their brain mechanisms.

Behavioral Comparisons

Naturalistic and experimental investigations of chemoreception in insects show that this sense is highly developed and of extreme importance to many of them. Most insects have antennae which are "almost unbelievably sensitive to airborne chemicals."[10] This sensitivity corresponds to the vertebrates' olfactory sense. There are also "contact chemo-

[10] James Case, *Sensory Mechanisms,* Macmillan, 1966, p. 67.

receptors" which detect odorous substances. This is somewhat analogous to the gustatory sense in vertebrates.

Many insects, for example ants, excrete alarm substances which have communicative significance for others. They sense the presence of strangers chemically, and they lay trails which others follow. The use of a chemical signaling system is observed in many insects, and the signals are called *pheromones*, from the Greek *pherein* (to carry) and *hormone* (to excite). The chemical substances involved are "secreted by an animal to the outside and cause a specific reaction in a receiving individual of the same species."[11]

The senses of taste and smell are well developed in all vertebrates studied experimentally. Some investigations show that fish distinguish other species and each other on the basis of smell, and there is evidence that minnows "discriminate phenol compounds about twenty times more accurately than can man."[12] Mammals have good olfactory sensitivity and possibly good taste sensitivity as well, although not much research has been done on the latter sense. There is no doubt that rats have a good sense of smell. This has been shown by numerous studies of olfactory discrimination.[13] The acute olfactory sensitivity of dogs, including their ability to follow olfactory trails, is well known. A great deal is also known about olfactory sensitivity in other domestic mammals, including cats, cattle, sheep, and horses, all of which in their sexual behavior react to olfactory stimulation.[14] Naturalistic observation and a few experimental studies based on the response of gustatory nerves to sweet,

[11] From Peter R. Marler and William J. Hamilton III, *Mechanisms of Animal Behavior*, Wiley, 1966, p. 293. This book is a good source of more detailed information on all aspects of sensory functions in a wide variety of organisms.

[12] Eckhard H. Hess, in Waters, Rethlingshafer, and Caldwell, *Principles of Comparative Psychology*, p. 96.

[13] See the writer's *Handbook of Psychological Research on the Rat*, Houghton Mifflin, 1950, pp. 168–174.

[14] A good source of information on this is E. S. E. Hafez (Ed.), *The Behavior of Domestic Animals*, London: Baillière, Tindall & Cassell, 1962.

sour, and salty substances leave no doubt that all mammals have a sense of taste and that this plays an important part in selection and rejection of foodstuffs.

THE OTHER SENSES

Vision, hearing, and the chemical senses are the ones most obviously involved in the adaptations of animals, and they are of peculiar importance because they enable organisms to respond to objects at a distance from the body—that is, they are *distance receptors.* But there are other senses specialized for body contacts and for feedback involving the moving parts of the body and movements of the body as a whole.

The senses based on body contacts are those which underlie responses to noxious stimuli (such as cuts and electrical currents) and the experience of pain, body contacts such as light or heavy pressure, and variations in temperature. Together, these are known as the *cutaneous,* or skin, senses.

All vertebrates and most of the lower organisms have receptors specialized for noxious stimuli, although very intense stimulation of any kind of receptor will arouse withdrawal reactions that suggest pain. Other forms of cutaneous sensitivity, including response to temperature changes, are evident in most animals. Experiments have shown that some of the lower mammals, including rats and squirrels, discriminate relatively small differences in temperature. Nest-building in rats, and possibly in many other mammals, is controlled to some degree by changes in temperature.

The body senses involved in feedback are called *proprioceptive* (meaning self-stimulating) because the organism's own activities provide the stimulation. One of these, *kinesthesis,* depends upon pressure applied to receptors in the muscles, tendons, and joints during movement of a limb, for example. Resulting nerve impulses are transmitted to centers in the spinal cord and brain. These impulses convey information about the limb's position at the time, and they automatically arouse return impulses which control its next movement. Thus, activities such as crawling, flying, walking, and reaching for objects may be coordinated automatically, with or without awareness. Kinesthetic sensitivity is certainly present to some extent in all animals that move around in and manipulate aspects of their environment by using appendages. This would include all of the vertebrates and most of the invertebrates.

The other proprioceptive process, the *static sense,* or *sense of equilibrium,* was touched on in our discussion of the structures of the ear. There we mentioned the statocyst, a primitive mechanism which informs the animal of its position in space, and the semicircular canals which later evolved to mediate this sense. Static sensitivity is evident to some degree in all animals with a statocyst or comparable organ of equilibrium. The antigravity reactions of snails, the ability of a crab to right itself, and the ability of a cat to land on all fours when dropped from any position are all examples of body control through static sensitivity and related feedback. The cat, like ourselves, has an elaborate static receptor consisting of the three *semicircular canals* and an associated structure referred to as the *vestibule,* which may be a more direct carry-over of the statocyst.

The semicircular canals have hair-like projections which are moved by changes in the liquid of the canals which surrounds them. Their movements initiate nerve impulses which travel to the thalamus and the cerebellum, the part of the brain particularly concerned with the integration of body movements. The three semicircular canals are especially sensitive to rotary movement—as in turning around, doing cartwheels, or performing front or back somersaults. The vestibule, on the other hand, is specialized for rectilinear motion—as in going up and down, forward and backward, right and left. It contains hairs weighted with calcium particles (*otoliths*) which bend with changes in motion; as the hairs bend, they set up nerve impulses which initiate behavioral responses that will aid in maintaining balance.

The inner structures of the body—such as the throat, stomach, bladder, and intestines—have receptors which, in human beings, underlie experiences such as thirst, hunger, and abdominal cramps. Sexual arousal is believed to have a similar basis. Experience arising from such internal receptors is referred to, in general, as the *organic sense*. The evolution of the receptors involved in such experiences has not been studied sufficiently to warrant more than this passing reference. As we said in Chapter One, there is no way of knowing what animals experience, so nothing can be said about their organic sensitivity from that standpoint. However, there are also behavioral manifestations of organic sensitivity, usually studied within the context of physiological drives, or motives. Such sensitivity is assumed to play a role in initiating drinking, eating, and mating activities, for example. Viewed in this way, organic sensitivity must exist, in some form, throughout the animal kingdom. From the lower vertebrates up there is certainly a great deal of similarity in internal organs and, presumably, in their receptor mechanisms. Among the mammals we observe still greater similarity, not only in their internal organs, but also in physiological drives and modes of expression—that is, in the ways such activities as elimination, drinking, eating, and mating occur.

MOTOR EVOLUTION

Some degree of motility is present in all animals. In the amoeba and some other relatively simple organisms motility is unspecialized—any part of the body can move. Later, we observe animals whose cilia and whiplike organs propel them through water, for example, the paramecium and euglena (illustrated, p. 101). Some marine organisms have tentacles, sometimes with suckers, as in the octopus. Squids move by jet propulsion, by squirting water. Crustaceans have legs, for walking and grasping, and also other movable parts. The lobster's tail, for instance, helps to propel it through the water. Insects have wings and legs. Fins, wings, legs, and arms are the most common motor organs of vertebrates, although some (e.g., the elephant) have a trunk and others (e.g., the monkeys) a prehensile tail.

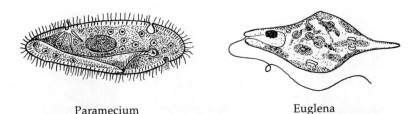

Paramecium   Euglena

By taking to the trees, man's primate ancestors started a process which led, over many millions of years, to the specialization of hands for activities that are almost exclusively prehensile, such as grasping and manipulating objects. Our arboreal ancestors used their hands in swinging from tree to tree and from limb to limb, as well as in grasping, manipulating, scratching, picking, slapping, and perhaps even throwing.

For reasons unknown to us, some primates left the trees and assumed an upright posture; thus, their hands were freed from locomotor duties. One outcome of this was that man is the only organism whose hands are not needed for locomotion. Another is that the thumb evolved so that it could be actively opposed to the rest of the hand.[15] As the illustration (p. 102) suggests, an ape's thumb is relatively small and plays largely a passive role in grasping and other prehensile activities. Man's thumb, by contrast, is relatively large, and it can be moved in opposition to the palm and to each of the fingers separately. Human beings can, of course, also manipulate objects with their feet and mouths. They can even do this with great skill if deprived of their hands. Freeing the mouth from manipulative needs beyond those

[15] Strangely enough, the American opossum's hindfoot is somewhat like a human hand. Dr. C. G. Hartman says, "The similarity to the human hand is heightened by the opposability of the great toe or 'thumb' . . . with its tip the animal can touch the tips of the other digits. Only man and the apes —and opossums—have opposable first digits." From *Opossums*, University of Texas Press, 1952, p. 40. On page 34 of Hartman's book there is a picture showing the remarkable similarity between the opossum's great toe and a human thumb.

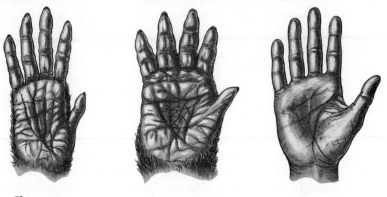

Chimpanzee   Gorilla   Man

The hands of chimpanzee, gorilla, and man. Note that the ape's thumb is relatively small. For the most part it is a passive structure, seldom used alone or in opposition to the fingers. Man's thumb, by contrast, is capable of active movement in opposition to the hand as a whole and to each finger separately.

of eating was perhaps another result of the specialization of the hands for manipulation and grasping.[16]

The evolution of the human hand, and a nervous system competent to initiate, control, and integrate the activities of which it is capable, had a significance for human life that could hardly be exaggerated, for it was the beginning of almost everything that makes man different from other animals. It led to the ability to make and control fire, to make and use tools and weapons, and to pass on the fruits of experience to others through written records.

Spoken language is no doubt also a result, in part at least, of the freeing of the hands and mouth from such activities as fighting, tearing things apart, and moving them from place

[16] The word *manipulate* is usually defined as "to move things with the hands," since it is derived from the Latin noun *manipulus,* a handful. However, its meaning is often extended, as in this discussion, to represent comparable prehensile activities involving the mouth and feet.

to place. This freeing of the mouth contributed to the emergence of a more delicate and dextrous musculature of the mouth and throat than exists in other primates. More will be said about this in later discussions.

It is obvious, then, that civilization itself, in both its good and evil aspects, is an outcome of the evolution of the hand and the brain that controls it, neither of which would be effective without the other.

THE EVOLUTION OF NERVOUS SYSTEMS

The brief description of the human nervous system presented in the first chapter provided some basic information about neural aspects of human mental life. Here we shall consider some antecedents of man's nervous system. The basic specialized function of any nervous system is conduction—transmitting the effects of stimulation to parts of the body capable of responding. In the amoeba there is no specialized conduction. Just as any part is sensitive to stimulation and any part can respond, any part can also conduct. Thus, the effects of any kind of stimulation to which the amoeba responds are diffuse.

ELEMENTARY NERVOUS SYSTEMS

If stimulation of receptors in one part of an organism is to produce particular responses in another part, there must be insulated conduction channels such as nerve fibers. This does not mean, however, that the earliest specialized response mechanisms were neurally activated. In some sponges, for example, cells contract when stimulated directly by mechanical contact. Responses of muscles to direct stimulation by pressure also occur in vertebrate embryos, even before nerve fibers have grown out from the spinal cord to make functional contact with these muscles.

The first neural structure was a fiber going from a receptor to the responding structure, the effector (see illustration, p. 104). This meant the effector could react without direct

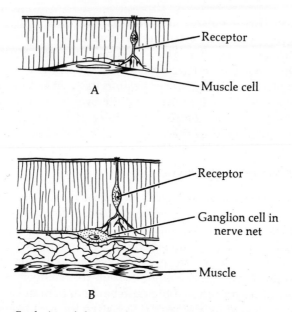

*Evolution of the nervous system. A. Muscle cell
below the surface but connected to it by means of
a receptor. B. Receptor-effector nervous system
found in parts of the sea anemone.*

stimulation—the nerve impulse activated it. One feature of
the evolution of the nervous system is the development of a
less direct, more complicated linkage between receptors and
effectors. In some of the lower organisms the nerve fibers
coming from receptors terminate in a net of fibers (nerve net)
rather than in effectors directly. Thus, the impulses are
spread to various parts of the body more or less simultaneously, and many effectors respond together. The result is a
diffuse response, involving the whole organism rather than
some part of it, as in a reflex.

Reflexes did not appear until a synaptic nervous system
had evolved. In a synaptic nervous system, found in all
vertebrates and in many lower organisms, including worms

and mollusks, there are, as we have seen, many relatively discontinuous units known as neurons. These are anatomically separate structures which make functional contact at synapses, where their impulses may be stopped from going further or may be switched in this direction or that, depending upon their location and functional conditions at the moment.

In all vertebrates there are basically three kinds of neurons —sensory, association, and motor. We considered these in discussing the human nervous system. The reader will recall that sensory neurons convey nerve impulses from the receptors to the spinal cord or brain, where they make synaptic connection with motor neurons directly, or indirectly via association neurons. Direct synaptic connections between sensory and motor neurons are commonly found among invertebrates with a synaptic nervous system. They also occur at the vertebrate level to some extent, even in man. However, the predominant feature of the vertebrate nervous system, especially at higher levels, is an indirect linkage between sensory and motor neurons through synaptic connections with association neurons. Nevertheless, impulses originating in receptors, or elsewhere within the vertebrate nervous system, follow channels that are more or less specific. The result is not a diffuse response such as characterizes animals with a nerve net, but rather responses of parts of the organism, which, when integrated, are attuned to the stimulating circumstances.

CENTRAL MECHANISMS

After neural links between receptors and effectors had appeared, the next important step in the evolving of a human brain was the appearance of central switchboard mechanisms to integrate activities in various parts of the organism. The nerve ring of the starfish, pictured in our illustration (p. 106), is a simple mechanism of this type. It is, in effect, the brain of this animal. Nerve fibers in the five rays send impulses

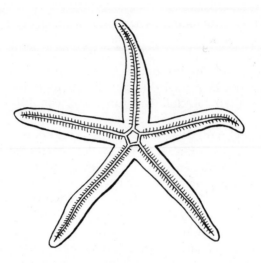

Nervous system of the starfish.

to the ring, where they are integrated so that movements of the body as a whole can be coordinated. Thus, when the starfish is turned on its back, each of the rays plays its proper part in relation to the others and the animal soon rights itself. The importance of the nerve ring becomes apparent when it is cut in two opposite places. Then some rays act in opposition to the others, and the animal is literally torn apart.

The nerve ring of the starfish is only one of the many different kinds of neural organization that exist in the animal world today, all of which have as their basic function the integration of incoming and outgoing nerve impulses in such a way as to serve the adaptive needs of the organism as a whole.

The starfish, with its relatively simple brain, is little more than a reflex machine, albeit a well integrated one. It reacts only in terms of present stimulation. What it does is determined by built-in mechanisms of reception and response which are triggered, as it were, by stimulation. There is no clear evidence that the animal stores information and acts in terms of this as well as the immediate stimulating conditions.[17]

Brains of greater complexity than the nerve ring do store information and use it. Worms have a sufficiently complex brain to mediate simple learning, such as avoiding a roughened pathway that leads to electric shock.[18] The octopus, an animal whose brain and behavior have been studied in great detail, exhibits a still higher order of complexity. It learns to discriminate between various visual and tactile stimuli when one stimulus is followed by food and the other by an electric shock, and it learns to move a lever to release a piece of food.[19] It has been said that "*Octopus* has a nervous system that does many of the things that our own does—the animal learns readily, to mention just one aspect of nervous organization that we should like to know about—but it is a great deal less complicated. The octopus collects much the same sort of information about the world as we can ourselves, but it apparently makes different and far more limited use of this information."[20] It has been demonstrated, moreover, that octopuses have a dual memory system analogous to that of human beings—a "representation, in neural terms, of the learned situation" and "a mechanism that enables that representation to persist."[21] The neural mechanisms of the octopus which underlie its short-term and its relatively long-

[17] There is some evidence of learning in the starfish, but it has been questioned by Norman R. F. Maier and Theodore C. Schneirla in *Principles of Animal Psychology,* McGraw-Hill, 1935.

[18] See the studies by Robert M. Yerkes and others, reviewed in the writer's *The Evolution and Growth of Human Behavior* (2nd ed.).

[19] The discrimination studies are reviewed by M. J. Wells, "What the Octopus Makes of It: Our World from Another Point of View," *American Scientist,* 1961, Vol. 49, pp. 215–227. On lever movement, see P. B. Dews, "Some Observations on an Operant in the Octopus," *Journal for the Experimental Analysis of Behavior,* 1959, Vol. 2, pp. 57–64.

[20] M. J. Wells, "What the Octopus Makes of It," p. 227.

[21] Brian B. Boycott, "Learning in the Octopus," *Scientific American,* 1965, Vol. 212, pp. 42–50 (quotation from p. 44).

term memory have received intensive investigation by Boycott and others.[22]

The brains of vertebrates evolved independently of the brains of mollusks such as the octopus—one of many instances where different kinds of brains evolved independently to perform similar functions.

THE BRAIN FROM FISH TO MAN

From fish to man there has been an increasing elaboration of the parts of the brain concerned with what might be called *higher-level integration*—information storage and integration based on this (see illustration, p. 109). The spinal cord has not changed a great deal except to become relatively smaller than the brain. In the frog it is even larger than the brain. The cord's primary function is to provide a channel for incoming and outgoing impulses and to mediate simpler integrations. Integration at higher levels of complexity—the sort of integration mediated by acquired information, insight, and reasoning processes—depended upon an increase in the size and complexity of the brain beyond that required for sheer sensorimotor functioning.

The weight of the brain is far greater than the weight of the spinal cord in animals which have the capacity for such higher-level integration. An ape's brain is 15 times as heavy as its spinal cord, and man's brain is 55 times as heavy as his spinal cord. Generally speaking, as bodies have grown larger, the brain weight also has increased.[23] One might expect this because a larger body has more sensorimotor mechanisms to be controlled by its brain. Thus, a large brain is not neces-

[22] See Boycott, above, and J. Z. Young, *A Model of the Brain,* Oxford University Press, 1964.

[23] The dinosaurs were exceptions to this trend. Diplodocus, weighing an estimated 40 tons, had a brain no larger than a man's fist, one of several possible reasons for its possession of a sacral enlargement which may have housed a nerve center about twenty times as large as its brain proper. The nature and function of this enlargement are controversial. See, for example, L. Sprague de Camp and Catherine Crook de Camp, *The Day of the Dinosaur,* Doubleday, 1968, pp. 139–140.

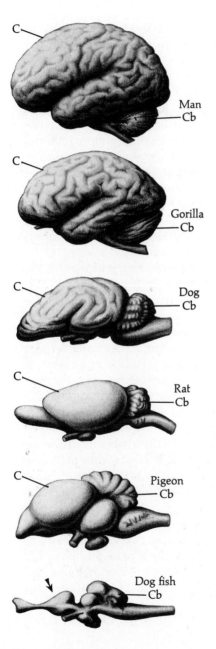

The brain from fish to man. Brains are drawn the same length to show adequate detail in smaller ones. Relative sizes are shown by approximate weights, in grams: man, 1500; gorilla, 400; dog, 130; rat, 2; pigeon, 2.2; and dogfish, 3. The cerebrum (C) not only grows heavier, it also enlarges in proportion to body weight. The dogfish has no cerebrum (arrow shows comparable structure). The gorilla, much heavier than man, has only about one-fourth the human brain weight. Note invaginations shown in the dog's brain; these are more pronounced in the gorilla and human brains. The smell brain, prominent at the left of the three lower brains, recedes in higher brains. Cb is the cerebellum. Note its prominence in the pigeon, which exhibits behavior notable for its complex coordinations. In the pigeon the optic thalamus is seen below the cerebellum.

sarily indicative of advanced mental ability. The elephant's 10-pound brain, more than three times larger than man's, is chiefly concerned with controlling the animal's bulk. One might say the same for the whale's 14-pound brain. (See illustration, p. 111.) In terms of brain weight/body weight ratios, the average human being has about one pound of brain to each 50 pounds of body weight. Comparable ratios for the elephant and the whale are, respectively, 1 to 500 and 1 to 10,000. Even the gorilla has only about one pound of brain to 250 pounds of body weight.

Vertebrate brains have a somewhat comparable pattern. Each is an elaboration of the head end of the spinal cord, and each receives stimulation from the ascending pathways of the cord and from those cranial nerves (olfactory, optic, auditory) which have an input function.

As shown in Chapter One, the ascending pathways of the spinal cord bring information to the cerebrum from receptors in the skin; in the muscles, tendons, and joints; and in the internal organs. The spinal cord merges with the brain stem (medulla, pons, midbrain, hypothalamus, and thalamus). We have observed that the thalamus, sometimes considered a basic cerebral structure rather than part of the brain stem, is a switchboard mechanism which receives sensory information and then relays it to the sensory projection areas of the cerebral cortex. This information comes from ascending fibers of the spinal cord and also from the optic and auditory nerves. Olfactory impulses bypass the thalamus. They go directly from the olfactory bulbs to that relatively primitive part of the cerebrum already referred to as the "smell brain." The reader may recall, from our earlier discussion, that this is part of the limbic system.

Nerve impulses also descend from the cerebral cortex and lower brain structures to the muscles and glands. Some of these, such as those which control the tongue and jaws, are transmitted via cranial nerves. Those which activate the limbs descend the spinal cord and connect synaptically with motor nerves.

It can be seen from our illustration (p. 109) that lower

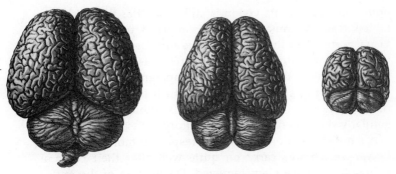

Whale   Elephant   Man

Some large brains. The whale brain weighs 14 pounds, the elephant brain about 10 pounds, and the human brain about 3 pounds.

vertebrates such as the fishes, amphibians, and birds have brains which consist primarily of brain stem, smell brain, optic thalamus, and cerebellum. The cerebrum does not become a prominent feature until the mammalian level is reached. Even in lower mammals like the rat and dog, the cerebrum is still overshadowed by the olfactory bulbs and the "smell brain" in general. When the primate level is reached, the "smell brain" has receded in relative size so much that one must look under the cerebrum to find it.

The cerebral hemispheres are smooth in lower vertebrates and even in lower mammals such as the rat, rabbit, and shrew. In dogs, cats, raccoons, and some others of about this level, the cerebrum has begun to extend its surface by folding inward, or invaginating. This process increases the area of the all-important cerebral cortex, the mantle of "gray matter" which covers the cerebrum. Invagination becomes increasingly evident as the primate level is approached.

Another aspect of cerebral evolution is an increase in the relative size and importance of the sensory projection areas of the cortex. The sensory processes of lower vertebrates are mediated primarily at subcortical levels. A bird's excellent vision, for example, is dependent upon its relatively large optic thalamus, so its vision is still good after the cerebrum is removed. Mammals' vision is more dependent on the visual cortex than that of birds. Rats and dogs have some visual sensitivity after their visual cortex has been destroyed. Human beings, on the other hand, apparently are completely blind following such destruction, which is sometimes incident to removal of brain tumors. Man's auditory sensitivity is similarly dependent upon the auditory cortex.

A similar situation exists with respect to motor functions. Lower vertebrates carry on quite well after their cerebral hemispheres have been removed. Destruction of the motor area of man's cortex is followed by paralysis, although this paralysis can sometimes be partially overcome by special training.

It may be recalled from our earlier discussion of the human brain that the cerebral hemispheres have associative functions, such as interrelating the information conveyed to them by the senses, storing information, and providing the neural basis of such stimulus-response connections as occur in the learning process. Such higher processes as recalling past experiences and reasoning are also associative in nature.

The brains of inframammalian vertebrates have relatively small association areas. They are concerned primarily with sensory reception and motor control, mainly on a reflex or instinctive level. These vertebrates are capable of learning, when suitably motivated, but learning plays a minor role in their adaptation. We shall see in a later discussion that they have no such higher processes as reasoning. From lower to higher mammals, however, associative functions become increasingly important, and there is a correlated enlargement of associative areas.

When the human level is reached, the association areas are larger than the areas given over to sensory and motor functions. This trend is illustrated by our schematic diagrams of the brains of the dog, chimpanzee, and man (p. 113). One will also observe that the frontal lobes of the human cerebral hemispheres are especially large. These are concerned with voluntary motor action and association. The left frontal lobe,

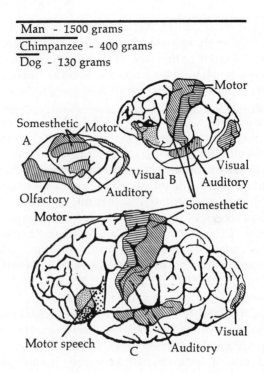

Man - 1500 grams
Chimpanzee - 400 grams
Dog - 130 grams

The left hemispheres of three mammalian brains drawn to scale to show the relative lengths. A more accurate measure of the size relations of these three brains is given by the scales at the top, which indicate the relative weights of entire brains, weighed fresh. A. The brain of a large adult dog. B. The brain of a young adult chimpanzee. C. A human brain somewhat below the average size. The positions of certain primary sensory centers are indicated. In the primate brain the small olfactory centers do not show in this view. The greater part of the visual area is on the inner side of the hemisphere so that it does not appear here. The region which corresponds to the human motor speech area in the chimpanzee (indicated by small dots) is quite uniform in structure as compared to the structurally complex motor speech area of man. (After Campbell, from S. W. Bartelmez, "Man from the Point of View of His Development and Structure," in The Nature of the World and of Man, *University of Chicago Press, 1926.)*

as we mentioned earlier, has an area specialized for motor speech. In the chimpanzee brain there is a motor region which corresponds to this (shown by dots in the illustration), but it has a much simpler structure than the human speech area. This area will be referred to again when the evolution of language is discussed.

The prefrontal region of the frontal lobes—the region in front of the motor areas—appears to play an important role in such symbolic functions as recalling, thinking, and reasoning. These processes are said to be *symbolic* because they represent, or substitute for, aspects of past experience. Thus, a visual image may represent something we have seen, and words may represent (serve as symbols for) any aspect of past experience. Thought processes are symbolic because they involve associations of images, words, or other substitutes for past experience. The prefrontal areas are believed to be of crucial importance for such processes because their destruction in animals is followed, in most instances, by marked impairment of ability on tests of recall and reasoning—tests to be described in the next chapter. However, the reason for this impairment is far from clear. Some investigators have assumed that it indicates the presence, in the prefrontal areas, of "centers" for memory and reasoning. This is hardly justified because there are many indications that the cerebrum functions more or less as a whole in mediating associative functions. Moreover, there is evidence from the animal experiments themselves that good performance on tests of symbolic processes requires close attention to what is going on, together with the ability to ignore distracting influences. Prefrontal destruction might, therefore, lead to poor recall memory and reasoning by making the animal less attentive, or more distractible, than when the prefrontal areas are intact.

In some human beings with brain tumors, the prefrontal regions have been removed without any consistent evidence of intellectual impairment. Cutting the connections to the prefrontal areas from the thalamus, an operation performed quite frequently some years ago to relieve psychotic symptoms, also has no consistent effect on intellectual functions such as those under consideration. The most frequent outcome of such operations is that the individual becomes less anxious, less self-conscious, and less concerned with the future. Professor Stanley Porteus has gathered information, based on his maze test of mental ability, which suggests that such individuals may suffer an impairment of the ability to moderate present actions in terms of anticipated consequences.[24]

It is of course possible that the prefrontal areas, in relation to others also concerned with associative functions, may be of greater importance in the accumulation of information during early life than in adulthood. Once information is accumulated, loss of these areas may not be as serious as it would be early in life.

It is impossible, at the present time, to give a definitive statement on the actual functions of the prefrontal areas. This will have to wait upon the outcomes of further research, of which there is much in progress. That these lobes have associative functions and that they are somehow crucially involved in symbolic processes, there is no doubt, but the particular nature of their involvement in such processes is the question so far unanswered.

This chapter has been concerned mainly with the evolution of structures involved in mental life. In the next chapter we shall consider the evolution of mental life as revealed by studies of behavior.

[24] See Stanley D. Porteus, *Porteus Maze Tests,* Pacific Books, 1965, pp. 30–54.

CHAPTER FOUR

THE RISE OF
ANIMAL INTELLIGENCE

In our earlier discussion of the animal mind we called attention to the role of unlearned behavior (tropistic, reflex, instinctive) in the adaptations of animals to aspects of their environment. Tropisms are especially prevalent in insects, although they are also found in many other animals, even lower mammals such as the rat. All animals with a synaptic nervous system have reflexes. These relatively automatic responses of particular organs play an important part in adjustment, even at the human level. Reflexes may be modified (conditioned). Pavlov and others have made the claim that all learned behavior has, as its base, the conditioning of reflexes. Instinctive behavior, often defined as an unlearned patterning of reflexes, is also evident in all animals having a synaptic nervous system, except possibly the higher primates. The presence of instincts in humans is seriously questioned, because learned behavior (habit) dominates so many aspects of human life.

Unlearned behavior is, for the most part, highly adaptive.

It often suggests the presence of intelligence, and at a level which the animal could not conceivably have reached. But this is "built-in" intelligence, if we can call it intelligence at all, and not an outcome of individual achievement. Moreover, the behavior is more stereotyped than variable, flexible, or versatile. It has evolved in relation to relatively fixed conditions of life, and environmental changes tend to disrupt it. Individually acquired intelligence, on the other hand, is characterized by versatility in adjusting to changed conditions.

Every organism that is not dominated completely by innate modes of response can acquire new responses—that is to say, it is capable of learning. But learning capacity varies a great deal. It is basically dependent upon inheritance, hence it varies from species to species and, within a particular species, from one individual to another. What is learned also depends upon the opportunities provided. Some of the lower animals in whom learning has been demonstrated experimentally may not have learned anything before psychologists so changed their environmental circumstances that they were induced to do so—like the cockroach that learned to avoid darkness when its tropistic light avoidance was followed by an electric shock.

Although there are undoubtedly unlearned aspects of mind (and intelligence), our best evidence of mental evolution comes from the ability of organisms to depart from unlearned modes of adjustment by adopting learned adaptations (in this connection see pp. 37–42).

TESTS OF LEARNING ABILITY

In efforts to compare the learning ability of animals at different levels of evolution, psychologists have devised a large variety of tests. Some of the simpler ones are reversal of a tropism (as in the cockroach), modification of reflexes (as when an animal is conditioned so that light evokes salivation), inducing the animal to press a lever which releases food (as in operant conditioning), training the animal to discriminate (light versus dark, triangle versus circle, and so on), and maze training on paths varying in complexity from a single T or Y unit to a succession of such units with many blind alleys between entrance and exit.

The use of such tests as these has shown that most of the animals tested are capable of learning. It is some of the simpler invertebrates whose learning capacity is in question. The behavior of many of these, even the paramecium, has been modified by experimental procedures designed to test for learning ability, but there is considerable controversy as to whether learning has been demonstrated, or whether the modifications are unlearned reactions to changed environmental conditions.[1] Many vertebrates, representing fishes, amphibia, reptiles, birds, and mammals, have been successful in conditioning, discrimination, and maze learning tests. Generally speaking, there is more rapid learning (fewer trials and less time required) as we go from lower vertebrates to mammals. In discrimination learning and maze tests there are also fewer errors. Moreover, the complexity of what can be learned increases as the mammalian level is approached.

From lower mammals like the rat up to man we find that discrimination problems and mazes do not make very good tests of intelligence. They involve such elementary aspects of learning that they do not sufficiently differentiate between the more and less intelligent animals. In maze learning, for example, all the animal must do is make the proper turn, in response to the proper stimuli, at the proper time, and in the proper sequence. The reader may be surprised to learn that white rats can even best college students in this sort of learning; in fact, they have done so repeatedly. We know that college students are more intelligent than rats, so we are forced to conclude that while mazes are good tests of sheer modifiability, there is much about mental capacity that they do not reveal.

<hr>

[1] See the writer's *The Evolution and Growth of Human Behavior* (2nd ed.), Houghton Mifflin, 1965, pp. 131–137; W. N. Kellogg, "Worms, Dogs, and Paramecia," *Science*, 1958, Vol. 127, p. 166; and M. S. Katz and W. A. Deterline, "Apparent Learning in the Paramecium," *Journal of Comparative and Physiological Psychology*, 1958, Vol. 51, pp. 243–248.

SYMBOLIC PROCESSES

With the coming of mammals something beyond sheer ability to be modified and to make adjustments is added to mental life. This has already been referred to as the *symbolic process*, a process enabling organisms to recall something previously experienced but now absent. The ability to learn is a necessary antecedent, as is the ability to retain what has been learned.

A symbol is something which represents or can serve as a substitute for an object, a situation, or an event. Such an association between a symbol and what it symbolizes must be learned, as when the child learns that such and such an object is a *cat*. Human beings learn to associate images and gestures, as well as words, with particular experiences. Then they use these substitutes to recall (or think of) the experiences after they have passed. Thus, a man may recall the wife he left at home, the women he might have married, or anything else that he has experienced. This ability to acquire symbols which represent past experience is the basis of all higher mental processes. Its emergence was a great forward leap in mental evolution.

The Delayed Reaction

Rudimentary aspects of the ability to recall past experiences are revealed in the so-called *delayed reaction test*. What we find out in a delayed reaction test is whether the animal can respond *to*, or *in terms of*, something that has been present but which is now gone. If it does respond in terms of absent stimuli, we must assume that something within it, perhaps some modification of its brain, *represents* the absent stimulus. A necessary precaution in such experiments is to make certain that no present stimulus is guiding its response, for response to stimuli present at the time of response is not only easy for most animals but also no evidence that a symbolic process is involved.

In one test of delayed reaction the animal is placed in a restraining cage made of wire mesh. Facing this are three identical exit doors, each with its own electric grid and light

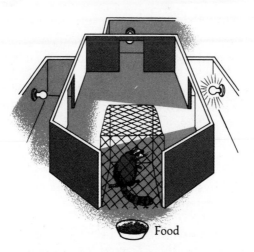

Hunter's delayed reaction apparatus. This particular form of the apparatus was used with raccoons. See text for further explanation.

bulb, as illustrated above. In each test, only one bulb is lit. The light may appear in any one of the three positions, its location on a particular trial being determined by chance, so that the light, and not the position in which it appears, will be associated with the correct exit. The animal responds when the restraining door is lifted. What it must learn initially is that going to the light gives access to food, while responding to the unlighted exits is followed by an electric shock. After the lighted exit has been selected consistently for a time, a series of delayed-reaction trials is given.

So far we have considered only the situation in which the light was lit at the time of the animal's release and it thus served as an external cue telling the animal where to go. In delayed reaction tests, however, the light is turned on for a moment, then off, and it is off at the moment of release. What we want to know at this point is whether the animal remembers where the light was.

When tested in this way, a rat goes to the correct exit so

long as it can point its head toward it while waiting for release and then follow its nose. This could mean that the stimuli guiding the response are muscular—that muscle tensions rather than symbolic processes are bridging the interval from the time the light goes off until release occurs. The animal could therefore be responding to stimuli (muscular cues) present at the time of response even though the light itself is off. Such cues may be broken up by turning the animal around before releasing it. In the case of the rat, this is followed by no better than chance accuracy, so we are forced to conclude that, in this test, the animal has failed to demonstrate the presence of a symbolic process.

The raccoon, comparatively a very wise animal, has passed the same test with flying colors, with delays of up to 25 seconds. Instead of pointing, a raccoon spends the delay interval pacing back and forth. Upon release it goes directly to the exit where the light was. Something other than muscle tension, something in the raccoon's nervous system which represents the absent light, must bridge the interval. But it cannot do so for longer than 25 seconds. Intervals longer than this are followed by chance accuracy.

Although rats have failed this delayed reaction test, they have been successful on somewhat simpler tests involving the same principle. In a delayed alternation test, for example, the basic problem is to turn to the right or left after emerging from a central alley of a T-shaped box in a sequence such as *right, left, right, left,* and so on. If a delay is introduced after each turn, for how long an interval can the animal remember the preceding turn? Rats have responded correctly in this type of situation with delays as long as 10–15 seconds.

Many other tests of delayed reaction have also been used with rats, dogs, cats, and raccoons as well as primates. Rats, cats, and dogs have, in some types of delayed reaction tests, delayed successfully for several minutes, but the methods of testing them have differed so much that there is no basis for comparing their performances.

Below the mammalian level there is no good evidence of

the type of memory involved in delayed reaction tests. The octopus has failed such tests. One experiment with minnows seemed to show evidence of delayed reaction, but a repetition of the experiment, in which additional controls were introduced, yielded negative results. Naturalists sometimes observe what appears to be delayed response in animals, but the absence of experimental controls makes it difficult to know whether the response is truly symbolic or whether the animal is reacting to stimuli not evident to the observer.

Monkeys and chimpanzees do exceptionally well on tests of delayed reaction. Moreover, they can be tested more directly, without preliminary training (see illustration, p. 123). The animal sits in its cage. In front of it are two cups which look and smell alike, one to the right, the other to the left. After getting the animal's attention, we slip a piece of food under one cup, then introduce a screen which hides the cups during the delay interval. During this interval, the animal may sit in its cage, sleep, or be taken for a walk. Later the screen is removed and the animal is released. If the monkey selects the correct cup, it gets to eat the food. Selection of the incorrect cup is unrewarded. From trial to trial the baited cup varies in right-left position according to a chance sequence. Since the cups look alike, since both are smeared with the same food so as to smell alike, and since they vary in random sequence from right to left, there is no external cue to guide the animal. In order to respond correctly, it must remember where it saw the food placed. Monkeys remember correctly for intervals up to 24 hours. In a slightly different situation, chimpanzees have remembered for as long as 48 hours.

The problem is sometimes complicated by using several pairs of cups. After seeing the food placed under one cup of each pair, a monkey goes from one pair to the next, selecting the correct cup in each. When monkeys and chimpanzees are compared on this test, the chimpanzees come out way ahead. They remember more pairs than the monkeys, and they remember them after longer intervals.

What is perhaps more interesting than the fact that a

A direct test of delayed reaction. The monkey sees the food placed, then a screen cuts off its view until the test. Several cups may be used. From "The Evolution of Mind," N. L. Munn. Copyright © 1957 by Scientific American, Inc. All rights reserved.

monkey or chimpanzee remembers the correct position of the food is the fact that it also remembers *what* was hidden. The monkey takes and eats whatever it saw placed under the cup. But what will happen if we surreptitiously substitute a less preferred food—say, lettuce, after banana has been placed under the cup? When such a substitution is made during the interval, the monkey picks up the correct cup, rejects the lettuce (which is accepted when the animal has seen it placed), and hunts around for the missing banana. Quite often it also has a temper tantrum.

The ability to retain a symbolic representation of past experience is an extremely important step in mental evolution because it prepares the way for understanding and thinking. Once the organism can *think of* an object or event, it can begin to "put two and two together," to solve problems by reasoning instead of by overt trial and error. The difference between a haphazard or trial and error solution and a solution based on understanding, or *insight,* is illustrated by detour problems.

Detour Problems

In a relatively simple detour test the animal is placed behind a wire mesh or glass screen through which it can see food on the other side, as illustrated (p. 125). To reach the food the animal must go around the barrier, which involves turning away from the food at first. A chicken or rat responds directly to the barrier, as if trying to get through it to the food. After this approach fails, there is much random running about. Sometimes the animal runs back and forth along the screen and reaches the food accidentally in the course of such activity. Put back behind the screen, the chicken or rat behaves pretty much as before making direct approaches to the screen. However, it may get to the food a little faster than before by relinquishing some of its inadequate responses. After repeated tests, the animal learns to circumvent the barrier without loss of time and effort.

Contrast this with the behavior of a monkey or a chimpanzee tested in a similar situation. It goes around the barrier to

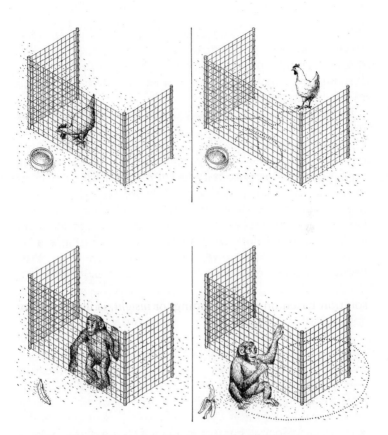

The chicken does not go directly to food behind a wire fence. After trying to reach the food through the fence (upper left), it moves about at random and may accidentally find the food (upper right). A chimpanzee in the same situation will go directly to the food. From "The Evolution of Mind," N. L. Munn. Copyright © 1957 by Scientific American, Inc. All rights reserved.

the food without delay. It can do this because it is not bound by what is physically present but can reconstruct the situation while looking it over and, one may assume, in some way thinking about it. It "puts two and two together" and perceives possible moves. Primates thus learn by observing and thinking about what they observe as well as by acting. They demonstrate what Wolfgang Köhler, the famous Gestalt psychologist, called *insight*.

Consider a detour problem of greater complexity. Professor Köhler put a banana high above a chimpanzee in a cage which also contained possible aids with which to reach this delicacy. These included sticks, boxes, and a hanging rope. The question was: Will the chimpanzee have sufficient insight to make effective use of such objects? Sometimes it does. Chimpanzees have been known to stack boxes, use long sticks somewhat as a pole vaulter does, and to swing on a rope Tarzan fashion. One chimpanzee got the banana by suddenly scrambling up on the Professor's shoulder. Professor Yerkes, who considered chimpanzees almost human, liked to tell about a chimpanzee to whom he presented a problem having, in his opinion, three possible solutions, only to have the animal solve it by a fourth way.

Chimpanzees have been known to join two bamboo poles by poking one into the end of the other to make a stick long enough to reach otherwise inaccessible objects (see illustration, p. 127). They are very fond of ants, and it is not uncommon for those in captivity to lick a piece of straw, put it down until ants swarm over it and get stuck, then lick the ants off. Jane Goodall has observed wild chimpanzees poking sticks into termites' nests, leaving them there for a moment, then drawing them out covered with termites, which are then removed with lips and tongue (see illustration, p. 127).[2] She also reports observations made by others showing that chimpanzees use sticks to get honey out of an underground bees' nest and use a stone to break open the kernel of the palm nut. In their ant-seeking activities, chimpanzees break sticks to make them of suitable length. Here, according to Jane Goodall, are "the first examples of free-ranging non-human primates actually *making* very crude tools."[3]

[2] Jane Goodall, "Chimpanzees of the Gombe Stream Reserve," Chapter 12 in Irven DeVore (Ed.), *Primate Behavior*, Holt, Rinehart and Winston, 1965.

[3] Goodall, "Chimpanzees of the Gombe Stream Reserve," p. 473.

Use of instruments by chimpanzees.

All of these examples involve some form of detour behavior where the animal circumvents the barrier either by locomotion around it or by using instruments of one kind or another. Various mammals, from the rat up, have been credited with some degree of insightful behavior in certain relatively simple situations, but no lower animal has even approached the level of insight and resourcefulness exhibited by the primates.

The Double Alternation Test

Even more convincing proof of symbolic ability in animals is found in problems designed to be impossible of solution except through reasoning. One of these, Walter S. Hunter's double alternation problem, has been used to test a large number of animals ranging from rats to human beings. There are various forms of this test, but the one most widely used is that illustrated (p. 129). Note the T-shaped arrangement of alleys. The subject starts at the foot of the T, goes to the head, and, turning into the right or left arm of the T, returns by a passage to the starting point. In order to earn a reward (and avoid electric shocks for making wrong turns), the animal must go through the run four times, making a right turn at the head of the T the first time around, another right turn on the second trip, a left turn on the third trip, and another left turn on the fourth trip. This *right, right, left, left* sequence of alternations is arbitrarily set.

Under certain circumstances this would be a simple problem which any mammal might solve. We could, for example, have two lights at the choice point, a bright one for right turns and a dim one for left turns. Then the animal would only need to learn the meaning of these signals. We would have a bright, bright, dim, dim sequence, and most animals would soon learn to respond right, right, left, left. In the problem under consideration, however, there are no such lights. Indeed there are no external signs of any kind which could signal the turn to be made. In order to solve this problem the animal has no alternative but to learn the principle involved.

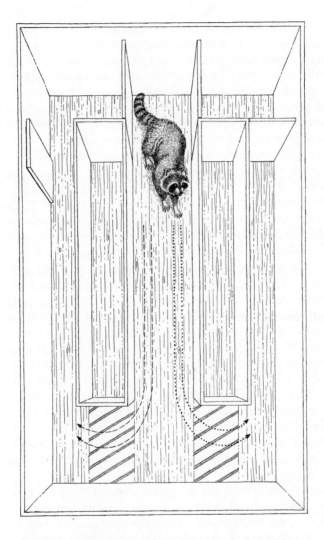

This T-shaped pathway was used to test whether various animals could learn to generalize the relationship RIGHT, RIGHT, LEFT, LEFT, . . . , *thus escaping punishment and getting a food reward. From "The Evolution of Mind," N. L. Munn. Copyright © 1957 by Scientific American, Inc. All rights reserved.*

Note, moreover, that there are no muscle cues which might guide the animal. If the sequence were *right, left, right, left*—single alternation—there might be such cues. Having gone to the right could leave muscle tensions which might serve as stimuli for a left turn. Having gone to the left could provide the cue, similarly, for a right turn. But in the double alternation problem there are no such cues. The *same* muscle tensions precede now a right turn, now a left.

Thus, if an animal is to learn this problem at all, it must *figure it out,* using something to represent the sequence required. Human beings use words, saying something like, "Oh I get it. You go twice to the right and twice to the left." We do not know what symbols are used by animals which solve this problem, but it is inconceivable that they could succeed without using symbols of some kind. We say this because it is necessary to remember the preceding turn, as well as what the sequence calls for, while approaching the choice point.

On this test a rat fails completely, even after 1000 trials spread over several months.[4] Raccoons, on the other hand, solve the problem in 500 to 800 trials, and cats and dogs do about as well. Monkeys and chimpanzees learn this type of problem in about 100 trials. Children under three years of age have failed it, but beyond this age, it is learned with fewer trials in successively older groups of children. The average number of trials required by a group of 38 children ranging in age from three to thirteen was approximately 15. On the same test, 25 college students required an average of 6 trials.

Ability to extend the *rrll* series of turns beyond one cycle is another indication of the level of mastery achieved. After learning the *rrll* sequence, some raccoons extended the series to *rrllrr*. Dogs and cats failed to do this. Monkeys appear to

---

[4] Rats have performed the double alternation when gradually "educated" to it by subsidiary procedures, but they do not succeed on the test described here: On this point, see the writer's *Handbook of Psychological Research on the Rat,* Houghton Mifflin, 1950, pp. 210–212.

have no difficulty extending the series up to at least 8 additional turns, or *rrllrrllrrll*. Human subjects can continue giving the appropriate turns until stopped. They say to themselves, "right, right, left, left, right, right, left, left," and so on.

Language is not essential in learning and extending the double alternation problem. If it were, animals could not learn it. But language certainly helps. As we said earlier, words are excellent substitutes for past experiences. They not only represent experiences, but they also bridge gaps to establish relationships and to formulate principles, such as that of the double alternation problem.

Acquiring Learning Sets

Another widely used test of animal intelligence involves discrimination procedures, but it goes beyond mere discrimination to investigate what Professor Harry Harlow calls *learning sets*. The development of such sets is sometimes so rapid as to suggest that the animal has insight into what is required of it.

The use of discrimination procedures in studying animal sensitivity has already been discussed. Our earlier interest in such procedures was limited to the question of whether or not the animal could discriminate between brightness, colors, figures, odors, or other stimulus pairs. We were not concerned with discrimination learning as such. If we had been, we should have discussed such aspects as trials to learn and the number of errors made prior to mastery. Actually, this would not have led us far, since discrimination learning, like maze learning, does not change significantly as we go from the lower vertebrates to primates. All of these animals learn discrimination problems easily, providing they have the requisite sensory capacity. Thus, discrimination learning in itself is too elementary to serve as a basis for comparing the intelligence levels of different vertebrates.

However, in testing for learning sets we begin with a discrimination problem. This may be a visual one in which positional cues are controlled so that the animal must discriminate in terms of what it sees.[5] Suppose we begin with a problem requiring the animal to select a triangle instead of the cross that is paired with it. After our subject has learned this discrimination to an accuracy of 90 per cent in 20 consecutive trials, we present another pair of stimulus patterns, say a vertically striped versus a horizontally striped figure. When this is learned, another stimulus pair is presented, and so on, with many different stimulus pairs being presented. What we want to know is how rapidly the animal can learn new pairs. If the number of trials required is reduced as successive discriminations are learned, then we have evidence that the animal is developing a learning set—that it is "learning to learn." This presupposes that the stimulus pairs are not themselves successively easier to discriminate.

The ultimate level of achievement in this type of test is reached when each new pair of stimuli is consistently discriminated after the first trial. One trial is necessary to indicate which pattern is correct. The animal with insight into what is going on makes a selection and then, in terms of the outcome, continues selecting on that basis. If its first selection is correct, it thereafter selects that stimulus pattern; if incorrect, it subsequently selects the other.

In the experiment with an Indian elephant (illustrated, p. 133), 330 trials were required to master the initial discrimination—between a black circle and a black cross. As new pairs of stimulus patterns were introduced, the number of trials required was reduced. Only 10 trials were required for the fourth pair. With sixteen more pairs, the elephant could do no better than it did on its fourth test. Tested similarly, monkeys often achieve one-trial learning after many stimulus pairs have been learned.

In the examples given, each discrimination was mastered to a given level of proficiency before the next stimulus pair was introduced. A more widely used procedure is to present

[5] This is important because experiments on learning set in which positional cues can be learned do not reveal much difference in ability from lower to higher vertebrates.

Indian elephant discriminating visual patterns. The animal was required to remove the correct cover, under which a piece of bread was found. Here we see the elephant discriminating narrow from broad horizontal stripes.

one stimulus pair for a particular number of trials (perhaps 50), then present another pair, regardless of how well the animal is doing. This continues, with a substitution being made after each block of trials, until the animal's maximum level of performance can be ascertained. When this procedure is used, the investigator is interested in observing whether accuracy improves in successive blocks of trials. Cats, raccoons, and other mammals have shown slight improvement.

For example, in later blocks of trials, cats have reached an accuracy of 70 per cent and raccoons 60 per cent. Monkeys, on the other hand, reached an accuracy of 90 per cent. Some of them exhibited one-trial learning after the first few stimulus pairs were presented. Chimpanzees and gorillas do no better than monkeys on such tests.

Concepts

Discrimination problems like those already described may be extended still further to provide tests of abstraction, generalization, or concept formation. The more complicated of such tests call for a high level of reasoning ability. Concepts represent the basic similarities between somewhat diverse things. Thus, many figures which differ from each other in color, size, and overall configuration have in common the characteristic known as triangularity. This characteristic is abstracted from the many particulars, hence all are called "triangles." Human beings have words like "triangularity" to represent such concepts. Animals do not have words, but some of them have been induced to respond on a conceptual basis, as when an equivalent response is made to many different figures which have in common three sides and three angles. When an animal does this, we say that it has developed a concept of triangularity.

Rats, dogs, raccoons, monkeys, and chimpanzees have demonstrated ability to respond in this way when given a sufficient amount of suitable training. However, no infra-primate has learned concepts at a higher level of abstraction. It is with such concepts that we now concern ourselves. All of the tests to be considered here were carried out in Professor Harry Harlow's primate laboratory at the University of Wisconsin, using the Wisconsin General Test Apparatus.

One of the simplest concepts involved in these studies is the "oddity" concept. As shown in the illustration (p. 135), a monkey is presented with three test objects, in this case two circular and one T-shaped, or one circular and two T-shaped objects. In the first instance the monkey is rewarded if he selects the T; in the second, if he selects the circular

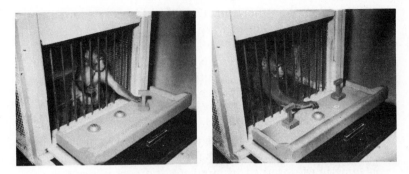

Two oddity tests solved by monkeys. This is one form of the oddity test, where the monkey must move the odd object, regardless of its color, shape, position, and the nature of associated objects.

object. From one presentation to another the items may differ from those illustrated—the size may be odd, the color odd, or the form odd, and the odd object will be in different positions relative to the other two objects. Learning to select the non-odd from such arrangements of objects is an even more difficult problem.

A further complication of the oddity-nonoddity problem is as follows: The test tray, let us say, holds three objects—red triangle, red cube, and cream cube. From the standpoint of color, the cream cube is odd. In terms of shape, the red triangle is odd. However, the test tray itself differed in color from one trial to another. If the tray was cream-colored, the odd form was correct. If it was orange, the odd color was correct. Thus, the type of oddity to be selected was conditional upon the color of the test tray on which the objects were presented. Monkeys learned this problem, but they often required as many as 6000 trials before seeing the point and responding appropriately. Chimpanzees have not done as well as monkeys on such tests, but this is attributed to personality differences rather than to lower intelligence. It has been said that "chimpanzees are extremely sensitive to the slightest changes in an otherwise familiar situation, a new pair of shoes worn by the regular caretaker may temporarily transform the animal's attitude from friendly, confident approach to one of wary avoidance."[6] There is also an "enormous effect" when the stimulus is displaced an inch or so from its usual position. No doubt all of this is, in itself, a mark of high intelligence, although distracting when there are problems to be attended to.

Some Aspects of Social Behavior

Social interaction at a relatively high level of complexity involving imitation and various forms of cooperative behavior is sometimes observed in monkeys and apes. Since this reveals an advanced animal intelligence, it also has a place in the present context.

Even animals as low in the scale as rats may be taught to imitate simple acts, as when one animal learns to follow another in order to get a reward. Cooperation at an elementary level may also be learned. Rats, for example, have learned to take turns on a platform connected with a shocking device, in this way being able to avoid shock while eating. However, spontaneously aroused imitation and cooperation have not been elicited experimentally except at the primate level.

When one imitates, he learns something by observing another's performance, and when this takes place more or less suddenly, without special training—that is to say, spontaneously—it is usually regarded as a sign that higher processes are involved. The animal must observe a performance and, after such observation, use a symbolic representation of what it has observed as the basis for imitation.

Observational learning of this nature was studied in rhesus and cebus monkeys by Professor Carl J. Warden of Columbia University. He used two identical cages side by side, with one monkey in each. Everything which happened in one cage could be seen from the other. Each cage contained a puzzle device which the monkey could open by pulling a chain, turning a knob, lifting a latch, or carrying out some

[6] L. P. Gardner and H. W. Nissen, "Simple Discrimination Behavior of Young Chimpanzees: Comparisons with Human Aments and Domestic Animals," *Journal of Genetic Psychology*, 1948, Vol. 72, p. 161.

relatively simple act. The monkey in one cage had already been trained to perform the necessary act. The question was: Would the untrained monkey, after observing such an act, immediately open its puzzle box in a similar fashion? As one test was completed, a new opening device was slipped over the front of the puzzle boxes. In this way, 24 different tests were given. Rhesus and cebus monkeys imitated within 60 seconds of seeing the trained animal's performance. One of the rhesus monkeys was successful in 23 of the 24 tests.

Viki, a home-raised chimpanzee, imitated problems of greater complexity than the above when told "Do this," then given a demonstration. Some problems were: inserting a pencil in a pencil sharpener and turning the handle, taking the lid off a can with a screwdriver, and displacing a string by leverage with a stick, thus opening a puzzle box. Professor and Mrs. Keith Hayes, who reared Viki, report that her performance equaled that of two- to three-year-old children given a comparable test.[7]

Two types of cooperative problem solving were observed in chimpanzees by Dr. Meredith Crawford. One of these involved pulling on ropes in unison so that access to food could be gained (see illustration, p. 138). The ropes were attached to a box loaded with pieces of iron so that it was too heavy for a chimpanzee to pull in alone. Preliminary training was given, such as teaching both chimpanzees to pull on command. However, the real test came when a pair were on their own. Under these circumstances each chimpanzee coordinated its pulling by watching the other. But it sometimes happened that one chimpanzee failed to pull until solicited and induced to do so by the other, more enthusiastic member of the pair. Often, when both were pulling, one suddenly let go of the rope. When this happened, the partner, acting surprised, gave a sideward glance in its direction, then by various gestures, tried to induce it to pull. Sometimes this was successful and sometimes not. The soliciting chimpanzee could not indicate what it wanted

[7] A popular presentation of the experiments with Viki appears in Cathy Hayes' *The Ape in Our House*, Harper, 1951.

*Communication in chimpanzees.
Top: Bula touches Kambi near the
mouth and turns her head toward the
grill. Middle: Bula's hand is on top of
Kambi's, pushing it down toward a
rope. Bottom: Bula and Bimba pull
together.*

from the other, and chimpanzees do not point. So the gestures and attempts of the soliciting animal to turn its partner around when he was headed away from the rope were saying nothing more specific, if anything, than "Help me do something."

The other test of cooperative behavior required that yellow, green, red, and blue panels be pushed in that order to release food. Each animal was trained to push the panels, then the partners were separated by a grill with yellow and red panels on one side and green and blue on the other. First the chimpanzee with the yellow panel had to push it. Then the partner had to push its green panel. This had to be followed, in order, by pushing of the red and blue panels. Four of the chimpanzees given this test cooperated, each watching for the appropriate response from its partner before responding itself. Two of them solicited when the partner did not respond. They did this by reaching through the grill and turning the animal in the proper direction, or by pushing him.

LANGUAGE

Soliciting behavior of the kind observed in the foregoing experiments comes as close to language as any animal has been able to achieve with its own untutored resources.

In their natural state, chimpanzees vocalize when emotionally aroused, and they communicate with gestures, but for some reason they have never been known, without special training, to bridge the gap between these limited forms of communication and conventionalized vocal or gestural signals such as all languages use. While their vocalizations cover a wide range, these have no symbolic reference to aspects of the environment or to the animal's past experience.

This deficiency goes back, in the first instance, to the animal's failure to *invent* a language as primitive men did. But it is apparent, also, in the chimpanzee's failure to imitate, without elaborate training, an already given language. The normal human child acquires the language of those around it with apparent spontaneity, but a chimpanzee, even with the intelligence of a two- to three-year-old child and treated like a child in a human family situation, makes no progress in this direction unless subjected to an elaborate conditioning program. Even then, progress is slow and extremely limited. One chimpanzee has been trained to use a few sounds resembling words, another has been taught to communicate with human beings by using conventionalized gestures selected for this purpose, and still another has learned to communicate with its trainers by arranging variously colored plastic shapes in certain sequences.

Some problems involved in inducing chimpanzees to communicate linguistically are brought out in the following discussion, which also compares linguistic acquisition in chimpanzees and children.

LINGUISTIC ACQUISITION IN CHIMPANZEE AND CHILD

Viki, the chimpanzee whose imitation has already been mentioned, was taught to "say" a few "words," but teaching her to do so was a very arduous process (see illustration, p. 141). The chief difficulty, at the outset, was to get her to make any sounds other than inborn reflex vocalizations elicited by excitement. Except when emotionally aroused, Viki was silent. A human infant of the same age would have been babbling for months, spontaneously and without any obvious relation to what was going on around it.

Since Viki had no urge to vocalize, Dr. and Mrs. Hayes decided to make her "speak" for her supper, as a dog might be taught to bark for it. This met with no success at first. When asked to speak, Viki looked at the milk held in front of her but said nothing. If Mrs. Hayes moved away, however, she gave worried little sounds (oo oo). This vocalizing, although only an emotional reaction, was immediately rewarded: Viki got some milk. While drinking the milk, she made "sputtered food barks," which brought more milk. After five weeks of further training, a new sound (ahhh),

Teaching Viki to say "Mama." As described in the text, the lips were first moved while Viki was making an "ahhh" sound. Then, as the lips began to move without aid, touching with a finger was sufficient. When the finger was removed, Viki would put her lip to the trainer's finger, as illustrated, or touch the lip with her own finger while she spoke.

accompanied by facial contortions and a tense, preoccupied look, began to appear. When she made this sound, Viki reached for her milk, and she was rewarded. Thereafter, the command to speak brought an *ahhh*. Now Viki was ready to learn her first word, *Mama*. Mrs. Hayes trained her to say this by pressing her lips together and releasing them as she said *ahhh* for food. After a few weeks of such training, it was no longer necessary to touch Viki's lips, she was saying *Mama* by herself. The word *Papa* was laboriously added to her vocabulary after she had learned to imitate a Bronx cheer. Softer and shorter *p*'s with relaxed lips were required, then the repetition of two *p*'s in succession. This produced something approximating the sound *Papa*. The word *cup* was acquired by learning to repeat the sounds *k* and *p* in rapid succession. Later still, Viki learned *ch* for a drink. She also learned to click her teeth for a ride in the car. This is as far as Viki went in learning to speak. Moreover, she never came to use her words for social purposes or for egocentric expression. She spoke only when there was no other way of getting what she wanted. There was no evidence that she had any insight into the meaning of language.

How different it is when children learn to speak! It is not necessary to subject them to special training. They not only vocalize spontaneously (babble), they also learn to imitate, with gradually increasing accuracy, the words used by those around them. This process is aided by the favorable responses of others to their vocalizing and by the fact that as their imitations get better, they are able to communicate their wishes more easily. But nobody has to command them to speak, move their lips in appropriate ways, or provide special rewards. Children soon "catch on" to the fact that everything has a name and that they can use words to represent aspects of their world.

The sudden insight which is often a part of this process was dramatically revealed in Helen Keller's learning of her first word. Helen had two handicaps—blindness and deafness—but she was a very bright child. Her teacher, Anne Sullivan, communicated with her tactually, through a manual alphabet. One morning during Helen's seventh year she made an extremely important discovery, and her brightness enabled her to capitalize on it almost immediately.

Anne Sullivan tells how the child asked the name for water by pointing to it and patting the teacher's hand. Miss Sullivan spelled the word in the manual alphabet. Later, when they went out to the well for water, she made Helen hold her mug under the pump spout while she spelled "w-a-t-e-r" into the child's free hand. Says Miss Sullivan:

The word, coming so close upon the sensation of cold water rushing over her hand, seemed to startle her. She dropped the mug and stood as one transfixed. A new light came into her face. She spelled "water" several times. Then she dropped on the ground and asked for its name and pointed to the pump and trellis, and suddenly turning round she asked for my name. I spelled "Teacher." Just then the nurse brought Helen's little sister into the pump-house and Helen spelled "baby" and pointed to the nurse. All the way back to the house she was highly excited, and learned the name of every object she touched, so that in a few hours she had added thirty new words to her vocabulary.

The next day Helen was like "a radiant fairy," going from object to object naming it. Everything had to have a name, and if she didn't know it, she asked.[8]

The discovery that everything has a name is "like an intellectual revolution," as the German philosopher Ernst Cassirer pointed out in his *An Essay on Man.* "The child begins to see the world in a new light. It has learned the use of words, not merely as mechanical signs and signals, but as an entirely new instrument of thought."[9]

Insight such as this is beyond the reach of any animal. Animals react only to sounds, not to the symbolic meaning of words. The late Professor Edward L. Thorndike once demonstrated this point with an experiment on cats. He had trained the animals so that when he said "I must feed those cats," they dashed to the food box, even when he put no food in it. One day, to test their understanding of his words,

[8] Helen Keller, *The Story of My Life,* Doubleday, 1903, p. 315.

[9] Ernst Cassirer, *An Essay on Man,* Yale University Press, 1944, p. 35.

he exclaimed at the cat's mealtime: "Today is Tuesday." The cats instantly sped to the box. The words "My name is Thorndike" evoked the same response.

Here, then, is an important and puzzling question. Why did the apes get so far in symbolic development, as revealed by delayed reaction, double alternation, and other such tests, yet fail to bridge the gap between nonlinguistic symbols and those of speech? Why are they "almost human," yet without speech or anything comparable with it? Have they nothing to say? This is a possibility, but one linguist has pointed out that having nothing to say does not stop us from speaking! The difficulty does not lie with the ape's vocal range. This does not lend itself readily to the making of human sounds, but it includes enough sounds to serve a linguistic function. There is no evidence, however, that apes have a vocal language of their own. As suggested earlier, in speaking of Viki, apes make no sounds at all except emotional ones. These would have no communicative significance beyond telling another of their kind that its mate is angry, frightened, or on the prowl.

Some importance may be attached to the fact that apes fail to vocalize spontaneously, as babies do when they babble by the hour. Recall that Viki could not be trained to "speak" until she had first been induced to vocalize unemotionally. Man probably vocalized in a babbling fashion until he got the idea that sounds can be used to represent objects and events and are thus useful for communicative purposes.

The ape's linguistic backwardness may be attributed to insufficient insight and relatively poor symbolizing ability. If it were to develop into a talking animal, it would need a very high level of insight, exceptional ability to store and retrieve information, and great versatility in reasoning—in "putting two and two together."

There are no doubt several neurological and anatomical reasons for the ape's failure to invent a language. Recall that the ape's brain weighs only one third as much as our own, yet it has an equally large (or larger) body to control.[10] This means that its brain is largely concerned with sensory and motor functions. The association areas are small in comparison with the areas specialized for sensory and motor processes. Even the frontal lobes, so prominent in the human brain, are relatively small.

TEACHING SIGN LANGUAGE TO A CHIMPANZEE

Chimpanzees gesture spontaneously, although their movements have no known linguistic significance under natural conditions. Professor Winthrop N. Kellogg[11] asks whether this spontaneous use of gestures by chimpanzees could not be developed into something more. Might not "an intelligent animal learn a series of regular or standardized signals—as a sort of semaphore system?" Kellogg continues by pointing out that "Even though a chimp may lack the laryngeal structure or neural speech centers of man, it does not necessarily follow that it has deficiencies in general motor activity" which would make it unable to "communicate back and forth in a series of hand movements, arm signals, and postures." When Kellogg's statement appeared, two investigators at the University of Nevada had already begun an experiment designed to teach a chimpanzee a selected group of signals from the American Sign Language (ASL), which finds wide use in communication among the deaf. These investigators, R. Allen Gardner and Beatrice T. Gardner, selected for their experiment a wild-born female chimpanzee estimated to be eight to fourteen months old. They named her Washoe.

After a period of adaptation to a human environment, Washoe was gradually trained, by various "friends and playmates" as well as "providers and protectors," to use the se-

[10] It is interesting to observe that human infants of 15 months, an age when speech development is normally well under way, have an average brain weight of 944 grams, while the brain weight of a mature chimpanzee is no greater than 450 grams. Human brain weights at various ages are given in J. L. Conel, *The Postnatal Development of the Human Cerebral Cortex*, Vols. 1–8, Harvard University Press, 1939–1967.

[11] Winthrop N. Kellogg, "Communication and Language in the Home-Raised Chimpanzee," *Science*, 1968, Vol. 162, pp. 423–427 (quotation from p. 426).

lected signals, which were introduced into games and other activities calculated to "result in maximum interaction." Each of the participants had already learned the signals, and these, rather than oral communication, were used in the interactions with Washoe.

Part of the training comprised "Do this" games. (See illustration, p. 147.) One of the rewards for correct imitation of a signal was tickling. Imitation on command was difficult to obtain. The Gardners say:

It was not until the 16th month of the project that we achieved any degree of control over Washoe's imitation of gestures. Eventually we got to the point where she would imitate a simple gesture, such as pulling at her ears, or a series of such gestures—first we make a gesture, then she imitates, then we make a second gesture, she imitates the second gesture, and so on—for the reward of being tickled."[12]

A prompting method was also used to introduce new signals and to correct errors. This involved "repeating in exaggeratedly correct form, the sign she had just made," until she repeated it herself "in more correct form." Pressing too hard along these lines, however, made Washoe depart from what she had been doing—to "ask for something entirely different, run away, go into a tantrum, or even bite her tutor."

Delayed imitation also played a role in Washoe's acquiring of appropriate signs, for example, the sign for "toothbrush."

A part of the daily routine has been to brush her teeth after every meal. When this routine was first introduced Washoe generally resisted it. She gradually came to resist with less and less fuss, and after many months she would even help or sometimes brush her teeth herself. Usually, having finished her meal, Washoe would try to leave her high chair; we would restrain her, signing "First, toothbrushing, then you can go." One day, in the 10th month of the project, Washoe was visiting the Gardners' home and found

[12] R. Allen Gardner and Beatrice T. Gardner, "Teaching Sign Language to a Chimpanzee," *Science*, 1969, Vol. 165, pp. 664–672 (quotations from p. 666).

Washoe learning to give the "drink" sign.

her way into the bathroom. She climbed up on the counter, looked at our mug full of toothbrushes, and signed "toothbrush." At the time we believed that Washoe understood the sign but we had not seen her use it. She had no reason to ask for the toothbrushes, because they were well within her reach, and it is most unlikely that she was asking to have her teeth brushed. This was our first observation, and one of the clearest examples, of behavior in which Washoe seemed to name an object or an event for no obvious motive other than communication.[13]

By the 14th month, after imitative prompting and other procedures, she called for her toothbrush by making the proper sign when the meal was finished. Delayed imitation also appeared in acquisition of the sign for "flower." Early in the experiment, when Washoe showed an interest in flowers and pictures of flowers, the sign for flower was given by her tutors, and she was induced to imitate it. But there was no spontaneous use of the sign until the 15th month, when she made it as she and a companion approached a

[13] Gardner and Gardner, p. 667.

flower garden. The investigators capitalized on this spontaneous signing, as they had done in the case of "toothbrush," and the sign eventually appeared quite reliably in response to a variety of flowers and their pictorial representations.

A gestural form of babbling was encouraged and utilized in teaching new signs. Take, for example, acquisition of the sign for "funny." In this, as used by Washoe, the tip of the index finger touches the nose and a snort is given. This sign first appeared "as a spontaneous babble that lent itself readily to a simple imitation game—first Washoe signed "funny," then we did, then she did, and so on. We would laugh and smile during the interchanges that she initiated, and initiate the game ourselves when something funny happened. Eventually Washoe came to use the 'funny' sign spontaneously in roughly appropriate situations."[14]

Instrumental conditioning with successive approximations to a desired response also played a part in sign acquisition. As an illustration of this, take the sign for "more." As we have already said, Washoe liked to be tickled and was rewarded by tickling. When tickling stopped, she often indicated that she wanted more by taking the tutor's hands and placing them in the appropriate positions on her body. The Gardners say that:

The meaning of these gestures was unmistakable, but since we were not studying our human ability to interpret her chimpanzee gestures we decided to shape an arbitrary response that she could use to ask for more tickling. We noted that, when being tickled, she tended to bring her arms together to cover the place being tickled. The result was a very crude approximation to the ASL sign for "more." Thus we would stop tickling and then pull Washoe's arms away from her body. When we released her arms and threatened to resume tickling, she tended to bring her hands together again. If she brought them back together, we would tickle her again. From time to time we would stop tickling and wait for her to put her hands together by herself. At first, any approximation to the "more" sign, however crude, was rewarded. Later, we required closer

14 Gardner and Gardner, p. 667.

approximations and introduced imitative prompting. Soon, a very good version of the "more" sign could be obtained, but it was quite specific to the tickling situation."[15]

Later, the Gardners attempted to extend the "more" sign to a wider range of situations. It came to be used for more pushing across the floor in a laundry basket, more swinging of Washoe in the arms, for more feeding, and so on. Finally, Washoe "transferred the 'more' sign to all activities, including feeding. The transfer was usually spontaneous, occurring when there was some pause in a desired activity or when some object was removed. Often we ourselves were not sure that Washoe wanted 'more' until she signed to us."[16] In a somewhat comparable way, Washoe learned the sign for "open," using it first as a request to open the door, then to open many things—as well as turn on the water faucet.

After subjection to such procedures for 22 months, Washoe had acquired a vocabulary of 34 signs. In addition to those already mentioned there were the signs for *open, tickle, go, out, hurry, hear-listen, drink, hurt, sorry, please, food-eat, cover-blanket, you, napkin-bib, brush, hat, shoes, pants, clothes, cat, come-gimme, key, baby,* and *clean.* These were all used frequently, in appropriate contexts. Acquisition was initially slow, but it accelerated as training continued. For example, there were 4 spontaneously aroused signs in the first seven months, 9 new ones in the second seven months, and 21 additions in the third seven months. Some difficult differentiations were involved, like the difference between "flower" and "smell." Transfer from one context to other appropriate contexts has been common, like the "dog" sign for a real or pictured dog to the sound of a dog barking. After she had acquired a repertoire of about 10 signs, Washoe began to use combinations of them, such as "gimme drink please," "go in," "open key" (locked door), "listen eat" (alarm clock signaling mealtime). Acquisition of "I-me" and "you" has led to combinations resembling short sentences.

This experiment continues, and the eventual outcome re-

---

[15] Gardner and Gardner, p. 669.

[16] Gardner and Gardner, pp. 669–670.

mains to be seen. Concerning this, the investigators say, "In terms of the eventual level of communication that a chimpanzee might be able to attain, the most promising results have been spontaneous naming, spontaneous transfer to new referents, and spontaneous combinations and recombinations of signs."[17]

Why did Washoe do so much better than Viki in acquiring and using linguistic symbols? It seems unlikely that she was that much more intelligent. It seems unlikely, also, that better training techniques were used with Washoe, except for the fact that gestures are more readily shaped than vocalizations. The chimpanzee is limited when it comes to spontaneous vocalization, as we saw in the case of Viki, but the range of gestures and their spontaneous arousal is not so limited, and it appears that this gives the answer to our question. Vocally, a chimpanzee appears to have relatively little to say. Gesturally, however, it can, with appropriate training, be given the wherewithal to "say" a great deal. It can also be taught to communicate through appropriate use of visual signs.

USE OF VISUAL SIGNS BY A CHIMPANZEE

Sarah, a seven-year-old chimpanzee, learned to communicate with Professor David Premack and his assistants by using chips of various shapes, sizes, colors, and textures.[18] The chips were made of plastic and backed by metal so that they would adhere to a magnetized "language board" on which the chimpanzee had to place them, sometimes singly and sometimes in meaningful combinations, in order to "say" what was required to get a reward. Some of the most easily described chips and the words represented by them were: blue triangle (*apple*), small purplish square (*banana*), blue star (the verb *insert*), a yellow figure shaped somewhat like an arrow (*equal to*), the same shape colored red (*not equal to*), a blue propeller-like shape (*yes*) and a similarly shaped

[17] Gardner and Gardner, p. 672.

[18] David Premack, "The Education of Sarah," *Psychology Today*, September, 1970, pp. 54–58.

gray chip (*no*). The chips represented various verbs, personal names, colors, foods, objects, concepts, adjectives, and adverbs.

First Sarah was presented with a readily accessible banana, then she was required to learn that an otherwise inaccessible banana could be gained by putting a nearby chip on the language board. When she had learned to "ask" for the banana in this way, she was presented with other fruits and their chips. After having learned to use these signs appropriately, Sarah was taught to use chips representing verbs like *insert* and *give* as well as various additional nouns. The next step was to require an appropriate sequence, such as "Mary give apple Sarah," "Sarah insert banana pail," and so forth. That is to say, the chips representing *Mary, give, apple,* and *Sarah* had to be placed in this order on the language board. A further step was to teach such things as "*Apple name of. . . .*" and "*Apple not name of. . . .*" in relation to the presented fruit.

This experiment had run for two years and was continuing when the brief report so far available was written. It appears that during this time Sarah had learned 120 "words" and also such language functions as construction of sentences and asking and answering questions. According to Professor Premack, Sarah not only used the chips in meaningful combinations but also "understood" what she was doing, as evidenced by the fact that she at one time devised a "sentence-completion test" for her trainer.

There is an obvious gap between man's *invention* of language, oral, gestural, and written and the ape's failure in this respect. And there is a marked difference in the ability of an ape and a child of normal intelligence to acquire the linguistic symbols already available in a human environment. The child picks up these symbols quite readily, and its vocabulary grows apace. The ape, on the other hand, acquires very few of the symbols available to it, and even these it acquires only after laborious tutoring. All of this is relevant to an issue with which we shall end this chapter on the evolution of intelligence.

CONTINUITY OR DISCONTINUITY?

Was mental evolution a process in which successive small increments built one upon another until the level of human mentality had been achieved? Theorists who argue for the continuity of mental evolution say that it proceeded in just that way. But there are others who hold that mental evolution moved ahead in leaps rather than, or in addition to, continuous increments. In the succeeding discussion we shall see that evolution, in its various aspects, reveals both continuities and discontinuities. We shall see, too, that the invention of language as a means of communication comes as close as anything to supporting the argument for discontinuity.

The continuity viewpoint is clearly expressed by Professor Harry Harlow, who says; "If we are to explain learning in terms of modern evolutionary theory, there should be continuity from the simplest to the most complex forms of learning. The appearance of a radically new kind of learning at any evolutionary point or period, including that during which man developed, is not in keeping with modern gene theory," which Harlow interprets as the theory that "evolution takes place by natural selection among multiple mutations, each of which produces some small organic change."[19]

But gene changes may be small or large. When small, they may not become evident structurally until enough of them, or a certain combination, sufficiently changes the genic balance. Then the structural outcome may be markedly divergent from previous structure even though each gene mutation is, in itself, very small. We must also keep in mind that many mutations are recessive, hence they do not find structural expression unless the animal carrying them breeds with others having a similar genetic constitution. When this happens, there may be a suddenly appearing change in struc-

[19] Harry F. Harlow, "The Evolution of Learning," in Anne Roe and George Gaylord Simpson (Eds.), *Behavior and Evolution,* Yale University Press, 1958, pp. 277–278.

ture; even a large one.[20] If inbreeding does not occur, the mutations may never become apparent. Moreover, many mutations which found structural expression in the past may have been lost, as suggested by the many extinct animals. Such a loss would produce gaps in the line of descent. Thus, we are *not* forced by modern gene theory to suppose that mental evolution was marked by continuity. There appears to be much continuity interspersed with discontinuity at certain points.

The presence of discontinuity was stressed by Professor D'Arcy Thompson, who saw particular evidence of it in the transition from invertebrates to vertebrates. The problem exists, to a degree, even as we go from one vertebrate level to another. According to Thompson, "Darwinian evolution has not taught us how birds descend from reptiles, mammals from earlier quadrupeds, quadrupeds from fishes, nor vertebrates from the invertebrate stock." But he was not presenting an argument against evolutionary descent, for "we may fail to find the actual links between the vertebrate groups, but yet their resemblance and their relationship, real though indefinable, are plain to see; there are gaps between the groups, but we can see, so to speak, across the gap." However, "We *cannot* transform an invertebrate into a vertebrate, nor a coelenterate into a worm, by any simple and legitimate transformation, nor by anything short of reduction to elementary principles." Thompson says that his argument "indicates, if it does not prove, that . . . mutations, occurring on a comparatively few definite lines, or plain alternatives, of physicomathematical possibility, are likely to repeat themselves; that the 'higher' protozoa, for instance, may have sprung not from or through one another but severally from the simpler forms; or that the worm-type, to take another

[20] Inbreeding and its effects on mutations are exceedingly complex, even under the relatively restricted conditions imposed upon laboratory colonies of mice. For a detailed discussion of the mutations observed in mice and the effects of various breeding systems upon their transmission, see Earl L. Green (Ed.), *Biology of the Laboratory Mouse* (2nd ed.), McGraw-Hill, 1966.

example, may have come into being again and again."[21]

Commenting on Thompson's views, the late Professor Henry W. Nissen said that "this emphasis on large and abrupt variations in evolution is representative of most modern biological thinking," and "its implication for comparative psychology is that in behavior also we may expect to find discontinuity—qualitative rather than merely quantitative changes—as we pass from the lower to the higher animal forms."[22].

In discussing the problem before us, Professor Dobzhansky, who sees both discontinuity and continuity in evolution says:

Man is not simply a very clever ape. On the contrary, he possesses some faculties that occur in other animals only as rudiments, if at all. Quantum evolution, emergence of novel adaptive designs, may involve breaks in the evolutionary continuity when the differences between the ancestors and the descendants increase so rapidly that they are perceived as differences in kind. Antecedents of the new designs may, nevertheless, be detected in the old one. We must equally resist the temptation to regard man either as something completely unlike any animal or as something devoid of all novelty. . . . For example, legs in land-living vertebrates were new organs, since fishes from which the land vertebrates descended had no legs. Comparative anatomy shows, however, that the extremities of the land vertebrates arose from the paired fins of their fishlike ancestors.[23]

Modern evolutionary theory thus lends support to the idea that there was continuity in the evolution of some psychological processes and discontinuity in the evolution of others. What aspects of intelligence, then, appear to fall into the continuous category and what into the discontinuous?

[21] D'Arcy W. Thompson, *On Growth and Form*, Cambridge University Press, 1942, pp. 1093–1095.

[22] Henry W. Nissen, "Phylogenetic Comparison," in S. S. Stevens (Ed.), *Handbook of Experimental Psychology*, Wiley, 1951, p. 348.

[23] Theodosius Dobzhansky, *Mankind Evolving*, Yale University Press, 1962, p. 203.

We see the clearest evidence for continuity in the simpler, or basic, processes—those upon which sheer survival is contingent. The natural environment, in itself, places limitations on the kinds of mutants that can survive. Survival requires at least minimal sensitivity to environmental changes and ability to respond to aspects of the environment in such a way as to satisfy basic physiological needs, such as the need for food, water, and shelter from the elements. Therefore one would expect to find all animals with some degree of sensitivity. We know, in fact, that there is a more or less continuous line of development from the unspecialized sensitivity of the amoeba to the specialized sensitivity of human beings. In some respects, this trend can be considered purely quantitative—as increasing increments of the same sort of sensitivity. There is gradually increasing sensitivity to brightness. An increasing amount of detail in visual configurations becomes evident to the organism. Sounds of decreasing loudness can be heard. And so on, with many other aspects of sensitivity. On the other hand, discontinuity is suggested when color vision emerges. This suddenly-appearing sensitivity to the wavelength properties of light cannot, it seems, be derived from some quantitative transformation of brightness vision.[24] The emergence of a depth dimension in the vision of primates is perhaps another example of sensory discontinuity.

In motor functions there is likewise a certain degree of continuity and also discontinuity. Adaptation requires locomotor ability, and all animals move around to some extent, although with different degrees of facility and by use of different locomotor mechanisms. Thus, in some respects the evolution of locomotor ability from amoeba to higher forms is continuous. One will recall the previously mentioned

---

[24] One must keep in mind that some processes have undergone independent evolution in different evolutionary lines. For example, different mechanisms underlie color vision in insects, birds, and primates. Spatial vision in owls has as perhaps its only similarity with that of primates the fact that the eyes, being toward the front of the head, can get overlapping images of what lies before them.

structural change from fins to legs, a transformation regarded by Dobzhansky as basically continuous and quantitative. But when a terrestrial animal gives rise to one which moves through the air, we have something essentially new in locomotion, despite the similarities (homologies) in limb and wing structures.

Some psychologists see evidence of discontinuity between unlearned and learned behavior, i.e., between instinct and habit. Professor Gaston Viaud, referring to discontinuity in mental evolution, says "The milestones in the evolution of intelligence are the emergence from instinctive reactions and the appearance of conceptual thought."[25] The emergence from instinctive reactions is cited as the beginning of intelligence. However, the idea that there is a basic dichotomy between instinct and intelligence, or between instinct and habit, has been defended and refuted many times. The argument seems rather fruitless because both learned and unlearned behavior persist throughout most of the animal world, with inborn modes of response predominating at lower levels and acquired ones at higher levels. Learning itself may be viewed as a modification of unlearned reactions and earlier learned reactions. Thus, there is no clear break between instinctive and learned behavior.

The evolution of learning ability is marked by apparent continuity, at least up to the mammalian level. Pavlovians and many others regard learning as reducible, in the last analysis, to conditioning, which is viewed, essentially, as the acquisition of new stimulus-response connections. We have already observed that the ability to learn discrimination habits and avoidance of blind alleys in a maze shows more or less gradual improvement until the mammalian level is reached. This is a quantitative development, evidenced by faster learning, fewer errors, decreased effort, and an increase in the complexity of sensorimotor skills that the animal can learn. In this elementary type of learning, with its dependence upon conditioning and trial and error, there is

[25] Gaston Viaud, *Intelligence: Its Evolution and Forms*, Harper, 1960, p. 116.

no further advance from rat to man. This does not mean that the simpler learning processes ceased to exist beyond the rat level, but only that they were supplemented by processes essentially different in kind and more characteristically mammalian. These processes have been referred to, in general, as symbolic: more specifically, as insight, recall memory, concept formation, generalizing, and reasoning. All have in common the fact that, to some degree, they transcend the immediate stimulating circumstances by bringing to bear upon them the fruits of past experience. In their more complex aspects they comprise what Professor Viaud and many others refer to as conceptual thought.

It is possible that the emergence of symbolic processes had to wait upon the evolution of the cerebral cortex, which first became clearly apparent in mammals. In lower vertebrates, as was pointed out in earlier discussions, the cerebrum is rudimentary and so largely involved in olfaction that it is often referred to as a "smell brain."

Professor Bitterman and collaborators at Bryn Mawr College believe that they have found evidence for discontinuity in learning between the fish and bird levels, with birds (pigeons) behaving at a typically mammalian (rat) level despite the absence of a well developed cerebrum. These investigators used several learning problems, but we shall consider the one which comes closest to being a test of insight—that involving successive reversals of a visual discrimination. This will be recognized by the reader as a learning-set (or learning-how-to-learn) problem. Our earlier examples of learning set involved successive pairs of stimulus patterns, and the animal was credited with insight if it showed more or less sudden improvement in its learning of successive discriminations. In reversal learning, on the other hand, the same stimulus patterns (for example, vertical versus horizontal black and white stripes) are used throughout. The animal is trained with one pattern rewarded (say, horizontal), then the other (vertical) is rewarded, making the former incorrect. When training with the vertical pattern rewarded is finished, another reversal occurs, making the horizontal again correct. Such reversing of cues continues, and the investigator seeks evidence of progressive improvement with successive reversals. On problems like this, monkeys sometimes reach a one-trial level of performance. As in learning successive discriminations, they make no more errors after the first trial with the new reversal. This is taken to mean that they have insight into what is going on. On the other hand, animals which show progressive improvement, even though they do not reach the one-trial level, may be credited with a certain degree of insight.

On problems involving reversal of visual cues, fish and turtles showed no progressive improvement. In fact, after 18 reversals their performance was poorer than in the original learning and earlier reversals. The situation was quite different with pigeons. Their performance got progressively worse in the early reversals, then began to improve, until after 18 reversals they were making relatively few errors. Rats also demonstrated progressive improvement after the first few reversals. Thus, Bitterman concluded that his experiments had tapped "an intellectual capability of higher animals that is not at all developed in the fish."[26]

Psychologists have had little or no success in finding evidence of recall memory and reasoning below the mammalian level. This is a clearer discontinuity than can be found in the development of learning sets based on reversal problems. Our earlier discussion of symbolic processes showed that rats have what might be called rudimentary symbolic processes, as revealed in delayed reaction and reasoning tests. These processes become increasingly evident as the primate level is approached. They also reach high levels of complexity, as in the solving of complex delayed reaction, double alternation, and conceptual learning problems by monkeys and chimpanzees.

Although apes have symbolic processes basically compar-

[26] M. E. Bitterman, "The Evolution of Intelligence," *Scientific American*, 1965, Vol. 212, p. 96. For a more detailed report of these experiments, see M. E. Bitterman, "Phyletic Differences in Learning," *American Psychologist*, 1965, Vol. 20, pp. 396–410.

able to man's, their failure to invent speech is perhaps the most evident discontinuity in the evolution of mental life. Nevertheless, Professor Harry Harlow questions whether this difference is as large as it seems. He refers to the "common error of assuming that the particular human traits of language and culture imply the existence of some vast intellectual gap between man and other animals." Harlow believes that "a relatively small intellectual gain by man over the anthropoid apes" may have given rise to "the development of symbolic language and also culture."[27] He does not profess to know what this "small intellectual gain" may have been, but reference is made to the possibility that the ape's "language inadequacies basically result from the failure to possess certain unlearned responses." More specifically, apes fail to engage in spontaneous vocalizing, or what, in human beings, is called babbling. We have seen from the researches of the Gardners and David Premack, however, that certain unlearned gestures and visual signs may be utilized by the chimpanzee for linguistic communication when suitable training procedures are used. This is a "small intellectual gain" not found in the *vocal* behavior of chimpanzees, but it still leaves a large gap between the communicative abilities of apes and men. Indeed, Noam Chomsky thinks that human linguistic communication is based on "entirely different principles" and "associated with a specific type of mental organization" not possessed by subhumans. "There seems to be no substance," he says, "to the view that human language is simply a more complex instance of something to be found elsewhere in the animal world. This poses a problem for the biologist, since, if true, it is an example of true 'emergence'—the appearance of a qualitatively different phenomenon at a specific stage of complexity of organization."[28]

[27] Harry F. Harlow, "The Evolution of Learning," in Roe and Simpson, *Behavior and Evolution,* p. 278.

[28] Noam Chomsky, *Language and Mind,* Harcourt, Brace and World, 1968, p. 62.

CHAPTER FIVE

THE EMERGENCE
OF MAN

In its basic aspects, the evolution of the human mind was dependent upon the evolution of the human body, particularly the brain. The brain alone makes possible the reception and storage of information, functions which underlie all mental processes. In tracing mental evolution, however, we find neither minds nor brains. We are limited to fossilized skeletons, sometimes with a skull and sometimes without. When skulls are found, we have evidence of cranial capacity, hence of brain size. By making a cast (endocast) of the inside of the skull we may also discover the general shape of the brain.

There is at least indirect evidence of mental evolution as brains grew larger and approached the shape of present-day human brains. This evidence is limited by the absence of a direct correlation between brain size and mental capacity. It is limited, also, because the size and shape of the brain give no indication of mental content—of knowledge, ideas, concepts, and other aspects of mental life. But despite such limitations, the study of fossil skulls tells us a great deal about the evolution of the human brain and provides some indirect information about the mental processes of our remote ancestors.

Information on some aspects of behavior is provided by fossilized bones. Those of the lower cranium show whether the head was characteristically held erect, or thrust forward, as in apes. The structure of the pelvis provides information on posture and locomotion. Bones of the lower leg and foot reveal the presence of a plodding, shuffling, or striding gait. A hand skeleton can show whether the individual had only a power grip, or whether he could grip with his thumb and fingers opposed. It can also show whether the knuckles were used in apelike locomotion. The brain of course integrates an organism's locomotor and prehensile activities, and the evolution of these functions depended upon the evolution of the brain as well as that of potentially versatile mechanisms for locomotion and manipulation.

Here we trace the evolution of the human organism as revealed by fossils and, in doing so, gain some indirect evidence about the evolving human mind. Incidental references are made to such artifacts as tools, but these and other products of human activity are dealt with more fully in the following chapter.

Our account begins with the primate ancestors of man, but it is concerned chiefly with the transition from manlike primates to man himself. This transition occurred during the Pleistocene (see Geologic Time Scale, p. 67), an epoch which began some two to three million years ago.[1] It is customary to divide the Pleistocene into three stages, lower, middle, and upper, and each of these in terms of its glacial

[1] A relatively conservative estimate of 2,000,000 years is given by Kenneth Oakley, in *Frameworks for Dating Fossil Man* (Aldine, 1968, p. 292), but Dr. J. R. Napier (in personal correspondence) says that the date is now considered to be at least 3,000,000 years ago. Uranium fission-track dating of volcanic glass, Oakley says, yields a date of 1,500,000 to 2,500,000 years ago, and the potassium-argon method a date of around 1,700,000 years ago. Quite obviously, the date cannot be pinpointed at the present time.

and interglacial stages. A manlike creature, if not man himself, emerged during the lower Pleistocene, when the Günz glaciation was advancing in the northernmost latitudes. In view of the coldness of the northern hemisphere at that time, it should not be surprising to find that man and his immediate ancestors evolved in the more hospitable southern hemisphere, in particular, Africa.

The dates given in this account are those at present estimated from geological strata in which fossils and artifacts have been found and from the new methods of dating which utilize what is known of the fixed rates at which radioactive isotopes decay (see Footnote 1, opposite). Such estimates are, as we have seen, subject to revision as new evidence comes to hand. However, the assignment of new dates to the fossils and artifacts considered here will not alter the sequential order of events (as revealed by geological strata) or the evolutionary trends which these indicate.

MAN AS A PRIMATE

Man is a primate. He stands at the head of a sequence which includes, in our own times, the tree-shrews, lemurs, tarsiers, monkeys, and apes. That does not mean that he descended from some modern manlike (anthropoid) ape such as the orang-utan, chimpanzee, or gorilla. It means, rather, that some ancient and now extinct primate stock produced variations which started new branches of the primate family tree, two of which evolved to become such divergent yet related and basically similar organisms as apes and men. The more apelike primates (pongids) are late representatives of a line whose other members became extinct (see figure, p. 169). The extinct members are known to us through their fossilized remains. Fossil men as well as men living today belong to the other (hominid) branch. Earlier hominids have become extinct, leaving our own kind of man as their sole representative. All living human races belong to the species *Homo sapiens*—"wise man."

The pongids and hominids formed separate branches of

the primate family tree millions of years ago. Remains classified by some as hominid take us back 14,000,000 years. An advanced hominid, certainly almost human, lived in Africa an estimated 2,000,000 years ago. He was possibly the first maker of stone tools. There is evidence that he existed for 1,500,000 years and, toward the end of that time, lived contemporaneously with men who had evolved from his earliest ancestors. Then, 500,000 years ago, primates of a clearly human type had appeared. These and later types of men became extinct except for the modern type, which was clearly in evidence 30,000 years ago.

As we proceed with our discussion of the fossil record, filling out certain details of what has been so briefly sketched, it will become apparent that fossil primates are relatively rare. This is especially true of the more advanced types with which this discussion is concerned. There are a number of reasons for this scarcity, but most important of all is the relatively high level of primate intelligence, going, as it does, with advanced locomotor ability and manual dexterity. Most animals that become fossils are trapped in water, in bogs and natural asphalt pits, or by volcanic lava or falling rocks. They are not sufficiently perceptive and resourceful to escape floods and other catastrophic events. The tree-dwelling primates escape more frequently not only because of their intelligence but also because their arboreal life removes them from many terrestrial dangers. When they die, they usually do so in trees or on solid ground. This means that their bodies are destroyed by scavengers and the elements. Those whose bodies become fossilized are usually trapped by events that they cannot escape, such as sudden floods or collapsed caves. Human fossils are sometimes found in ancient burial grounds. In any event, the body which becomes a fossil must be covered before it is destroyed. Then, as sediment builds upon it and turns to rock, it gradually becomes mineralized so that its form is preserved. Eventually it is overlaid by layer upon layer of rock and forever hidden from view unless some upheaval, or the cutting action of a river, exposes the strata, as in places like the Grand Canyon of the Colorado. But after fossil-bearing stratification is thus revealed, the fossils lie there unknown to science unless some interested person, such as a paleontologist, discovers them or has them called to his attention. Thus, while primate fossils are relatively rare, there are no doubt many more than have yet been discovered or will ever be found.

MISSING LINKS

Because man descended from an apelike primate, there has been much discussion of missing links. However, as pongids and hominids are on different branches of the ancestral tree, one should not expect to find a primate that is half ape and half man—an "ape-man" or "man-ape." On the other hand, the early pongids and early hominids might be expected to resemble each other more than modern apes resemble modern men. In fact, we shall see that the remains of an ancient primate may be apelike in some respects and manlike in others, thus giving rise to considerable controversy as to whether it should be classed as pongid or hominid.

One difficulty in resolving such an issue is the close resemblance of present-day apes and men, particularly in their skeletal characteristics. There are, of course, some very clear differences—in cranial capacity, teeth, hand and foot bones, to mention only a few. But complete skeletons of the most ancient pongids and hominids are rarely found. Sometimes there are just bits and pieces, such as a fragment of a cranium, a few limb bones, or a few teeth.

The transition from terrestrial mammals through monkey-like primates to the pongids and then to the hominids involved the adoption of arboreal life and a return to terrestrial life. Mammals below the primate level are predominantly terrestrial, moving along the ground on all fours. Those that became primates lived predominantly in the trees, and this arboreal existence became extremely important in their further evolution. It led to marked anatomical changes which, as Professor Frederic Wood Jones and others have pointed out, were steps toward man.[2]

There were changes in sensory emphasis which led to alterations in the brain. Smell, for example, was not as important in the trees as on the ground, so the smell brain became relatively smaller. Vision and hearing became more important than they had been, and more advanced visual and auditory mechanisms evolved, leading to changes in the size, shape, and relative importance of corresponding areas of the brain. The increased significance of kinesthesis and the sense of balance for tree-living animals no doubt produced changes in the brain as well as in the associated sensory mechanisms.

The feet, and later the forearms, became better adapted for grasping as well as for locomotion through the trees.[3] In many of the primates both hands and feet became so well adapted for grasping that we could call these animals "four-handed." As the forelimbs developed hands in place of paws, there were corresponding changes in the motor mechanisms of the nervous system. The hand became an organ for exploring, examining, and manipulating as well as grasping and walking. There were also changes in the hind limbs and feet which, in time, facilitated upright locomotion in the trees and on the ground.

Some primates eventually became less tied to an arboreal environment. Chimpanzees and gorillas, for example, became as much at home on the ground as in the trees. It was from some such arboreal and terrestrial primates that men evolved. To them we owe our advanced sensitivity, our locomotor ability, and our great manual dexterity. Manual dexterity (and of course the brain which controls it) became of the utmost importance. The pongids have clumsy hands

[2] Frederic Wood Jones, *Arboreal Man,* London: Arnold, 1926.

[3] One may recall from our earlier discussion (p. 101) that the American opossum has a thumblike great toe which may be used much as the thumb is used by primates. Apart from primates, this is the only animal with such an appendage.

compared to our own (see illustration, p. 102), partly because their thumb is relatively small, weak, and not effectively opposed to the rest of the fingers, either singly or as a group.

The greater flexibility of the human hand is related to the fact that man's arboreal ancestors left the trees and assumed an upright posture. At first, like modern apes, they probably walked upright only part of the time, alternating this with locomotion on all fours. The first hominids, however, walked upright. We know this from their bone structure, as revealed by fossils. Bipedal locomotion freed the hands from locomotor duties, thus facilitating their further evolution.

Our arboreal ancestors used their hands to make nests and, in time, implements of various kinds. Some, like the present-day chimpanzee, could use sticks or other objects as ready-made implements, and they could no doubt improvise, as by fitting pieces of bamboo together. But man's superior brain, controlling a much more flexible hand than that of any other primate, made it possible for him to invent relatively complicated tools and weapons, and eventually to produce and use fire and to draw, paint, and write.

Although chimpanzees sometimes improvise tools, these are relatively simple. It would be beyond this animal's intelligence, and also its manual skill, to use one instrument to modify another, as men do when they make tools. Even the simplest human artifact, as illustrated (p. 168), would be beyond the limits achieved by any ape. The discovery of such an implement, with or without accompanying fossils, would suggest the presence of a human or near-human hand and brain.

With the assumption of an upright posture and the evolution of manual skill there was a decreasing need to use the mouth for crude manipulative duties, as in fighting and tearing tough foodstuffs apart. Thus freed from crude manipulative functions, the mouth, the jaws, and structures of the throat evolved into a set of organs adapted for speech. Again, the brain was crucially important, for it alone could formulate the message to be conveyed by manipulation of the speech mechanisms.

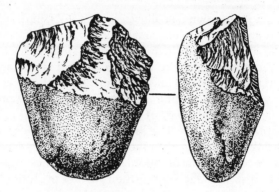

Pebble tool from Africa. From L. S. B. Leakey:
The Progress and Evolution of Man in Africa
published by Oxford University Press.

FROM APE TO MAN

From the comparative anatomy of living primates and the fossilized remains of those now extinct it is evident that the transition from a tree-shrew type of primate to the human type followed a course like that diagrammed (p. 169) and that a period of some 75 million years was involved. The pongid line, represented as branching off at point E, is believed to have appeared 25 to 30 million years ago. This line is represented today by the apes of southern Asia (gibbon and orang-utan), the apes of equatorial Africa (chimpanzee and gorilla), and man. We do not know when and where the hominid line branched off from the pongid, but there is good evidence that it did so in Africa and that it was an offshoot of the line now represented by chimpanzees and gorillas.

Evidence that the hominid line originated in Africa comes from the fact that the most ancient remains which are clearly hominid have been found there, the fact that this is the location of the various controversial "man-ape" or "ape-man" fossils, and the fact that there is an especially close biochemical affinity between humans and the African apes. This affinity has been revealed by analyzing hemoglobins

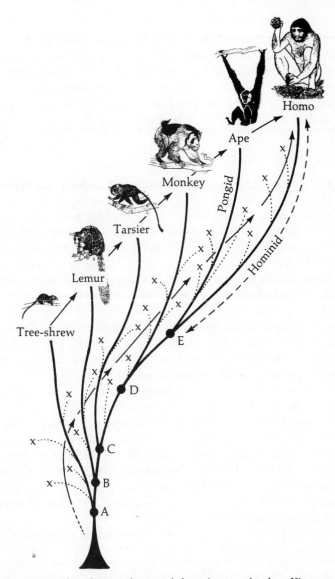

Homo

Ape

Pongid

Monkey

Hominid

Tarsier

Lemur

Tree-shrew

E

D

C

B

A

The presumed evolution of some of the primates of today. X's represent extinct (fossil) lines. Redrawn by permission of Quadrangle Books from The Antecedents of Man *by W. E. LeGros Clark, copyright © 1959 by Edinburgh University Press.*

and serum proteins.[4] According to Ernst Mayr, in *Animal Species and Evolution*, such analysis "proves conclusively" that "the hominid line branched off from the line of African apes (chimpanzees and gorillas) at a comparatively recent date, long after the pongid line had split into an Asiatic (*Pongo*) and African (*Pan + Homo*) branch."[5]

SOME ANCIENT APES

The most ancient apelike primates yet known are represented by fossils discovered in Egypt. *Propliopithecus*, estimated to have lived more than 30 million years ago, was first represented by a jawbone, the teeth of which included five-cusped molars. Molars of this type are found in apes and men but not in Old World monkeys, hence *Propliopithecus* is judged to have been an ape, possibly ancestral to the gibbon. A more recently discovered type, referred to as *Aegyptopithecus*, has been given an estimated date of 28 million years ago. It is represented by an almost complete skull and some partial jaws with teeth. According to Professor Elwyn L. Simons of Yale University, this "new genus of upper Oligocene primate could have evolved from a species of *Propliopithecus* during the several million years or so separating it from the fossil remains of the earlier genus. The evolution has been in a direction that gives the younger animal a close resemblance to the still later apes of the genus *Dryopithecus*, which were a major element of the Old World primate population in Miocene times." The characteristics of this animal were such that it could "occupy an early position in man's lineage and even perhaps be the direct forebear of apes such as the modern gorilla as well."[6]

[4] See the papers by Morris Goodman ("Man's Place in the Phylogeny of the Primates as Reflected in Serum Proteins") and Emil Zuckerkandl ("Perspectives in Molecular Anthropology") in Sherwood L. Washburn (Ed.), *Classification and Human Evolution*, London: Methuen, 1964.

[5] Ernst Mayr, *Animal Species and Evolution*, Harvard University Press, 1966, p. 628.

[6] Elwyn L. Simons, "The Earliest Apes," *Scientific American*, December 1967, pp. 32–33.

Another type of African ape, already referred to as *Dryopithecus,* is believed to have existed some 20 million years ago. Fossils of this early primate were discovered in Kenya about 40 years ago by Dr. L. S. B. Leakey. Many others have been found since that time, some as far away as Asia and Europe. The original find, a skull and part of a skeleton, led to the belief that it was the remains of a primeval chimpanzee, which at that time was given the name *Proconsul* (meaning before Consul, a noted performing chimpanzee). As additional fossils became available, it was apparent that some dryopithecines were as large as gorillas. There now appears to be little doubt that these apes were the forerunners of the chimpanzee and possibly also the gorilla.[7] According to Sir Wilfrid Le Gros Clark, the dryopithecines may represent the ancestral stock which in time diverged to produce the modern pongids in one direction and the hominids in another.[8]

A creature apparently more hominid than pongid lived in places as widely separated as India (where part of a jaw was discovered by G. E. Lewis of Yale University) and Africa (where another piece of jaw was discovered by L. S. B. Leakey). Both specimens were found at approximately the same geological level, and their possessors are estimated to have lived some 14 million years ago. These have been given the name *Ramapithecus brevirostris.*

The proper classification of *Ramapithecus* is not yet agreed upon, but Professor Elwyn L. Simons says that this primate possessed "several characters in the upper dentition and maxilla which significantly approach the dental conformation of Pleistocene species of tool-using man." Some of "the characters, which distinguish these forms from typical pongids and suggest hominid ties, are a parabolic (not U-shaped) dental arcade, an arched palate, a canine fossa, low-crowned cheek teeth, small incisors and canines, a low degree of prog-

[7] See the discussion by F. Clark Howell in *Early Man,* Time Inc., 1966, p. 37.

[8] Paraphrased from *Man-Apes or Ape-Men?,* Holt, Rinehart and Winston, 1967, p. 128.

nathism, and a short face. Separately, almost all of these features can be found among pongids, but their occurrence in combination in R. *brevirostris* is a strong indication of hominid ties."[9] Professor F. Clark Howell refers to *Ramapithecus* as possibly "man's oldest known direct ancestor."[10]

AN ALMOST HUMAN HOMINID

The most ancient relics which authorities generally regard as hominid come from South and East Africa. They represent a near-human who is estimated to have existed for possibly two million years. The oldest fossils are believed to take us back two million years; the most recent, perhaps no more than 500,000 years. Although all of these near-men have been given the same generic name, they varied greatly in size and certain other characteristics—so much so, in fact, that at least two species are generally recognized.

The first specimen came to light in 1924. This was embedded in limestone rock which was blasted out of a quarry near Johannesburg, South Africa. Professor Raymond Dart of the University of Witwatersrand, to whom the rock was sent, chipped away at it until the complete facial skeleton and partial skull of a juvenile were revealed. A full set of milk teeth and partially erupted molars suggested an age of six years. The teeth, jaw, and relatively flat face (see figure, p. 173) were more like those of a human than an ape, yet the cranial capacity was too small to be human. The brain would have been no larger than that of a chimpanzee of comparable age. This juvenile thus appeared to be "an ape with human features," and Professor Dart named it *Australopithecus africanus*, the South African Ape.

Since this discovery, Dr. Robert Broom, Dr. L. S. B. Leakey, and others have found the remains of more members of this species, juvenile and adult, male and female. These finds include skulls, vertebrae, jaws, teeth, pelvic structures, and

---

[9] Elwyn L. Simons, "Some Fallacies in the Study of Hominid Phylogeny," *Science*, Vol. 141, September 6, 1963, p. 888.

[10] F. Clark Howell and The Editors of LIFE, *Early Man*, p. 38.

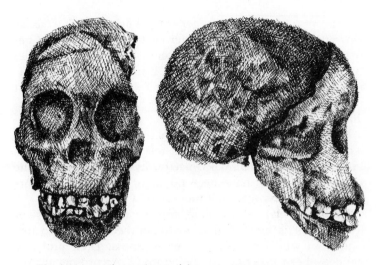

The first juvenile specimen of AUSTRALOPITHECUS AFRICANUS *to be discovered. From* Man-Apes or Ape-Men? *by Wilfrid LeGros Clark. Copyright © 1967 by Holt, Rinehart and Winston, Inc. Redrawn by permission of Dr. Raymond Dart and Holt, Rinehart and Winston, Inc.*

fragments of the limbs, including bones of hands and feet. Some specimens have been found at various places in South Africa and others at the Olduvai (Oldoway) Gorge in what is now the East African country of Tanzania. The cutting action of an ancient river created this gorge and exposed the stratified rock in which the fossils were found.

Comparative studies demonstrate that some of these early African hominids were relatively small and slender (gracile), with a height of perhaps 4 feet and a weight of less than 100 pounds, while others were relatively robust, with large jaws and teeth, a height of possibly 5 feet, and a weight of 130–150 pounds. The robust type was discovered by Dr. Robert Broom, who gave it the name *Paranthropus* (akin to man).

Today there is rather general agreement among those who have examined the various South and East African fossils that they are variations of a single genus and, although they inhabited both regions, Dart's designation "Southern ape" has been retained in the generic name, *Australopithecus.* However, the smaller and larger australopithecines are believed to represent separate species. The smaller (gracile) type, which was what Professor Dart discovered first, is referred to now as *Australopithecus africanus.* The robust type (*Paranthropus*) is now generally referred to as *Australopithecus robustus.*

From their fossils it appears that these types were contemporaneous. Both species had relatively small brains, as indicated by their cranial capacity. Even the brains of the robust type would have been no larger than those of a gorilla, which is less than half the size of a human brain.

From the pelvis, thigh bone, and structures at the base of the skull, it is evident that australopithecines walked upright, but with less than human erectness. Their probable gait has been described as "plodding." According to Professor John Napier, who studied their foot structure, these hominids could not stride. His study of their hand structure leads him to conclude that they had a power grip but probably not the precision grip characteristic of humans. That is to say, they could grasp with the hand as a whole but not with the fingers opposed to the thumb. Nor could they have had the dexterity of man in opposing the thumb to the index finger and to each of the other digits separately.[11]

We have seen that chimpanzees use natural objects as tools and that they sometimes make simple modifications of sticks, even to the extent of joining those which may be fitted together. There is every reason to believe that the australopithecines also used natural objects as tools and weapons, but there could be no proof of this, for used and unused natural objects are indistinguishable. If they modified sticks or other perishable materials, there could be no proof of this either.

The modification of stones in ways which make them distinguishable from the modifications produced by natural

[11] John Napier, "The Locomotor Functions of Hominids," in Washburn, *Classification and Human Evolution,* pp. 178–189. Also in "The Antiquity of Human Walking," in *Scientific American,* April 1967, pp. 56–66.

forces is quite a different matter. Such stones (see earlier illustration, p. 168) have been found in the regions of Africa inhabited by the australopithecines. They are chipped on two sides to produce a cutting or scraping edge. In some instances they have been found in places quite removed from the natural location of such stones, suggesting that they were transported to these places by hand. But were these pebble tools made by the australopithecines or by some more nearly human creature, with a larger brain and more dextrous hands? There could be no clear answer to this question unless such artifacts were located in close association with australopithecine remains, and under conditions where only the australopithecine could have been responsible for their manufacture. In 1957, an authority on man as a toolmaker pointed out that "no deliberately chipped stones or bone artifacts have been recognized with any certainty in the deposits containing remains of *Australopithecus.*"[12] However, two years later, chipped pebbles of the type illustrated earlier (p. 168), were found with australopithecine remains.

Pebbles like these were discovered by Dr. and Mrs. L. S. B. Leakey in the Olduvai (Oldoway) Gorge over a long period, but without associated australopithecine remains. Nevertheless, they referred to them as products of the "Oldowan culture" and as "Oldowan pebble tools." In 1959, however, they found what they thought was a possible maker of such tools. Its upper jaw and numerous skull fragments were embedded in a layer of rock at the edge of the stratified gorge, a layer presumed at the time to be 600,000 years old. Excavation revealed a living floor with Oldowan tools and the scattered remains of small animals in close proximity to the hominid remains. When the pieces of skull were fitted together (see illustration, p. 176), the cranial capacity was seen to be smaller than that of any known human find, but the teeth were seemingly human and, what was more important, here were tools made "to a set and regular pattern."

[12] Kenneth P. Oakley, *Man the Tool-Maker,* University of Chicago Press, 1957, p. 14.

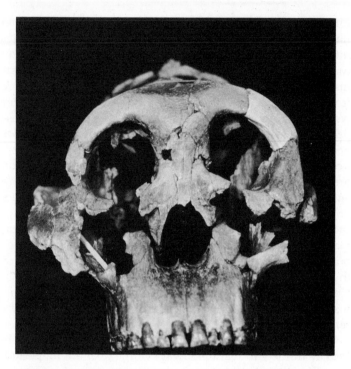

Zinjanthropus, *now considered to be a representative of* Australopithecus robustus. *Copyright © 1960, Courtesy, National Geographic Society.*

The making of such tools has always been regarded as a peculiarly human accomplishment. It is not surprising, therefore, that Dr. Leakey named this find East African Man, or *Zinjanthropus.*

In subsequent years there were other finds nearby, again with associated tools. One of the most important of these included an almost complete foot skeleton and some hand bones. Various considerations, including the foot bones, small teeth, and estimated cranial capacity of some of these newer finds, convinced Dr. Leakey and his collaborators[13]

[13] L. S. B. Leakey, P. V. Tobias, and J. R. Napier, "A New Species of the Genus *Homo* from Olduvai Gorge," *Nature,* 1964, Vol. 202, p. 7.

that they had discovered an even more clearly human type than *Zinjanthropus*. They called this type *Homo habilis* (skillful man). *Homo habilis* was found in the same layer as *Zinjanthropus*, hence may have been a contemporary. Presumably it was *Homo habilis* who made the tools found in this layer. The layer also contained volcanic rock, enabling it to be dated by the potassium-argon method referred to earlier. This indicates an age of 1,700,000 years. The fission-track method gives a date of between 1,500,000 and 2,500,000 years ago.

Subsequent study of the zinj and habilis fossils led Sir Wilfrid LeGros Clark and some other paleontologists to question their classification as human. They regard them as unquestionably hominid, but insufficiently different from australopithecines to warrant the setting up of a new genus. Zinj is now generally regarded as a specimen of *Australopithecus robustus;* habilis, of *Australopithecus africanus. The* latter is sometimes referred to as an advanced australopithecine, and as the most likely maker of the Oldowan tools. *Australopithecus africanus* appears to have been a hunter and a meat-eater; *Australopithecus robustus,* a vegetarian. The latter might have had no particular need for tools and weapons.

Although the australopithecines were more human than apelike in several respects, including their facial structure, the arrangement of their teeth, and their locomotor mechanisms, they are regarded as less than human because of their relatively small cranial capacity, which ranged from 450 to 650 cubic centimeters. The cranial capacity of the great apes has a similar range—350 to 650 cubic centimeters. However, the most ancient humans clearly recognized as such had a cranial capacity ranging from 800 to 1000 cubic centimeters.[14]

The australopithecines no doubt communicated with each other in various ways, as the apes do today, but there is no evidence, from the size of their brains and their jaws and related structures, to indicate that they might have developed speech. The absence of hearths, charcoal, or any other

[14] See Mayr, *Animal Species and Evolution,* p. 635.

evidences of fire in the vicinity of their remains suggests that they may not have learned to make and use fire. Actually, they had no particular need of it. Evidence of its use is first found in northern Europe and Asia, where the cold climate made fire particularly useful.

There is no indication that australopithecines went outside Africa, or even that they got as far as the Sahara. As Sir Wilfrid LeGros Clark has so succinctly pointed out, they were neither physically nor mentally equipped to travel far from the territory familiar to them. He says:

They had as yet to develop an erect posture as efficient as that of *Homo* for running and walking; they had no powerful canine teeth for attack or defence; their hands were clumsily constructed and, although there is reasonable evidence that they used and even fabricated tools, the latter were very primitive and crude in design; and it may be inferred that their small brains would hardly have allowed them to cope with unexpected contingencies apart from those with which they had familiarized themselves in a relatively restricted type of environment. Only later, following a progressive development towards the *Homo erectus* phase of hominid evolution, with a larger brain (corresponding to a cranial capacity of perhaps 1000 cc or thereabout), with a perfected upright stance character-istic of the genus *Homo,* and with the manipulative ability to make more effective and more varied weapons and tools, only then would the possibility arise for adventuring into novel territories and eventually spreading over far regions of the Old World. Of course, this is no more than surmise, but it seems a reasonable surmise on the basis of the evidence at present available.[15]

THE FIRST MEN

Some authorities assert that the most ancient type of true man was the one whose remains were discovered at Trinil, Java, by Eugene Dubois about 80 years ago. What Dubois unearthed was a skull cap and thigh bone. The skull was larger than that of any known ape, yet apparently too small

[15] Sir Wilfrid E. LeGros Clark, *Man-Apes or Ape-Men?*, Holt, Rinehart and Winston, 1967, p. 50.

to be human. The thigh bone, however, appeared definitely human. It had belonged to an individual who stood erect. Believing that he had discovered the remains of an erect ape-man, Dubois referred to him as *Pithecanthropus erectus*.

About 30 years later an even larger skull cap of the same type was found in a cave deposit near Peking, China. Its discoverer, Davidson Black, called this find *Sinanthropus pekinensis* (see illustration, p. 180). Now the same region has yielded many specimens, some of them with tools and evidence that this Chinese man was a user of fire. Similar remains have since been found in Java (near the site of Dubois's original find) in various parts of Europe and in Africa. All are sufficiently similar to warrant the general designation "pithecanthropine."

The African finds are of special interest. Again, the Leakey and the Olduvai Gorge finds play a significant role, for, at a higher level of the gorge than that occupied by the australo-pithecines, both gracile and robust, these searchers found a skull cap which, in size and shape, appears to be that of a pithecanthropine. It has been referred to by some as *Homo leakeyi*.

All of the fossils referred to under the names *Pithecanthropus, Sinanthropus,* and *Homo leakeyi* are sufficiently similar to warrant use of a single designation, pithecanthropine or something else. In fact the use of so many names for specimens which have such a structural similarity was so confusing that a group of influential paleontologists decided to assign all to a common species, *Homo erectus,* while recognizing such subspecies as, for example, *Homo erectus pekinensis,* the relatively large-brained type found near Peking.

The discovery of the so-called *Homo leakeyi* at Olduvai Gorge, with *Homo habilis* and *Zinjanthropus (Australopithecus robustus)* at a lower level, suggests that man may have evolved from australopithecines. At one site (Swartkrans, South Africa) there are *Homo erectus* remains intermingled with those of australopithecines, which shows that *Homo* lived at the same time as late representatives of the species from which he may have evolved. The Swartkrans specimens and

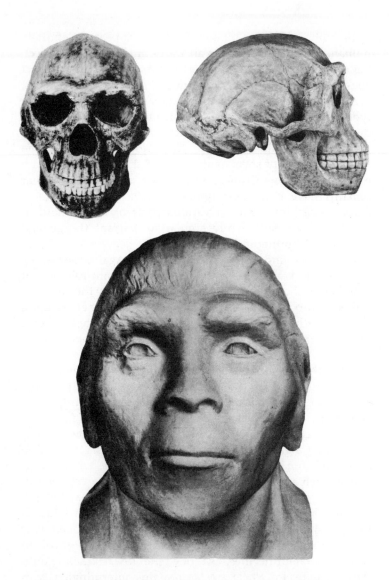

HOMO ERECTUS PEKINENSIS. *These reconstructions of what was earlier referred to as* SINANTHROPUS *are in the American Museum of Natural History. Courtesy of the American Museum of Natural History.*

those found at Olduvai Gorge "seem to reflect a transition from an australopithecine level to an *erectus* level about a million years ago."[16] If this were so, australopithecines would already have been in existence for a million years, since the most ancient fossils of this group are, as we have seen, dated at approximately two million years ago.

From the evidence so far available, it appears that *Homo erectus* may have evolved in Africa and then begun to travel as the australopithecines were not equipped to do. His superior brain, striding upright gait, skillful hands, and more effective tools and weapons would no doubt facilitate such travel. Social evolution may also have contributed to this. According to Dr. Bernard Campbell:

It could be that the evolution of cooperative hunting and its associated behavioral and anatomical adaptations enabled early *Homo* to spread from Central Africa north up the Nile Valley into Asia and east through the tropical zones of India and Southeastern Asia. In the absence of a constant environment throughout that area, the spread would have been made possible only by the evolution of a degree of versatility unique in the primate order, together with a very rapid assimilation of novel cultural adaptations. Men had arisen from nomadic scavenging bands, and his tendency to keep moving may have eventually led him into Asia, which was a vast area ready for occupation and exploitation, an area in which human evolution would further accelerate.[17]

Homo erectus had an average cranial capacity of about 1000 cubic centimeters, which is clearly human, yet he retained such apelike characteristics as heavy overhanging brows, a massive jaw, and absence of a chin. The most advanced members of this species may have been those whose remains were found in caves near Peking. Some had a cranial capacity of about 1300 cubic centimeters but retained primitive features like those of their predecessors. These people are estimated to have inhabited this region some 400,000 years ago.

[16] William H. Howells, "Homo Erectus," *Scientific American*, November, 1966, p. 53.

[17] Bernard Campbell, *Human Evolution*, Aldine, 1967, pp. 343–344.

The life of Homo erectus pekinensis, *as pictured by Maurice Wilson for the British Museum.*

An impression of what *Homo erectus pekinensis* and his living quarters may have looked like is given by the accompanying illustration. The general appearance of these people, as depicted, is purely conjectural, but their general configuration and posture is anatomically correct. The making of tools by chipping stone, the use of fire, and hunting are well established by what has been found in their caves. Deer meat, as evidenced by the preponderance of deer bones, was apparently favored. Human skulls, cracked open in a manner to allow extraction of the brains, suggest that this early man, like many after him, even up to the present day, may have been a cannibal.

THE TRANSITION FROM *ERECTUS* TO *SAPIENS*

The next step in human evolution takes us from *Homo erectus* to *Homo sapiens*, but this transition is "shrouded in mystery," and various fossil humans of possible transitional significance are veritable "bones of contention." Are these to be classified as *erectus* or *sapiens*? Are they in direct line of *sapiens* descent, or do they merely represent aberrant branches of the main evolutionary stream? One difficulty in answering such questions is that there is a scarcity of fossil humans dated between 300,000 years (when *Homo erectus* seems to have disappeared) and 70,000 years (when men classified as belonging to the *sapiens* type were clearly in evidence).

Another difficulty is that the apparently transitional specimens are fragmentary. Two of these are particularly interesting. Both appear to be somewhere in the neighborhood of 200,000 years old. One specimen is part of a cranium found at Swanscombe, in southeast England. This is usually referred to as female, because of the fineness of the bone, but its sex is not definitely established. The estimated cranial capacity is about 1,300 cubic centimeters, which is within the range of *Homo sapiens*. It is naturally puzzling to find such a large brain in this region of the world so long ago, although the upper level for Peking Man was comparable. The other seemingly transitional specimen comes from Steinheim, near Stuttgart, in southwest Germany. It comprises a cranium with part of the facial skeleton intact, and its sex is also judged to be female. Its cranial capacity has been estimated as about 1,200 cubic centimeters, again within the range of both *erectus* and *sapiens*. However, heavy supraorbital (eye) ridges, a low forehead, and other features seem to place this individual somewhere between *erectus* and *sapiens*. These structures resemble those of Neanderthal man, who did not enter the scene until an estimated 70,000 years ago. A study by Dr. Bernard Campbell[18] shows that the characteristics of

[18] Bernard Campbell, "Quantitative Taxonomy and Human Evolution," in Washburn, *Classification and Human Evolution*, p. 58.

the Swanscombe and Steinheim skulls are intermediate between those of Neanderthal man and more recent representatives of *Homo sapiens*. These skulls may also be considered intermediate between those of *Homo erectus pekinensis* and *Homo sapiens*. It is obvious, however, that the remains are too few and too fragmentary to provide a firm foundation for any conclusions concerning the transition from *Homo erectus* to *Homo sapiens*.

An opinion shared by several outstanding anthropologists is that a *sapiens* type represented by the Swanscombe and Steinheim skulls moved into northern Europe during a relatively warm period, when the glaciers were receding, and that this was replaced during a subsequent glacial period by the more robust Neanderthal race. These became extinct about 30 to 40 thousand years ago when superseded by men very much like ourselves.

NEANDERTHAL MAN

Neanderthal man, named after the valley in Germany in which his remains were first discovered, was almost as primitive as *Homo erectus* in appearance, yet his cranial capacity was as large as our own, averaging 1,400 cubic centimeters. He is classified today as *Homo sapiens,* subspecies *neanderthalensis.* Neanderthal fossils are widely and profusely scattered over Europe, together with a relatively advanced tool culture and evidences of ritualistic burial and a mystical outlook. This culture will receive attention later.

In appearance, *Homo sapiens neanderthalensis* was brutish, with a flattened but large skull, low forehead, heavy eyeridges which crossed the bridge of his nose, heavy protruding jaws, and hardly any chin (see illustration, p. 185). His average height was about five feet. He lived in caves heated by fire.

Neanderthal man was at first thought to be too brutish in appearance, and too late upon the scene, to have been a direct ancestor of modern man, but the discovery of other, somewhat similar specimens in various parts of the Old World,

Neanderthal man. An artist's conception, recon-
structed from skeletal remains. Note the absence of
a chin and the beetling eyebrows. From Life: An
Introduction to Biology, *Second Edition, by*
George Gaylord Simpson and William S. Beck,
copyright © 1957, 1965, by Harcourt Brace
Jovanovich, Inc., and reproduced with their
permission.

including North Africa, Iraq, Palestine, and Java, have led
to the conclusion that there were two Neanderthal types, a
European "classic" type and an Old World "progressive"
type. The latter is usually rated more progressive because its
features more closely approach those of the later appearing
Homo sapiens sapiens, our own kind of man, who did not put
in an appearance until some 30,000 years ago.

It seems unlikely that the classic type of Neanderthaler,
with his grossly primitive features, was ancestral to modern

man. The progressive type, on the other hand, might well have been.

Among paleontologists there is a widely held opinion that the progressive type came first and that the so-called classic type represents a population which made its way to Europe and there, under glacial conditions, developed its relatively gross features. It is also believed that members of the progressive type who came to Europe later, after the climate had moderated, were ancestral to modern man, as represented by European men of 30,000 years ago.[19]

THE RISE OF MODERN MAN

Humans of the modern type (*Homo sapiens sapiens*) were well established in various parts of Euope 30,000 years ago. They are usually referred to as *Cro-Magnon men* because the first specimen which received scientific attention was found in the Cro-Magnon rock shelter under an overhanging cliff of the Dordogne Valley in France. The specimen comprised a skull and some other bones, with a nearby hearth and flint tools of advanced design. Other Cro-Magnon remains have been found throughout France and in other parts of Europe. It is apparent that this man was as tall as men are today, held his head erect, and had a high-domed cranium, possessed a cranial capacity equal to or exceeding our own, and had other features which would make him indistinguishable from men now living (see illustration, p. 187). He is noted for his superior flint tools, his use of bones to make awls and needles, and his artistic achievements. The latter include sculptures as well as cave paintings which pictured the animals hunted and, in some cases, how they were killed. A comparison of the features of Cro-Magnon Man, Neanderthal Man, and *Homo erectus* is provided by the illustrated reconstructions.

[19] In this connection, see the discussions by John Buettner-Janusch, *Origins of Man*, Wiley, 1966; Theodosius Dobzhansky, *Mankind Evolving*, Yale University Press, 1962; and F. Clark Howell, *Early Man*, Time-Life, 1966.

Cro-Magnon man, the earliest known representative of HOMO SAPIENS SAPIENS, *could not have been distinguished physically from men living today. From* Life: An Introduction to Biology, *Second Edition, by George Gaylord Simpson and William S. Beck, copyright © 1957, 1965, by Harcourt Brace Jovanovich, Inc., and reproduced with their permission.*

THE DISTRIBUTION OF MODERN MEN

The fossil record, scanty as it is, shows the wide diversity of early humans. We have already referred to variations in their cranial capacity, size of jaws and teeth, eye-ridges, and overall stature. They also differed in other respects—round- or long-headedness, prognathism (how much the jaw protruded), and whether or not they had a chin. No doubt they also differed in such traits as hairiness and skin color, although the fossil record cannot reveal such things.

The wide range of differences within *Homo erectus* and within our own species has already been noted. Such differences led to the use of many names to represent specimens that are ·now lumped together as *erectus* or *sapiens*. This diversity has also led to controversies as to whether a particular specimen is to be regarded as *erectus* or *sapiens*.

Wide variation still exists among human beings, wherever they are found. It exists between individuals within any group we might specify and also between different racial, geographical, or cultural groups. In spite of such divergence, all human beings share a common gene pool, have a basically similar structure, and are capable of interbreeding. For these reasons they are considered to belong to the same species.

Some of the more obvious differences among living men— such as skin pigmentation, hairiness, head shape, and facial appearance—have led to the concept of race, or human subspecies. But the classification of *Homo sapiens sapiens* into races is largely a matter of convenience in discourse, for we can speak of this or that race more readily than of individuals. But there is actually so much overlapping among the various populations of mankind that racial distinctions are necessarily blurred. Thus, it is not surprising that anthropologists have difficulty in deciding upon a definitive classification of races. Some classifications include many "races," while others have only three to five main racial groups. The racial populations most widely referred to are Caucasoid, Mongoloid, Negroid, and Australoid. Many intermediate racial types are recognized and generally regarded as mixtures produced by interbreeding.

How the most clearly recognized racial populations originated is not known, but there are two major theories. According to one theory, *Homo erectus* evolved to *sapiens* level, as represented by the progressive type of Neanderthal

Man, then spread throughout the habitable parts of Europe, Asia, and Africa. Under the conditions prevailing in these regions, he gradually assumed the characteristics of the major racial populations living in those places.[20] Thus, the Caucasoid, Mongolian, and Negroid races are regarded as having evolved from a common ancestral line. The other theory supposes that at least four different ancestral lines were established at the *Homo erectus* stage, or earlier, and that these underwent parallel evolution which resulted in the major races of *Homo sapiens* living today.[21]

It is assumed that the Caucasoids, originally a European and Middle Eastern population but later also represented in India, originated from the progressive Neanderthal type. Indeed, fossils from Israel and Iraq show that this type existed in the Middle East some 45,000 years ago.

The origin of the Mongoloids is said to be *Homo erectus pekinensis* who, as we saw earlier, lived in China an estimated 400,000 years ago. Mongolians spread throughout East Asia, giving rise to the so-called "yellow race" and also, in more recent times, the Indians of the Americas, for Mongoloids appear to have crossed to Alaska from Siberia some 20,000 years ago, then gradually spread to the American plains and plateaus. They were apparently in these places 10,000 years ago, but their fossils are recognizably Indian.[22] Some pushed on into the South American continent, and there is evidence that they reached its southernmost region by 7,000 years ago.[23]

Negroid origins are not so clearly defined. However, there

[20] See William W. Howells, "The Distribution of Man," *Scientific American*, September 1960, pp. 113–127.

[21] Variations on this general theory have been presented by Franz Weidenreich in *Apes, Giants and Man* (University of Chicago Press, 1946), and Carleton S. Coon in *The Origin of Races*, Alfred A. Knopf, 1963.

[22] Howells, "The Distribution of Man," p. 114. See also Douglas D. Anderson, "A Stone Age Campsite at the Gateway to America," *Scientific American*, June 1968, pp. 24–33; and Anonymous, "Date for New World Man," *Science News*, 1968, Vol. 93, pp. 445–446.

[23] See Carleton S. Coon, *The Story of Man*, Alfred A. Knopf, 1954, p. 352.

are some African fossils with an age of possibly 40,000 years which suggest that the Negroes of Africa today may have evolved there from an advanced form of *Homo erectus* generally referred to as Rhodesian Man. But this type of man is assumed to have been ancestral only to the relatively tall and robust Negroes. The smaller people of Africa, such as the Bushmen and Pygmies, are believed to have had a different origin.

The Australoid race presumably had its remote origin in Java, where, in addition to the pithecanthropines, some more advanced types of fossil men have been found. One of these, who is generally believed to have reached the *sapiens* level, is represented by fossils discovered along the Solo River, hence his name Solo Man. His estimated age is 20,000 years. Some such man is believed to have entered Australia from Java or other parts of the East Indies. There may still have been a land bridge at that time (over which the marsupials entered Australia many millions of years earlier), but the islands are close together and might have been navigated in small boats. There are fossils and artifacts in Australia which provide evidence of human occupation by at least 20,000 years ago.[24]

The second of these theories rather neatly, possibly too neatly, ties together the scanty evidence that we have at present relating early man to the major races of *Homo sapiens sapiens* now living. The routes of entry into the Americas and Australia appear well established. But only future discoveries can possibly show whether all living men descended from a common line or whether there were separate lines for the major races.

Regardless of the line from which it originated, any given population would undergo further modification in its particular region, thus producing at least some of the racial diversity now evident. There are three important factors which underlie such modification. One of these is the smallness and relative isolation of the migrating populations, which would foster close inbreeding.

[24] See N. W. G. Macintosh, "Fossil Man in Australia," *Australian Journal of Science,* 1967, Vol. 30, pp. 86–98.

Another factor is what geneticists call "genetic drift." Of all of the genes in the original gene pool, any individual (or limited group of individuals) has only a restricted number. As Professor Dobzhansky presents the situation, "some genes of the original population may not be included in the sample, while others may be over-represented. The genes brought by the migrants will be impressed upon the new colony, tribe, and eventually, the race descended from the immigrant foundation stock."[25]

The other factor of importance in producing racial differences is natural selection. During migration, and after they had settled in a particular environment, those with physical variations which best adapted them to the conditions of life would survive in greater numbers, be represented by more offspring, and pass on a greater number of adaptive genes to their descendants than would those who were poorly adapted. Many of the latter would not have survived the migration or the early settlement.

All three of these factors, working together, would lead to changes differentiating the immigrant from the original stock. No doubt geographical conditions were important in the natural selection aspect of this process for, until recent times, the Negroids were largely restricted to Africa, the Caucasoids to Europe and the Middle East, the Mongoloids to Asia, the American Indians to the Americas, and the Australoids to Australia (see illustration, p. 192). The Australians, being most isolated, are sometimes cited as the purest of all races. The others all show a degree of intermixture at the fringes of their territories. This mixture is greatly increasing today, for travel is easier and racial restrictions are breaking down.

The various characteristics which differentiate modern men—such as skin color, hair texture, prominence of cheek bones, and slantiness of the eyes—are relatively superficial as compared with the basic human structure, including the size and shape of the brain. This basic structure has not changed appreciably in the 30,000 years or so since Cro-

[25] Theodosius Dobzhansky, *Mankind Evolving,* Yale University Press, 1965, p. 282.

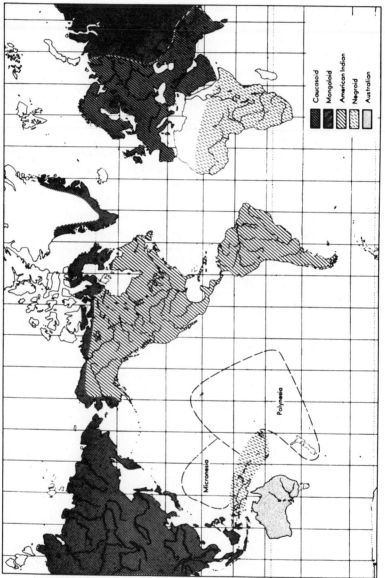

Magnon man made his appearance. Nor is there any evidence that man's basic mental capacity changed in all those years—his sensitivity, memory, and ability to learn and reason. What did change, however, was the content of his mind—the information available to him, with which his inborn mental processes could operate. This change came through cultural evolution, as we shall see in the next two chapters.

Locations of the major races before the population movements of modern times. Marston Bates, Man In Nature, Second Edition, © 1964, p. 40. Reprinted by permission of Prentice-Hall, Inc., Englewood Cliffs, N.J.

CHAPTER SIX

CULTURAL
EVOLUTION

The evolving human mind is revealed more by what man has done than by his skeletal remains. When partial skeletons alone are found, there may be some question as to whether these are the remains of apes or men. But manlike skeletons with objects which are undoubtedly hand-made tools, or even the tools alone, show that men, or at least near-men, have emerged. We have already observed that chimpanzees sometimes use natural objects as tools and that they may even improvise and modify to a certain degree. But, as Kenneth P. Oakley has pointed out, "to conceive the idea of shaping a stone or stick for use in an imagined future eventuality is beyond the mental capacity of any known ape." He goes on to say that "systematic making of tools implies a marked capacity for conceptual thought."[1]

[1] Kenneth P. Oakley, *Man the Tool-Maker,* University of Chicago Press, 1957, p. 4. This is different from selecting natural objects and carrying them to a distant locality, as when chimpanzees take stems to termite nests. See the earlier reference (p. 126) to the observations of Jane Goodall on wild chimpanzees. Also see Jane Van Lawick-Goodall, *My Friends, the Wild Chimpanzees,* National Geographic Society, 1967.

A well known paleolithic sculpture, the Venus of Willendorf. The original is in the Prehistoric Section of the Natural History Museum in Vienna, Austria.

Tools of increasing complexity mark the transition of man from *Homo erectus* to *Homo sapiens sapiens,* but there are additional evidences of man's departure from animal ways. Hearths reveal the cultivation and use of fire. Artistic productions give evidence of visual imagery and, in many instances, of a high level of creative imagination. Cro-Magnon men pictured not only the animals hunted but also weapons and trapping devices. Their pictures even suggest the use of magic, as we shall see later. Sculptures reveal what may well have been the ideal female form (see illustration above).

When human beings begin to bury their dead we see evidence of a possible reverence for human life. When they put weapons, utensils, and other objects in the grave, there is also a strong suggestion of belief in an afterlife. A consistent formal arrangement of bear skulls may reveal the presence of a cultish practice. Ornaments and decorations of various kinds show a departure from the making of purely utilitarian artifacts.

Language is the most typically human production of all, but when it began is not known. In all probability this can never be known, for language is without trace until written upon some medium which provides a permanent record. Such a record first appeared on the baked clay tablets of the Sumerians. Writing reveals the ways of men of the past as nothing else can. What, for example, could we have known of the laws of Hammurabi, without a written account?

Tools, the use of fire, art, and the ability to communicate ideas are important aspects of what we call "culture." Tools may have come first, or they may not have. If anything preceded them, it was some form of language. And this would have had to be an australopithecine language, for, as pointed out earlier, these most ancient hominids were probably the first tool-makers.

TOOLS

Whoever made them first, the Oldowan pebble tools (p. 168) and others of their kind stand at, or near, the beginning of material culture. They are the simplest instruments that can be differentiated from naturally chipped or eroded stones. Tools of this kind have been found in various parts of the world, including Africa, Europe, and Asia. They were made by holding the pebble in one hand while striking near its edge with a hammer stone held in the other. The pebble was turned over and similarly treated on the other side. This procedure produced a jagged but relatively sharp edge which could be used to skin an animal, scrape the skin, and cut up the flesh.

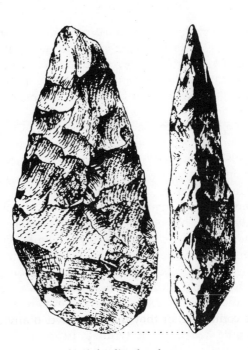

An Achuelian hand-axe.

The idea of producing such a tool would have occurred to the more intelligent or inventive members of a group. Then it would have been copied by others. This invention may have occurred independently in different groups and at different times, but there is no doubt that the idea of making such tools would also have diffused from one group to another.

From such simple beginnings there developed a number of increasingly complex stone tools and weapons. Many of these implements were first discovered in Europe and named after the location in which they were found. One such tool, a hand-axe like that illustrated above, was first discovered at Saint Achuel, in France; all others of its type, wherever found, are referred to as Achuelian. Some were found in the Olduvai

Gorge at a level above that containing the earliest known pebble tools. Others were found in various parts of Asia, India, and the Americas. They were probably used for digging, skinning, scraping, and chopping. Attached to a wooden haft, they could have been used as axes, for chopping or fighting.[2]

The complexity of the tools made by early Chinese Man (*Homo erectus pekinensis*) falls between that of the Oldowan pebble tools and the Achuelian hand-axes. These tools included choppers and scrapers, as illustrated (p. 199). Some were made by chipping around a rock (core) at the edges, while others were made from flakes chipped from the core. These flakes were sometimes chipped to produce a sharper edge. Bone and antlers were also chipped and used as tools.

Tools of the kind already discussed and illustrated belong to the Lower Paleolithic, which began one million years ago, or possibly earlier. Although the older tools continued to exist in various places, better tools began to make their appearance during the Middle and Upper Paleolithic.

The Middle Paleolithic is typified, in the main, by tools first discovered in the French village of Le Moustier and therefore designated Mousterian. These were made by that earliest of *Homo sapiens*, the classic Neanderthal Man who entered Europe some 70,000 years ago during a relatively warm period preceding the Fourth Glaciation. These men remained in Europe as the ice advanced and did not become extinct until possibly 30,000 years ago, when they were either killed off or absorbed by Cro-Magnon Man.

The Mousterian tools came relatively late in the culture

[2] The Australian aboriginals use somewhat comparable stone tools in this way. In Central Australia, until iron axes became available, the native bent a piece of green wood back upon itself, placed the stone axehead inside the bend, used a gummy form of resin to help hold the stone in place, and bound the handle at its upper end with string made from human hair. The axe was then used to chop trees, shape wood, or fight at close quarters. See Baldwin Spencer and F. J. Gillen, *The Native Tribes of Central Australia,* London: Macmillan, 1938, p. 589.

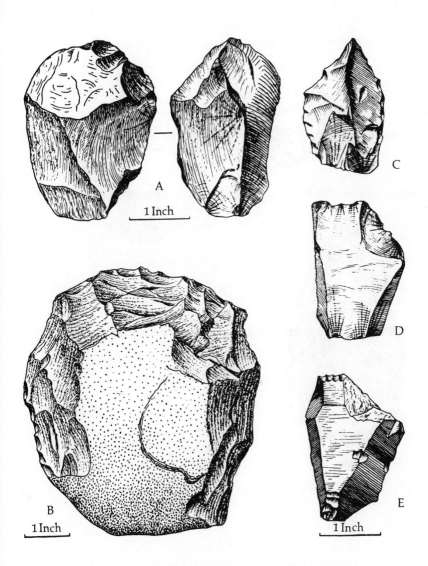

Stone tools of Peking Man. A. Quartz chopper-tool.
B. Boulder of greenstone flaked into chopper form. C. Pointed
flake of quartz. D. Bipolar flake of quartz. E. Bipyramidal
crystal of quartz utilized as a tool.

Some typical Mousterian tools.

Flint drill

Hammerstone

Flint cleaver with
lateral handhold

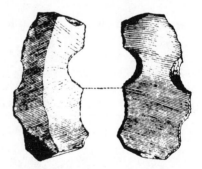

Flint spokeshave

of Neanderthal Man, making their appearance about 50,000 years ago. At this time the Neanderthalers were living in caves heated by fire; hunting mammoth, rhinoceros, and bear; and wearing clothes made from animal hides. Their tools, as illustrated above, were mainly cutting, skinning, and scraping devices, although they also used wooden spears, the tips of which were perhaps hardened by fire, as are those of the Australian aborigines.[3] Some stone scrapers were chipped only along one side, leaving the other side as a lateral handhold. Spokeshaves like the one illustrated were apparently used to shape wood into spear shafts. There were flint drills and hammer stones used for chipping flints. Bones were used as chopping blocks and for pressure-flaking of flint.

The upper Paleolithic began with the appearance of Cro-Magnon Man and continued, in Europe, until the last glaciation was drawing to a close some 10,000 years ago. Various stone industries are recognized and named in terms of their location, but these technical details need not concern us here. It will be sufficient, for our purpose, to show the increasing complexity and usefulness of the typical instruments devised during the Upper Paleolithic.

One new type of flint instrument invented early in this period was a slender blade (illustrated, p. 202) that was so designed that "the forefinger could press without discomfort against the retouched right margin of the blade while the left margin was made use of as a cutting edge."[4] Among other stone tools associated with the Upper Paleolithic were flint arrowheads, flint spearheads, awls, engraving instruments (burins), and a wide variety of cutting devices. Some of the spearheads, made with a pressure-flaking technique, were exceptionally thin and beautifully chipped, as illustrated (p. 202). Instruments made from bone and antler became increasingly prevalent and more elaborate as the Paleolithic drew to a close. These included awls, needles, fish hooks, and points for spears and harpoons. The latter were barbed. Antler spear throwers similar to those which Australian aborigines make from wood were also used. Weapons were sometimes engraved with the heads of animals.

[3] See Oakley, *Man the Tool-Maker*, p. 25, for evidence that spears were used.

[4] George Grant MacCurdy, *Human Origins*, Vol. 1, Appleton, 1924, p. 162.

A blade of the type discussed in the text.

A laurel leaf point made by pressure-flaking.

Cro-Magnon Man's cave paintings provided a new kind of record to supplement that hitherto provided only by tools and fossils. They portrayed the animals hunted—mammoth, wooly rhinoceros, wild boar, bison, and deer—and also something of how these were hunted. Spears, bows and arrows, and artificial pitfalls for trapping the mammoth are shown.

In trapping and killing large animals the hunters must have acted cooperatively. This was no doubt true of earlier stone-age men.

Did these men engage in warlike activity? We do not know, but late stone-age paintings in a Spanish cave show groups of men engaged in combat with bows and arrows.

The French cave paintings suggest that man may have attempted to enhance the effectiveness of his weapons by magical devices. He perhaps attempted to facilitate his control over the animal by picturing it, and even by using sympathetic magic, as when the pictured animal was speared before the live one was tackled. There is some basis for inferring the use of such practices.[5] Cave paintings also show pictures assumed to be those of simple dwellings. The accompanying illustration (pp. 204–205) reproduces some of the above features of Upper Paleolithic cave paintings.

A stone tool culture which immediately followed the Paleolithic in Europe is designated Mesolithic. Tools typifying this culture involve the use of microliths, small pieces of flint and other substances, such as obsidian and rock crystal, shaped to form points, trapezoids, and triangles. Points could be used to pierce the eye of a bone needle. Other microliths became arrowheads, points and barbs on javelins, and sawlike edges on knives and other tools. They were embedded in wood, bone, or horn for this purpose. Wooden sickles with microliths of flint to provide the cutting blade were used in the Near East about 7,000 years ago.[6] Some instruments involving microliths are shown in our illustration (p. 206).

[5] See Oakley, *Man the Tool-Maker*, pp. 105, 130, 133.

[6] Henri Frankfort, *The Birth of Civilization in the Near East*, Doubleday, 1956, p. 30.

Some paleolithic art.

Wounded bison

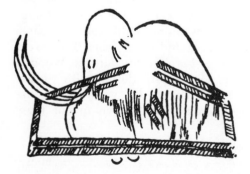

Trapped mammoth

Stag facing a trap

Reindeer

Fighting with bows and arrows

Dwellings

How microliths were used.

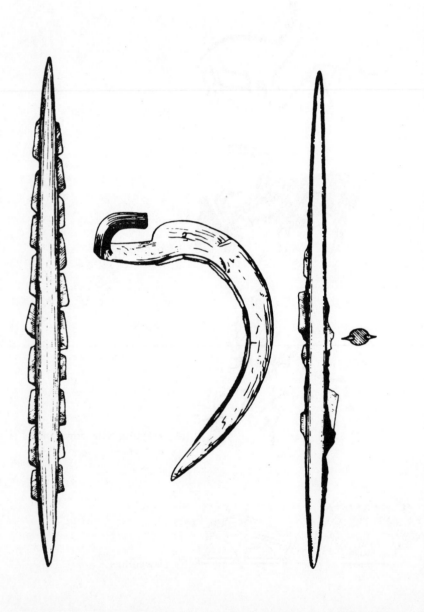

A NEW WAY OF LIFE

The Mesolithic led into the Neolithic—the New Stone Age. This was an age marked more by a new way of life than by newer stone tools. Hitherto man had been a food-gatherer and a hunter. He had been completely dependent upon what nature had to offer in the way of plants and animals. With digging sticks and hand-axes he had grubbed for edible roots. He had eaten wild grain when it was available. And he had hunted and fished. When food gave out in one region, he had moved to another. His tools, up to this time, had merely improved his success in obtaining and processing the available food. He had not yet become a food-producer.

The most significant feature of the Neolithic was the change from a food-gathering to a food-producing way of life. This change was revolutionary in its significance, for it turned the "natural man," or "child of nature," in a new direction, from which he would emerge as a civilized human being. Up to now he had not been very far removed from an animal existence. Now, as he began to till the soil and domesticate animals, his preoccupation with food was lessened, and he had time for other pursuits. He settled in one place, built a food surplus for future needs, and used animal power to supplement his own power. Surplus food was in time traded for other commodities. This called for various specialties associated with trading, such as storage, transportation, and record-keeping. Houses became necessary. People gathered in villages. And thus what we call "civilized life" began to evolve.

This new way of life began in the ancient Near East some 10,000 years ago. Its appearance was apparently somewhat more recent in India and China. Each of these places had a river valley with rich alluvial soil—the Nile, the Tigris, and the Euphrates in the Near East; the Indus in India; and the Yellow River in China. In each of these valleys cereals had been growing wild; now they were cultivated. Cattle, pigs, and other animals were domesticated and used for food or as beasts of burden.

The Neolithic did not reach Europe until about 2500 B.C. It still has not appeared in many regions of the world today where native populations still eke out a mere existence by gathering what nature provides.

Neolithic tools were usually ground and polished so that the cutting edge would more easily fell trees, cut wood, gouge logs, as in making canoes, and so on. As one would expect, many tools were specifically designed for agricultural use. These included hoes, sickles, and saddle querns (stones used in grinding cereals).

Surplus grain required storage facilities, so woven containers and pots came into use. The potting industry was in time facilitated by invention of the potter's wheel.

Gradually, as an outcome of Neolithic economy, populations increased to the stage where cities began to appear. Where before all had been engaged in searching for or producing food, there were now many who were engaged in secondary pursuits. Professor Robert J. Braidwood provides an interesting description of what this Neolithic way of life meant for man. He says that, after food production had begun, man's meat

was stored "on the hoof," his grain in silos or great pottery jars. He lived in a house; it was worth his while to build one, because he couldn't move far from his fields and flocks. In his neighborhood enough food could be grown and enough animals bred so that many people were kept busy. They all lived close to their flocks and fields, in a village. The village was already of a fair size, and it was growing, too. Everybody had more to eat; they were presumably all stronger, and there were more children. Children and old men could shepherd the animals by day or help with the lighter work in the fields. After the crops had been harvested the younger men might go hunting and some of them would fish, but the food they brought in was only an addition to the food in the village; the villagers wouldn't starve, even if the hunters and fishermen came home empty-handed.

There was more time to do different things, too. They began to modify nature. They made pottery out of raw clay, and textiles out of hair or fiber. People who became good at pottery-making traded their pots for food and spent all of their time on pottery alone. Other people were learning to weave cloth or to make new tools. There were already people in the village who were becoming full-time craftsmen.

Other things were changing, too. The villagers must have had to agree on new rules for living together. The head man of the village had problems different from those of the chief of the small food-collectors band. If somebody's flock of sheep spoiled a wheat field, the owner wanted payment for the grain he lost. The chief of the hunters was never bothered with such questions. Even the gods had changed. The spirits and the magic that had been used by hunters weren't of any use to the villagers; they needed gods who would watch over the fields and the flocks, and they eventually began to erect buildings where their gods might dwell, and where the men who knew most about the gods might live.[7]

THE AGE OF METAL

The way of life begun in the Neolithic continued and expanded in all of its aspects to the point where it exists in modern civilizations. But the discovery and use of metal brought a vitalizing element, the importance of which continues to grow in many directions. When metals were put to use as substitutes for stone, they not only produced stronger and more versatile tools, they also accelerated man's advance toward civilized life as we know it today, with its fast moving vehicles on sea and land and in the air and its towering skyscrapers.

The Stone Age lasted at least one million years. It took that long for man to learn that he could extract metals from their ores and melt and cast them. This discovery was probably a chance one. According to George Grant MacCurdy, it may have happened in some such manner as this:

When by chance a lump of copper carbonate, tinstone, or hematite was used as one of the circle of stones surrounding the hearth and had become embedded in its embers, the lump would almost cer-

---

[7] Robert J. Braidwood, *Prehistoric Men,* Chicago Natural History Museum, 1957, pp. 122–123.

tainly be reduced to metal. Such a mass of metal would attract the attention of primitive man, and experimentation would soon disclose its properties of malleability and toughness, qualities designed to be of great utility. The campfire was in all probability the first metallurgical furnace.[8]

This would have been only the beginning, for after the metal had been extracted and its usefulness recognized, it would need to be remelted and shaped into useful forms.

Copper was being used in Egypt by 7000 B.C., but mainly for ornamental purposes. Its use in tool-making was not widespread until it had been mixed with tin to produce bronze, a much harder metal. Where bronze was available, this was preferred to stone in the making of tools and weapons. Bronze axes, daggers, swords, and other implements formerly made with stone became increasingly evident. Bronze vessels of various kinds also came into use.

[8] MacCurdy, *Human Origins*, Vol. 2, p. 176.

Centers from which major domesticated animals are believed to have originated. E. S. E. Hafez' The Behaviour of Domestic Animals *(London: Balliére, Tindall, and Cox, 1962) has the following information. The fertile crescent of southwest Asia, extending from Iran to Jordan, was the most extensive early center of domestication, especially of herd animals such as goats, sheep, cattle, and swine. Donkeys were domesticated in areas around the Near East. According to Hafez, the horse evolved in North America and migrated to the Old World in Eocene times. It was apparently domesticated initially in Asia. According to V. Gordon Childe (*Man Makes Himself, *Mentor Books, 1957, p. 103), horses were used as draught animals in the Near East by 2000 B.C. and were introduced into Egypt, harnessed to war chariots, in 1650 B.C.*

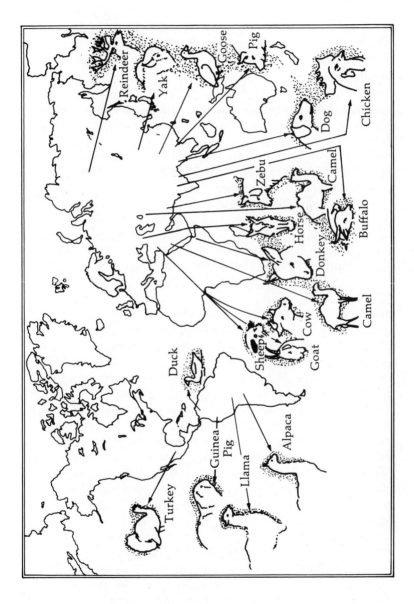

Before 2000 B.C. the Iron Age had begun in Egypt and China, where tools and weapons were being made from iron as well as bronze. Many implements previously made from wood, such as the plough and the wheel, were now made with iron. Oxen were tamed to pull ploughs as well as vehicles for transporting grain, and chariots drawn by horses were used by the Hyksos when they invaded Egypt in 1650 B.C. Iron, this "stranger from across the sea," as Aeschylus called it, gradually made its way into Greece and was commonly used there by 1000 B.C.[9] It became evident in other parts of Europe two centuries later.

Steel, an especially tough and versatile alloy produced by combining iron and carbon, was used by the ancient Greeks and Romans in making such weapons as swords and daggers, but it did not come into general use until about 200 years ago.

The Industrial Revolution involved a change from production by hand to production by power-driven machines. These machines were increasingly made of steel and were driven, at first, by steam.

Until he domesticated animals (see illustration, p. 211) and used some of them to do his work, man was dependent upon his own power. This was multiplied by group effort, including slave power. Limited help was gained from the wind, flowing water, the lever, a rolling log, and finally the wheel. The latter rotated clay in making pottery, facilitated transportation, and became a basic mechanism in power-driven machines. Animal power of course came into the picture as domesticated animals like the ox, the donkey, and the horse were utilized in various ways to substitute for or magnify human power. But the use of steam to drive boats, trains, and complicated industrial equipment marked the beginning of modern civilization—with mass production in place of individual craftsmanship, huge wealth concentrated in the hands of a few, and increased leisure.

The Industrial Revolution was greatly influenced by the introduction of complex technologies based on exact scientific knowledge. Many of the changes in tools and the utiliza-

[9] See James H. Breasted, *Ancient Times*, Ginn, 1935, p. 324.

tion of power which came with this revolution were applications of scientific findings. Such application continued, producing electrical and atomic energy as well as the computers which are increasingly substituting for man in the control of industrial machinery and also the control of his most sophisticated tool, the spacecraft.

Stone and then metal tools, the making and control of fire, cooperation in the hunt, a settled mode of life based on agriculture and animal husbandry, utilization of the lever and the wheel, magnification of manpower by domestication and use of beasts of burden, the use of steam and more potent kinds of power—all of these were landmarks in cultural evolution. But the most important invention, one which is no doubt inextricably bound up with all the others, was language and related operations with symbols in mathematics. For all we know, this may have come before any of the others.

THE EVOLUTION OF LANGUAGE

The higher primates are vocal to a high degree, but their vocalizations, as we pointed out earlier, are emotional expressions such as grunts, barks, moans, hoots, screams, and howls. They do not vocalize unemotionally, as a human infant does in vocal play, or babbling. A chimpanzee may be induced to vocalize for a reward, but this requires a long period of training. Chimpanzees gesture with apparent spontaneity—raising a hand toward others, reaching out with one or both arms, drumming with hands and feet, and so on. They also show a high degree of ability in imitating human gestures.[10]

There is no doubt that our hominid ancestors were endowed with a wide range of vocalizations and gestures and that these came to have significance for their fellows, whether or not they were made for this purpose. Used intentionally,

[10] See, for example, Vernon Reynolds and Frances Reynolds, "Chimpanzees of the Budongo Forest," pp. 404–409 in Irven DeVore (Ed.), *Primate Behavior*, Holt, Rinehart and Winston, 1965.

and in conventional ways so that they would be understood rather than reacted to reflexly by others, these signals would constitute a form of linguistic communication.

Our most remote hominid ancestors, the australopithecines, may well have developed some such form of communication. We cannot be sure that this happened, but their way of life provides some basis for the conjecture that it did. We know that they lived in open country and were hunters of small game. Presumably they hunted in groups, using natural objects and perhaps "deliberately prepared artifacts." All of this leads Sir Wilfrid LeGros Clark to suppose that

the coordination and cohesion of their group activities in the pursuit of game must have depended on a subtle system of communication (whether by vocalization or gesture) between members of each group. This is not to say, of course, that the australopithecines were capable of articulate language; there is no evidence at all that their mental faculties were advanced enough for speech. However, their use of gestures and different vocal sounds to guide each other in their hunting activities may have been the necessary prelude to the development of articulate language in the more highly developed hominids of a much later date.[11]

Professor Eric H. Lenneberg credits the australopithecines with "some potential for a primitive form of speech-like communication."[12] He points out that while modern apes cannot speak, and the australopithecine brain was actually no larger than theirs, it may have been relatively larger in view of their smaller physique.[13]

In all such conjectures, there is the assumption of a *potential* for articulate speech while recognizing the existence of some form of nonverbal communication prior to the realiza-

[11] Sir Wilfrid LeGros Clark, *Man-Apes or Ape-Men?*, Holt, Rinehart and Winston, 1967, p. 120.

[12] Eric H. Lenneberg, *Biological Foundations of Language*, Wiley, 1967, p. 258.

[13] Observe what was said earlier (footnote, p. 145) about the relative sizes of the brains of apes and humans when the latter begin to speak.

tion of the potentiality. We cannot know for certain whether any particular fossil hominid had either speech or the capacity to invent it. The capacity itself depends upon the vocal mechanisms and controlling centers in the brain. About all that fossils retain of the vocal mechanisms is a jaw, and this cannot tell us anything about speech or the potentiality to acquire it. Nor can the cranium tell us much. It gives some indication of the size of the brain and its general configuration, but it does not reveal in detail anything of the brain structure, which, in ourselves, is closely associated with speech. In modern man there is a parietal-temporal region, usually the one in the left cerebral hemisphere, which has to do with auditory and kinesthetic as well as storage functions involved in speech. Also in the left cerebral hemisphere is Broca's area, once thought to play a predominant role in the motor aspects of speech. However, recent research summarized by Eric H. Lenneberg in his *Biological Foundations of Language* makes it doubtful that Broca's area has particular significance for language. He points out: "The histological maps of cerebral cortices of subhuman primates have somewhat different lines of demarkation than man. This is true of cortical areas which in man have relevance to language; it is also true of Broca's area. The cytoarchitecture of Broca's area is also found in some roughly homologous areas in the cortices of some subhuman primates." He says, moreover, that: "It would be circular or meaningless to state that only man has a cortical speech area, because cortical language maps are based on observation of behavior. We cannot observe language interference in an animal that does not speak. Such an animal, by definition, lacks speech areas."[14]

After discussing the vocal and cerebral mechanisms involved, Bernard Campbell says that speech appears to be a "genetically determined character of modern man" which was probably "selected and evolved in the middle Pleistocene, at which time we know that man's cranial capacity very rapidly increased."[15] This was the time when *Homo erectus*

[14] Lenneberg, *Biological Foundations of Language*, p. 62.

[15] Bernard Campbell, *Human Evolution*, Aldine, 1967, p. 313.

appeared in Tanzania, Java, China, and Europe. The earliest appearance of this type is estimated to have been at least 500,000 years ago.

Whether or not articulated speech was used by *Homo erectus*, it is a reasonable assumption that Cro-Magnon man at least had the biological potential to use it. The basis for such an assumption is that racial diversification took place in Cro-Magnon times, and all races living today have a spoken language. As Lenneberg says:

We must assume that the evolutionary events favoring culture and language go back to the common ancestor of all modern races. This would mean that the age of language is no less than say, 30,000 to 50,000 years. Credence is lent to this hypothesis not only on the grounds of racial evidence; the cultures associated with the fossils of this period give evidence of the development of a symbolic medium other than language; graphic representation. The cave drawings of that time are extremely skillful and, what is more important, they are highly stylized and, in a sense, abstract. Thus, it is likely that the cognitive processes of Cro-Magnon had a number of characteristics in common with modern man.[16]

The biological potential (or capacity) to develop speech must depend upon the speech mechanisms and specialized cerebral structures for formulating and receiving messages and controlling these mechanisms. But capacity is one thing and actual speech something else. Without the capacity to acquire speech, there can be no speech. With the capacity to acquire it, there may still be no speech until someone has invented it. Moreover, it was invented innumerable times, for every isolated group of peoples has its own peculiar speech conventions—its own language. And twins are known to develop speech understandable only to themselves.

Some languages have common roots, but many have no discernible connection with other languages except certain "design-features" which characterize all speech—such as arbitrary connections between the objects and the sounds

---

[16] Lenneberg, *Biological Foundations of Language*, p. 261.

which represent them; reference to objects or events in the past, present, or future; and the coining of new utterances by combining elements already in use.[17]

INVENTION OF SPEECH

How speech was invented by our primitive ancestors is of course not known. The beginning could have occurred in many ways—sounds used to represent certain objects could be imitations of the sounds made by these objects (*bow-wow*, for dog); natural exclamations or ejaculations (*oh, ah*) could have been used to represent the situations which elicited them; vocalizations used in group effort (grunts) could have represented the situation involved; emotional expressions (cry, sigh) could have represented a situation, object, or activity associated with it.

Some writers have stressed the possibility that any chance association of a sound with an object could lead to subsequent use of that sound to represent that object. Children today vocalize a great deal, in an initially meaningless way, while playing. Primitive man may have acted similarly. In this "babble-luck" manner, sounds could come to signify objects for an individual. But before these sounds came to represent elements of a language, others would have to be induced to adopt and use this convention.[18]

Professor Otto Jesperson has called attention to the fact that the only essential condition for the development of a new language, given individuals with a potentiality to develop it, is isolation of a group without ready-made means of

[17] These and other design-features, as Professor Charles F. Hockett calls them, are discussed in "The Origin of Speech," *Scientific American*, 1960, Vol. 203, pp. 89–96.

[18] This discussion summarizes a more extensive consideration of the evolution of language in the writer's *The Evolution and Growth of Human Behavior* (2nd ed.), Houghton Mifflin, 1965, pp. 381–385. The babble-luck concept comes from Charles H. Judd, *The Psychology of Social Institutions* (Macmillan, 1926) and Edward L. Thorndike, "The Origin of Language," *Science*, 1943, Vol. 98, pp. 1–6.

communication. Like children under similar circumstances, members of the group will soon hit upon some means of communicating with one another.[19]

WRITTEN LANGUAGE

No doubt speech existed for a long time before it was represented in writing, and even today there are primitive tribes with a spoken language but without writing. The most ancient writing known to us is that of the Sumerians of 5,000 years ago, who impressed wedge-shaped characters on clay, which was then baked. Originally they used a stylized picture of the object represented, then this became more and more abbreviated. Finally it had no resemblance to the original. The same process was followed in the development of Egyptian, Chinese, and other written scripts.

In early Egyptian the word for owl was a picture of that bird. Later representation became less and less like the original (see the accompanying figure, p. 219). One will observe that the final letter (M) bears no resemblance to an owl, nor does it represent anything more than a letter to be combined with other letters to form words. Thus, what started out as a picture—a "pictorial word"—became a symbol without any specific reference. Later still, these symbols came to represent the sounds of speech. In Egyptian the spoken word represented by the stylized picture of an owl began with the m sound. Finally, the M no longer looked like or represented an owl, it represented only the sound m and had to be combined with other letters to form words.

The development of speech, especially its written form, was of an importance impossible to exaggerate. Before speech, the only basis of cultural transmission would be imitation of the old by the young. Social intercourse would be limited to overt behavior supplemented by gestural and other means of nonverbal communication. With speech there could be more versatile communication and transmission of the cultural heritage by word of mouth. Moreover, the

[19] O. Jesperson, *Language: Its Nature, Development, and Origin,* Holt, 1921.

From picture to letter. The Egyptian hieroglyph for owl looked very much like this bird. It was, in fact, a stylized picture. Successively, in the Egyptian, Phoenician, and Greek, it approximated our letter M. The significance of this transition is discussed in the text.

versatility of speech symbols would greatly increase man's ability to represent and think about the past, the present, and the future. When writing came, this not only facilitated communication between contemporaries, nearby as well as distant, but also communication to later generations than those with which man could converse orally. With the coming of specialized forms of writing, such as mathematical symbols with their highly abstract significance, the advance of science, which began with invention of the first artifact, would be given a tremendous impetus.[20] And, of course, written records mark the beginning of human history.

PERSPECTIVE ON THE PAST AND THE PRESENT

As Kenneth Oakley has so succinctly pointed out, "Modern civilization owes its present form to machine tools, driven by mechanical energy; yet these perform in complicated ways only the same basic operations as the simple equipment in the tool-bag of Stone Age man: percussion, cutting, scraping, piercing, shearing, and moulding."[21] To this should be added the invention of oral and written speech some time in the distant past, measurement (of length, weight, etc.), and the scientific revolution which began to have an important impact about 300 years ago.

Man perhaps required 1,000,000 years to attain his modern form, as represented by Cro-Magnon man in Europe. If we take 30,000 years as a conservative estimate of the age of modern man and represent this span as one hour on a clock, we can obtain some appreciation of the recency of major developments which led him from stone-age to modern civilization. On this scale, where each minute represents 500 years, the Neolithic Revolution in Europe began about five minutes ago; the use of iron less than two minutes ago; the Age of Science, perhaps one could say, less than one

[20] Sir William Cecil Dampier, *A Shorter History of Science* (Meridian Books, 1957), begins his history with the tool-making propensities of prehistoric man.

[21] Oakley, *Man the Tool-Maker*, p. 139.

minute ago; the Industrial Revolution, with its power-driven machines, about 30 seconds ago; and the Age of Steel some seconds more recent than that. On this scale, the release of atomic energy happened less than three seconds ago, with the age of computers and space flight following that.

Thus, man's control over his environment was slow at first, then took on an ever-increasing momentum. In recent times this control has grown at a rate which even one generation ago was inconceivable. Strange as it may seem, however, man's body today, including the shape and size of his brain, is not perceptibly different from that of his Cro-Magnon ancestors. For all we know, their capacity for mental development was no better nor worse than ours. How, then, does one account for the difference between their way of life and our own? How does one account for man's growing control over his environment when his brain and basic mental capacities have undergone no perceptible change at the same time? The answer is to be found in the accumulation of culture from generation to generation, facilitated by the advanced forms of communication made possible by written language.

Some living members of our species are as biologically advanced as ourselves, yet they live in what is for them the Stone Age. One need only step into parts of New Guinea, Australia, and South America to see them. They have been isolated during the advance of other members of the species, and their environment has been such as to provide little need for change, hence little motivation to move in civilized directions. When the motivation is provided, we see remarkably quick changes. One sees highly skilled Negro surgeons in a Harlem hospital whose ancestors only a few generations back were men living in the Stone Age. Motivation and opportunity, with a model to imitate, was all that was needed to make a cultural advance of 30,000 years.

Let us look at this in another way. Suppose that some drug were discovered which could make modern civilized man forget everything he had learned from the past but leave his biological potentialities and his basic mental faculties unaltered. Left to his own resources in this way, civilized man would be thrust back 30,000 years in his understanding of and ability to cope with his environment, even a natural environment uncluttered by the paraphernalia of the present day. His biological heritage would still be with him but he would have lost his cultural heritage.

Although the basic mental functions have apparently not changed since Cro-Magnon times, the contents of men's minds have changed almost inconceivably. But this change is not transmitted biologically—only the basic mental functions, including the potentiality to learn, are passed on in this way. Every shred of evidence that we have argues against the idea that what a man learns can be transmitted biologically to his offspring.[22] The vast amount of information accumulated since Cro-Magnon times is transmitted culturally, and it is obvious that only a limited sample of this can be acquired by an individual, especially when such information is channeled through different cultures and when there are various other limitations on the extent of educational opportunities.

The acquired contents of each person's mind are largely, if not entirely, cultural in origin. If the mind is initially a *tabula rasa*, a blank sheet, as John Locke claimed, then all of its contents come from experience. If, on the other hand, "stimulation provides the occasion for the mind to apply certain innate interpretive principles, certain concepts that proceed from 'the power of understanding' itself, from the faculty of thinking rather than from external objects directly," we must assume that the content of modern minds is a product of the interplay between innate propensities and the accumulated products of the cultural heritage.[23] However, any innate processing tendencies were presumably established in Cro-Magnon times, and the growth of mental content since then has resulted mainly from the accumulation

[22] On this issue see the evidence summarized by Norman L. Munn in *The Evolution and Growth of Human Behavior* (2nd ed.), pp. 71–72.

[23] Noam Chomsky, *Language and Mind*, Harcourt, Brace and World, 1968, p. 72.

of culture and its transmission through social intercourse. In these terms it may be maintained that the attitudes, ideas, and knowledge of modern man have been largely, if not entirely, shaped by his cultural heritage. The fact that mental content is shaped so differently in different cultures gives some idea of the impact of cultural transmission. In the next chapter we turn our attention to various aspects of the shaping of mental content by the social heritage.

CHAPTER SEVEN

THE SHAPING OF MODERN MINDS

Every normal human infant is inherently endowed with the basic structures, functions, and growth potentials which characterize *Homo sapiens*. These are outcomes of biological evolution. They are represented in the genes and brought to maturity by the internal and external conditions which are required for normal human growth.

Man's cultural heritage, on the other hand, is not biologically represented in the newborn. It is embodied in the inventions, languages, customs, beliefs, and ideas accumulated since man evolved. Every feature of this inheritance is external to the individual until educative processes, informal and formal, lead him to interiorize it—that is, to take it in and make it part of himself.

Although every normal human infant comes into the world with the basic sensory, neural, and motor mechanisms which characterize the species, his mentality is shaped, as he develops, by the cultural influences surrounding him. We could say that such influences are *focused upon him*. Thus, infants who develop in different cultural settings become adults with mentalities which differ accordingly. Historians refer, in fact, to "the Greek mind," "the Roman mind," "the Medieval mind," "the mind of Renaissance Man," and so forth. Thus, they highlight the fact that members of our species, all with the same basic mental mechanisms, differ in outlook, inventory of ideas, and way of life, depending upon the times in which they live and the impact upon them of associated cultural influences. The same infant, if reared in different cultural settings today, could be said to possess a "savage mind," a "fascist mind," a "communist mind," an "Asian mind," or a "democratic mind," to mention only a few possible designations. This point is well made by Dr. Robert Livingston, a noted neurologist, when he says: "In general we get committed to a cultural set . . . to a set of values and a world view that is profoundly culture-bound. Its entire vast inventory of images is peculiar to the place and time of the child's upbringing. Therefore these experiences will exercise a controlling influence on all future perceptions, judgments, motives and behaviors."[1]

Any particular human mind is shaped by an extremely limited segment of what the cultural heritage has to offer. Cro-Magnon men of some 30,000 years ago could perhaps learn all there was to know of their cultural heritage as it had evolved thus far. As cultural evolution continued, however, this heritage grew at an ever-increasing rate, aided eventually by written language and a growing communication between different cultures. When early historical times had been reached, it probably was no longer possible for even the most learned to know all that men of their own cultural background had learned so far. Today one can do no more than sample what the cultural heritage has to offer.

In some parts of the world, as in the highlands of New Guinea, there are still geographically isolated pockets of humanity. Cut off from the outside cultural heritage, these people are said to have a "savage" or "primitive" mind. Since

[1] In an address before the American Association for the Advancement of Science, as reported in *Science News*, January 18, 1969, p. 61.

we suffer no such geographical or cultural limitations, our minds are said to be "civilized." But the impact of what the past has to offer is also limited for us. Our potential heritage is filtered and channeled in terms of national, linguistic, and ideological predispositions. Whatever gets through such barriers is focused on the growing individual by the social milieu in which he develops, particularly as this is represented in parental example and admonition, the educational system, and mass media such as the press, radio, and television. As indicated in the quotation from Dr. Livingston, a further selection of social heritage and, indeed, of what any aspect of the environment has to offer the individual, is determined by a cultural set acquired early in life. What a person is attentive to, how his perceptions are distorted, what he wants to know—these are features of this selective process which further shapes and indeed forms what we think of as his mind.

It is possible to trace the impact upon the modern mind of many major cultural achievements of the past, such as particular religious systems, Greek philosophy, the scientific method, the theory of evolution, and the automobile. Thus, as Professor John Herman Randall, Jr., says in *The Making of the Modern Mind,* there is "a persistence of the past into the present," and the "ideas and beliefs, the aims and ideals of the California fruit-grower or the Pennsylvania coal-miner, the sheep-rancher of Queensland or the cultural club-man of Buenos Aires" are

a mosaic of bits and pieces gathered from here and there along the journey through the ages, set into new patterns to serve the needs and taste of America and Australia. A ramble through the mind of the modern man would reveal the same juxtaposition of beliefs that have endured unchanged for centuries, with ideas gleaned from the morning paper. . . . It is fascinating to explore the mind of the present generation, to unravel the many threads that enter its tangled fabric and to trace them back to their first appearance in the loom of history.[2]

[2] John Herman Randall, Jr., *The Making of the Modern Mind: A Survey of the Intellectual Background of the Present Age* (rev. ed.), Houghton Mifflin, 1940, pp. 4–5.

It would be beyond the scope of this book to attempt an excursion into the history of ideas which shape modern mentality, a task so well done by Professor Randall and others. What we shall do in this chapter, however, is to consider some basic aspects of the shaping process as exemplified in certain so-called "savage" and "civilized" societies. We shall observe, in this connection, the flexibility, modifiability, or adaptiveness of contemporary man, who may be lifted from savagery to civilization within the span of a single generation.

HUMAN NATURE

The newborn is not "clay in the potter's hands," despite its dependence upon others for survival and its typically human plasticity. Dependence and learning ability facilitate the shaping process, but nature imposes certain limits upon the degree to which human beings can be molded and the directions in which they can be modified. The organism has needs which cannot be eradicated or ignored, even though it may learn to satisfy them in a variety of ways. It is emotionally excitable, and, as development proceeds, a variety of emotions, such as fear, anger, and affection, normally make their appearance. The organism also has a repertoire of reflexes. These may be "conditioned," so that a certain reflex comes to be aroused by novel as well as "natural" stimulation. And they may be organized into more complex patterns of behavior.

Basic mental processes are likewise inborn. These include the capacity to learn, to remember, to perceive, to use symbols as in speech, and to attend to and be curious about aspects of the world around us. The shaping of these processes determines the direction in which they are applied and also their symbolic content. This sort of shaping is especially effective during early life.

Certain characteristics are usually considered to be inborn and ineradicable features of a "natural man"—one untouched by cultural influences. The earliest men, coming into a cultureless world, would be natural men in this sense. And any modern human being would behave like a natural man if reared without cultural contacts or if deprived in adulthood of everything that he had ever learned. A "natural man" would possess the sensory and perceptual capacities, the ability to learn and to remember, and the imaginative and reasoning powers with which evolution endowed human beings. He would possess and proceed to satisfy, as well as he was able, such physiological needs as hunger, thirst, and sex. He would have emotions—anger when frustrated, fear when life was endangered, and curiosity about his surroundings. It must be acknowledged, too, that this "natural man" came into the world a helpless infant who survived and developed only because others provided sustenance, shelter, and protection during the period of dependency. All of these—capacities, early dependence, and the need for social aid—are inherent in human nature. They are, so to speak, "inscribed in the nature of man."[3]

However, when it is suggested by some that certain aspects of human nature cannot be changed, they usually are referring more specifically to something else. They have in mind such allegedly universal and inborn motives as gregariousness (desire for human contacts), acquisitiveness (for example, the profit motive), and pugnacity or aggression (the urge to fight).

The most nearly universal of these motives is gregariousness. It appears in the higher apes as well as man. Chimpanzees separated from their group are often obviously disturbed. They emit mournful cries and make every possible attempt to regain social contacts. But we must not suppose that the presence of this motive in apes and its near universality in man are proof of its innateness. Actually, there is every reason to consider it an acquired form of motivation. Apes and human beings are all initially helpless. The infant ape or human must be cared for by older individuals throughout an early and impressionable period of its life. As a result

---

[3] An expression used by Claude Levi-Strauss in relation to monogamy, which, he says, is *not* so inscribed. See his chapter in H. L. Shapiro (Ed.), *Man, Culture, and Society,* Oxford University Press, 1956, p. 268.

the infant could well acquire close personal attachments by becoming conditioned to the presence and ministrations of those around it.

Acquistiveness is also an acquired motive. Some animals express this motive in their hoarding of food, but the higher animals lack such acquisitive tendencies. Nor is acquisitiveness universal in mankind. In many societies, including those of the Australian aboriginal, sharing is more characteristic than personal acquisition. In the Western world, however, acquisitiveness is clearly evident. It finds expression in what Professor D. C. McClelland refers to as the achievement motive. He and others have written at length concerning the cultural history of acquisitiveness and its variations within "achieving societies."[4] It is expressed in such aspects of social life as self-assertion, ambition to succeed, and prestige or status. There is no doubt that the profit motive, in its many ramifications, is a powerful factor in Western societies, but its obvious cultural basis removes it from the list of "ineradicable components of human nature."

Those who argue that there is an inborn urge to fight have been expecially vociferous in recent years, and their views have been attacked by sociologists and cultural anthropologists who regard aggression as cultural in origin. The issue is such an important one for modern society that it warrants a much more extended discussion.

AGGRESSION

Aggression is generally regarded as bad. Our hydrogen bombs and bacteriological weapons make it a threat to the continued survival of mankind. We would like to do away with it. But is this possible?

There are noted zoologists, psychologists, and psychiatrists who claim that aggression cannot be eradicated. They look upon it as the expression of an inborn urge which, like dammed up energy, demands an outlet. The best we can do,

[4] D. C. McClelland et al., *The Achieving Society*, Alfred A. Knopf, 1962.

they say, is to sublimate this energy—to redirect its expression from warlike activity into socially desirable channels.

Competitive sports are sometimes said to be an example of sublimated expression of the aggressive urge. Professor Konrad Lorenz argues that sports on the pattern of the Olympic games not only lower international tensions but "furnish a healthy safety valve" for the type of aggression found in what he calls "collective military enthusiasm."[5] Professor Tinbergen takes a similar stand when he suggests that we may "take the sting out of aggression" by focusing it on research. This, he says, "would seem to offer the best opportunities for deflecting and sublimating our aggression."[6] Like William James in an earlier day, these modern scientists are positing the existence of innate aggressiveness and seeking "moral equivalents" for its natural expression.[7]

Even if we accept the existence of an inborn aggressive urge, it is very doubtful whether such sublimations would be very effective. Dueling, boxing, wrestling, and other contact sports might provide an outlet for the few people involved in them. But what about the masses? Research on the causes of aggression would serve a very useful purpose, but research *as sublimation* could hardly be an equivalent, even for the very few people involved in it.

What basis is there for supposing that man is by nature aggressive? Recent discussions have leaned heavily upon the presence of fighting in animals and the concept of territoriality—or what Robert Ardrey has called "the territorial imperative."[8] Professor Lorenz shows that fighting among animals of the same species frequently is aroused when the territory which an individual has marked out for itself is invaded or threatened with invasion.[9] Professor Tinbergen

[5] Konrad Lorenz, *On Aggression*, London: Methuen, 1966, p. 242.

[6] N. Tinbergen, "On War and Peace in Animals and Man," *Science*, 1968, Vol. 160, p. 1418.

[7] William James, "The Moral Equivalents of War," *Popular Science Monthly*, 1910, Vol. 77, pp. 400–412. Reprinted in William James, *Essays On Faith and Morals*, Meridian Books, 1962.

[8] Robert Ardrey, *The Territorial Imperative*, London: Collins, 1967.

[9] Lorenz, *On Aggression*, p. 242.

also emphasizes the territorial backgrounds of aggression in animals when he says that "members of territorial species divide, among themselves, the available living space . . . each individual defending its home range against competitors." Moreover, "it is an essential aspect of group territorialism that the members of a group unite when in hostile confrontation with another group which approaches, or crosses into their feeding territory. The uniting and aggression are equally important." With respect to man, the most likely hypothesis, according to Tinbergen, is that "he still carries with him the animal heritage of group territoriality."[10]

The views of Lorenz, Tinbergen, and Ardrey are weakened considerably by the fact that territoriality is most evident in animals which are only remotely related to man—fish, birds, and some lower mammals. The great apes, our closest animal relatives, are not territorial, and their life in the wild is characterized much more by amiability than by aggressiveness. Even the gorilla, often ferocious in captivity, is normally a peaceful animal. What about our hominid ancestors, *Australopithecus* and *Homo erectus?* According to Professor Raymond Dart,[11] the former was a vegetarian-turned-carnivore who, in the process of change, became a bloodthirsty predator, even hunting his own kind as well as other animals. It is claimed that man's forebears stood on their hind feet so that they could wield a club and that they were more interested in weapons than in tools.

All of this is conjecture. Other paleontologists have taken issue with the proponents of this view, pointing out that Australopithecine remains, as well as those of *Homo erectus*, give no evidence of either aggressiveness or nonaggressiveness. It appears that cannibalism was practiced by early man, but this has no necessary bearing upon inborn aggression. As M. F. Ashley Montagu has pointed out, "The cracked

[10] Tinbergen, "On War and Peace in Animals and Man," pp. 1413–1414.

[11] Raymond Dart, "The Predatory Transition from Ape to Man," *International Anthropological and Linguistic Review*, 1953: 1,4; and, with Dennis Craig, *Adventures with the Missing Link*, Harper, 1959.

bones of Peking man may represent the remains of individuals who died during a famine and who may well have been eaten by their surviving associates. This sort of thing has been known to occur among most peoples of whom we have any knowledge. There is, however, no record of any people, prehistoric, nonliterate, or anywhere in the annals of human history, who made a habit of killing their fellow men in order to dine off them." Moreover, the fact that fire is associated with human remains does not mean that roasted human flesh was eaten, for "like some contemporary peoples, burning the corpse may have been Peking man's way of disposing of the dead."[12] In any event, it is difficult to see that "the loathsome cruelty of mankind to man" and the "blood-spattered, slaughter-gutted archives of human history, from the earliest Egyptian and Sumerian records down to the most recent unspeakable atrocities of World Wars I and II," could have had any connection with cannibalism.[13]

In *Man and Aggression,* Dr. Ashley Montague criticizes this "new litany of innate depravity and original sin" and gathers essays by other anthropologists, psychologists, biologists, and sociologists which refute the concept of human territoriality and also the idea that man has an inborn aggressive urge.

Even among men living today, territoriality and intergroup fighting are by no means universal, as they should be if these aspects of human nature are inborn. Dr. Ashley Montague points out, in this connection: "Among hunting peoples still living today, such as the Bushman of South Africa, the Pygmies of the Ituri Forest, the Eskimos of the Arctic Circle, and others, there is absolutely no sense of territoriality. As one would expect, some peoples are territorial, some only indifferently so, and others not at all.

[12] M. F. Ashley Montagu, *Man and Aggression,* Oxford University Press, 1968, p. 12.

[13] Dart and Craig, *Adventures with the Missing Link,* p. 201. The quotations are from this book, which attempts to tie in cannibalism with the alleged blood lust and innate aggressiveness of mankind.

What has happened to the 'animal heritage' of those people who are nonterritorial?" With respect to the "internal urge to fight," Ashley Montague continues, "if it is very difficult if not impossible to eliminate," how does it happen that "the Pueblo Indians, the Eskimo, the Bushman, the Ifuluk, the Australian aborigines, the Pygmies, and many other peoples have managed to avoid this. . . . By education, gene loss, or what? May it not be that the urge to fight is an acquired form of behavior? That anyone can *learn* to fight or not to fight? That the urge may become internalized through learning, that it is not innate?"[14]

FRUSTRATION, AGGRESSION, AND CULTURE

We have said nothing, so far, about the relation between frustration and aggression. An inborn urge to fight implies the need to fight *for fighting's sake*—a *dammed up aggressive urge* which demands direct or sublimated expression. This is quite different from the frustration-aggression hypothesis, which regards aggression as a response to anger which is elicited by interference with the satisfaction of needs or with ongoing activity.[15]

We know that frustration produces anger and that anger itself is an inborn response. Children born both blind and deaf, hence without an opportunity to observe emotional behavior, become quite obviously angry when their ongoing activity is hindered. But here anger is elicited—not something dammed up and demanding expression, not something free-floating and independent of circumstances. There is no innate *demand* for an aggressive outlet.

Where aggression exists, it could depend upon such circumstances as threatened injury—to oneself, one's mate, or the young—or actual or anticipated thwarting of the satisfaction of basic physiological needs, such as the need for

[14] M. F. Ashley Montagu, "Animals and Man: Divergent Behavior," *Science*, Sept. 6, 1968, p. 963.

[15] See, in this connection, John Dollard et al., *Frustration and Aggression*, Yale University Press, 1939.

food and drink. Such circumstances usually arouse anger, and this is characteristically expressed through some form of aggressive reaction—overt, as in fighting or struggling; verbal, as in threats or name-calling; or implicit, as when one fights his adversary in imagination, in fantasy. But these are not the only reasons for aggression. Cultural influences account for much of it, both individual and group aggression. Various groups have their "natural" enemies. Think of the feuding Scottish clans and the enmity between certain Kentucky mountain families of the not too distant past. Nations have their traditional enemies, and each child learns whom to hate. The group's antipathies are embodied in myths, legends, and history and kept alive through the mass media.

Except for societies in which aggression is rare or non-existent, each child is born into a situation where traditional antipathies—familial, political, religious, racial, and national —become part of his social heritage. He is endowed with various emotional mechanisms, among them those which produce reactions of anger when frustration occurs. The infant experiences such frustration when his ongoing activity is restricted or when the nipple is removed before his hunger is satisfied. In time he learns to anticipate frustrations of various kinds. Then, the fears and antipathies of his society come to him in its myths, legends, and history, and his attitudes are molded accordingly.

As a child growing up in Australia, I became aware of the "yellow peril" to the North, the "butchering Huns" in Europe, and certain nationalities that should be kept out of Australia because they can "live on the smell of an oily rag," hence endanger one's living standards. This is the stuff which provides a fertile soil in which aggressive impulses may develop. The only biological aspect is the anger which frustration arouses.

Anthropologists have provided us with important information on the cultural backgrounds of aggressiveness. Dr. Margaret Mead has shown, for example, how the education of children may shape them into either peaceful or aggressive individuals. The Arapesh of New Guinea provide admonition, and an example to imitate, which molds their children into peaceful, noncompetitive, cooperative adults. By contrast, the Mundugumor, another New Guinea tribe, educate children for aggression. The shaping process begins even in breast-feeding, where the baby is

kept firmly to his major task of absorbing enough food so that he will stop crying and consent to be put back in his basket. The minute he stops suckling for a moment, he is returned to his prison. Children therefore develop a very definite purposive fighting attitude, holding on firmly to the nipple and sucking milk as rapidly and vigorously as possible. They frequently choke from swallowing too fast; the choking angers the mother and infuriates the child, thus further turning the suckling situation into one characterized by anger and struggle. . . .[16]

As the child grows, the cultural pattern set for him is one in which "both men and women are expected to be violent, competitive, aggressively sexed, jealous, ready to see and avenge insult, delighting in display, in action, in fighting."[17]

A similar contrast is seen between the Zuni and Comanche Indians. The Zuni were a peace-loving, pastoral people who dressed in long flowing robes unsuited for fighting. These Indians belonged to the Pueblo group, already referred to as lacking an urge to fight. The Comanches, on the other hand, were warlike and showed this in their dress and other accoutrements. For them, the culturally fostered norm was an attitude of belligerence.[18]

If there were an innate urge to fight, our recruiting agencies would be swamped with volunteers for military service, especially in times of war. But nations find it necessary to conscript most of their forces, and they whip up aggressive

[16] Margaret Mead, *Sex and Temperament in Three Primitive Societies,* Morrow, 1935, p. 167.

[17] Mead, pp. 196–197.

[18] Ruth Benedict, *Patterns of Culture,* Houghton Mifflin, 1934; and Ralph Linton, "The Personality of Peoples," *Scientific American,* August, 1949, p. 15. The latter illustrates the difference in dress to which we have referred.

urges within the citizenry through propaganda which arouses fear and anticipated frustration.

We can expect human aggression to continue—unless man becomes extinct because of it, or unless he becomes so afraid of its consequences that he changes his ways soon enough to prevent extinction. If widespread aggression does continue, this will be because frustrations persist—engendered by competition between those who have and those who do not have access to the world's resources, to desired power, or to prestige. It will also be because racial, national, and other groups have not relinquished or modified the policies which frustrate others. It will not be because man is inherently aggressive.

THE SHAPING PROCESS

One of the most remarkable things about human beings is their modifiability. At the beginning they are quite helpless, with many reflexes but no preformed behavior patterns, or instincts, such as enable many other newborn animals to survive without the aid of others. Because instinctive behavior patterns are lacking, the human organism can survive on its own only if it learns to do so. Fortunately, it has sensory, neural, and motor mechanisms which provide an unexcelled readiness to learn. From simple beginnings in infancy, this readiness grows as the child matures and, through earlier learning, learns how to learn new things— as when linguistic skills enable him to understand instructions and to gather and convey information more easily.

Modification of behavior is at the beginning largely a matter of learning to satisfy physiological needs, as when the infant learns what to suck so that its thirst and hunger are satisfied. Increasingly complex modifications occur as the child develops. These include behavior such as crying to be picked up, avoidance of painful stimuli, and reaching and grasping. Then comes an increasing repertoire of motor, social, and verbal skills. All this time the child is acquiring a concept of self. His ego is developing. He is learning the ethical and moral ways of his group, thus developing a conscience, or superego. In all this learning the social element is everywhere apparent. Even the nipple must be made accessible by someone else.

Professor B. F. Skinner presents the general process of social learning, or conditioning, very succinctly when he says:

In general, the evolution of man has emphasized modifiability rather than the transmission of specific forms of behavior. Inherited verbal or other social responses are fragmentary and trivial. By far the greater part of behavior develops in the individual through processes of conditioning, given a normal biological endowment. Man becomes a social creature only because other men are important parts of his environment. The behavior of a child born into a flourishing society is shaped and maintained by variables, most of which are arranged by other people. These social variables compose the "culture" in which the child lives, and they shape his behavior in conformity with that culture, usually in such a way that he in turn tends to perpetuate it.[19]

The shaping of behavior involves various processes ranging from relatively simple conditioning to the intellectual grasping of complex conceptual information.

CONDITIONING

The conditioning process made so familiar by the work of Russia's Ivan Pavlov underlies much of a child's early learning. This process is involved when, for example, a baby learns to associate the sound of its mother's footsetps with the coming meal, so that it salivates and perhaps even sucks in anticipation. The associating of words with objects—such as "Mama" with the mother—involves the same type of conditioning process.

Another type of conditioning becomes increasingly im-

[19] B. F. Skinner, "The Design of Cultures," in Hudson Hoagland and Ralph W. Burhoe, *Evolution and Man's Progress*, Columbia University Press, 1962, pp. 128–129.

portant after the child has developed a repertoire of responses which allow it to do and say things—to "operate in or upon" its environment. Such responses bring rewarding or punishing (satisfying or annoying) consequences, and these play an important role in the further shaping of behavior.

Professor Skinner has focused a great deal of attention on "operant conditioning," as he has called it. The consequences of responding, which are referred to as *reinforcements,* are said to be positive if rewarding and negative if punishing. Candy, money, being allowed some privilege, getting an adult's attention, and obtaining praise all exemplify positive reinforcement. They are inducements to repeat the acts which elicit them. On the other hand, there are negative reinforcements, such as burning a finger, falling down, being smacked, being scolded, or having privileges withdrawn. Such outcomes do not favor repetition of the acts which preceded them.

Positive reinforcement is usually followed by an increase in the frequency of the reinforced response. This can be illustrated by an experiment with preschool children.[20] An experimental playroom had a lever arranged so that it would deliver a candy pellet whenever it was pressed. Upon being admitted to this room, a child looked the situation over and began to handle various accessible objects. He continued this for several minutes, then happened to press the lever. To his surprise, candy appeared. He pressed again and was rewarded again. Now the rate of pressing increased until, after 8 minutes, the child was operating the lever 20 times per minute. This is a typical instance of operant conditioning, although one need not reinforce every response. Indeed, a schedule of intermittent reinforcement often yields more persistent behavior than continuous reinforcement. For example: Reinforcement may be given for every fifth response, or it may come after every ten seconds, or it may follow a

[20] A. B. Warren and R. H. Brown, "Conditioned Operant Response Phenomena in Children," *Journal of General Psychology,* 1943, Vol. 28, pp. 181–207.

variable response or time schedule.[21] But such details are not our main concern in this discussion. Our aim here is to illustrate the conditioned focusing of response on a particular aspect of the environment and the increasing complexity of response as conditioning continues.

The focusing aspect may be shaped more directly than has been indicated so far. The child in the above-mentioned experiment probably would have learned to press the lever much sooner than he did if a procedure such as the following had been used: reinforcement when a move in the direction of the lever occurred; no further reinforcement until a closer approach was made; withholding of reinforcement until a still closer approach was made, and so on; then reinforcement only if the lever was touched; after that, reinforcement only when the lever was pressed. By reinforcing successive approximations to the desired behavior it is possible to develop quite complex performances in a relatively short time.

Any response may be shaped by appropriate use of reinforcement. In one experimental study, each one of a group of college students engaged in a protracted discussion with an experimenter who reinforced every expression of opinion, such as "I believe. . . ," and "I think. . . ." The reinforcement was verbal—the experimenter said "I agree," "That's right," "What you are saying is that. . . ," and so on. The effect of this was to increase the number of opinion statements over the number made during a control period in which no such reinforcement occurred. Twenty-four students were involved, and not one of them realized that his behavior was being shaped.[22]

Professor Skinner has written a great deal about the re-

[21] For a more detailed general discussion of operant conditioning procedures and schedules of reinforcement, see N. L. Munn, *Psychology* (5th ed.), Houghton Mifflin, 1966.

[22] W. S. Verplanck, "The Control of the Content of Conversation: Reinforcement of Statements of Opinion," *Journal of Abnormal and Social Psychology*, 1955, Vol. 51, pp. 668–676.

design of cultures through operant conditioning. In his *Walden Two*, a fictional account of a rationally designed culture, he tells how the child may be conditioned to persevere despite frustration. The children are in air-conditioned cubicles containing various toys. "A bit of a tune from a music box, or a pattern of flashing lights, is arranged to follow an appropriate response—say, pulling on a ring. Later the ring must be pulled twice, later still three or five or ten times. It's possible to build up fantastically perseverative behavior without encountering frustration or rage."[23]

Modern teaching machines are designed to shape the student's understanding of the subjects involved. Professor Skinner and his operant conditioning procedures have influenced the development of such machines.

The preceding examples illustrated positive reinforcement, but negative reinforcement is also a strong shaping influence. A child who puts his finger on a hot stove does not repeat this performance. The pain has taught him one thing *not* to do. The Mundugumor babies discussed earlier could suck on the breast only so long as they kept to the business at hand; as soon as they stopped sucking they were removed. Such a "time out" from feeding is negative reinforcement, and it engenders a tenacious fixation on the feeding response.

Margaret Mead provides us with still another example of negative reinforcement. In her study of the education of Manus children she describes how the baby is taught to sit astride its mother's neck and cling to her throat for security. When the baby slackens its grip, it is reseated with a "decisive, angry gesture," and this treatment develops an "alert and sure-handed" clinging which leaves the mother free to go about her business without worrying about the security of the child.[24]

Conditioning based on reinforcements of various kinds is, of course, not new. Most animals undergo conditioning in their everyday lives, and many of them have served as

[23] B. F. Skinner, *Walden Two*, Macmillan, 1948, p. 101.

[24] Margaret Mead, *Growing Up in New Guinea*, Morrow, 1930, p. 23.

subjects in conditioning experiments. Moreover, it can be maintained that virtually every human being who ever lived has had his behavior and his mentality shaped by conditioning, but not by conditioning that was premeditated—or rationally designed to shape behavior in particular ways. As with the Mundugumor and Manus peoples of our previous discussion, it came about by individuals' "doing what comes naturally."

Physiologists and psychologists now have a detailed understanding of the conditioning process—so complete, in fact, that they can use it as a tool to shape individual and group behavior, or to foster what Professor Skinner has called "cultural engineering." The possibility is held out that by these means we may design cultures free of the defects now evident. It has been argued that this is "mind-bending" or "brainwashing," and wholly unethical. Such a wholesale program of mind-shaping would be revolutionary indeed and akin to the sort of thing represented fictionally in Aldous Huxley's *Brave New World* as well as in Skinner's *Walden Two.* However, a deliberate programming of human life to replace the more haphazard shaping which takes place all the time may well be an aspect of man's future. Professor John H. Platt, a physicist and well-known writer on technological aspects of modern society says, "There have been many revolutions in our time, but I think that in the long run this psychological revolution that we see beginning here in the theory and practice of shaping behavior of the young will be the most important of all for the success and happiness of man on this planet."[25]

The conditioning processes play their most obviously important role in early childhood. Through these processes the child learns to differentiate aspects of its environment in terms of their satisfying or annoying effects; to develop favorable or unfavorable attitudes toward objects, situations, and persons; to form emotional associations, positive or negative, with the various aspects of his world; to repeat

[25] John R. Platt, *The Step to Man*, Wiley, 1966, p. 161.

and perfect forms of behavior required in locomotion and manipulation; and, in short, to "reality-test"—to learn what he can and cannot do, or must not do. In this process he develops a concept of self and, at the same time, a superego, or conscience. It is no wonder then, that conditioning processes are considered so important in the shaping of human minds.

In less obvious ways, conditioning may underlie all learning, including the acquisition of language, the learning of motor skills, and the acquiring of information. Indeed, Ivan Pavlov[26] claimed that "different kinds of habits based on training, education, and discipline" are nothing but chains of conditioned responses. This claim is perhaps too sweeping. Nevertheless, many of our motor and mental acquisitions, even when it is difficult to envisage them as conditioned responses, are doubtless dependent upon principles involved in the conditioning process, expecially those relating to reinforcement.

The most generally significant of the child's acquisitions is speech. This facilitates social intercourse with others; it provides symbols to represent objects and situations so that they can be thought about without the objects present; and it provides a tool with which information may be gathered— initially from the oral speech of others and later, from written speech. More than any other acquisition, speech makes the social heritage available to the individual and at the same time provides his society with an unexcelled medium through which to shape his mind in desired directions. The prerequisites are an ability to hear, mechanisms with which the sounds of speech can be made and patterned in accordance with a specific language, and the ability to imitate. Also required, of course, is a verbal community, a society which sets the speech pattern to be copied and reinforces conformity to this pattern.[27]

---

[26] Ivan P. Pavlov, *Conditioned Reflexes* (trans. by G. V. Anrep), Oxford University Press, 1927, p. 395.

[27] See B. F. Skinner, *Verbal Behavior*, Appleton-Century-Crofts, 1957.

ACQUIRING LANGUAGE

Although every normal human being is endowed with the basic biological requisites for language development, these must undergo considerable maturation before he can speak. Maturation usually continues for about one year before the first word is spoken. However, several significant antecedents of speech are present long before the first word is uttered. Basic sounds produced by the vocal mechanisms begin to appear at or soon after birth, and most of them are evident within a few months thereafter. These are the sounds of vowels and consonants. They are the same in babies of all races and cultures, although some are incorporated and others dropped in the various languages. Initially, however, these vocalizations have no linguistic significance. They are, as it were, building blocks out of which the languages of mankind are constructed. Babbling also precedes speech. It appears to be a necessary antecedent, as we pointed out in discussing language in animals. One will recall that animals do not babble. Neither do the congenitally deaf.

Whenever a child vocalizes, he is likely to bring attention to himself. And, since he can hear the self-made sounds, there is auditory feedback. The attention gained and the self-stimulation involved in vocalizing probably have reward value, serving as positive reinforcement of the vocalizing activities. Here we have the prerequisites for conditioned vocalizing: emission of a response (activation of the vocal mechanisms), an associated stimulation (the sound heard), and positive reinforcement (satisfying attention and/or self-stimulation.) There is a widely accepted theory which supposes that the sound made by the child becomes a conditioned stimulus for reactivation of the mechanisms which produced it. Thus, the sound *da* would elicit a repetition, and eventually, a repetitive sequence like *da-da-da.* . . . It appears, in any event, that the child is imitating itself. Such imitation might well be setting the stage for later attempts to copy the sounds made by others. Without such attempts the child could not learn to speak.

A child's first attempts to imitate words are poor copies of the models provided—"fant" for "elephant," "ite" or "yite" for "light," and so on. The important thing at this stage is that he *does* attempt to copy. Gradually his productions approximate the model. Successive approximations are re-inforced—by attention, praise, improved communication which brings faster results, self-satisfaction with accomplishment.

Association of words with things is, initially at least, a conditioning process. Any word frequently associated with an object comes to represent that object, even when the object is no longer present.

As the child's vocabulary grows, simple phrases and sentences are spoken. These, too, are attempts to imitate what is heard. They often fall short of the model at first, but they gradually conform to it. The proper sentence structure (syntax) is learned partly through imitation of models, but also, at a more advanced stage, by learning the rules of grammar. When the child begins to combine words on his own—that is, without imitating a model—he does not form random combinations but seems to have a syntax all his own. He says, "I hitted it," "Do it like this are," and the like. But again we observe the development of closer and closer approximations to the models provided. In time, the approved syntax prevails.

As one grows, the further acquisition of language is aided by an increasing ability to perceive similarities, differences, and relationships; to form concepts, both concrete and abstract; and to think about what is heard and seen.

In societies with a written language, the educated (or literate) individual learns to write and read, thus adding to his knowledge of the language and at the same time making himself a potential receiver of immeasurably more of the cultural heritage than is embodied in oral speech alone.

COPING WITH THE ENVIRONMENT

Children of every society must learn to cope with their worlds. Language helps a great deal, but there are many other skills to be acquired. These differ depending upon the society.

Certain skills are required in almost every society. These include avoiding dangers, dealing with elimination in approved ways, keeping acceptably clean, and knowing what to eat and how it should be eaten. Where clothing is worn, the child must learn to cope with this. Social skills must be learned, such as how to act toward parents, strangers, teachers, members of the other sex, and aggressors. How to use implements of various kinds, including the common tools and perhaps weapons, must be learned. In some primitive societies the child learns quite early such skills as differentiating animal tracks, using a digging stick effectively, and throwing a spear. In literate societies there is a more settled way of life, with little or no need for such primitive skills. Here the major emphasis is on formal schooling, athletic sports, and verbal skills. In both primitive and civilized settings, however, the chief aim of society is to shape the individual so that he can eventually take his place as a self-supporting and useful member of the group.

Skills like those mentioned depend upon conditioning, imitation, formal training, and what is often referred to as "trial and error." Trial and error applies most obviously in the learning of motor skills. Take spear-throwing as a relatively simple illustration. The child learns something about spears and their use by observing skilled performers, so his performance is not completely haphazard at the start. He knows what spears are for and, in general, how they are thrown. He is also told by an elder or playmates to "hold it this way," "tilt it so," "put your feet like this," and so on. Actual learning of many such skills occurs during play. The child's first performance is perhaps an attempt to copy what he has witnessed, or to follow instructions. The chances are that he misses the target on his first try. He tries again, this time saying to himself something like "I must throw it more in that direction." When he hits the target, perhaps after many tries, he might say, "That's it. I'll do it that way again." Reinforcement comes from satisfaction with progress toward the goal and perhaps from the approval of those who witness the performance.

INFORMATION

The individual begins to receive information as soon as he is born—for instance, where food and drink is to be had. Throughout life he receives various kinds of information about his world through the positive or negative reinforcements which accompany his activities—his reality testing, his attempts to imitate and, in general, his acquisition of motor and verbal skills.[28]

A tremendous amount of information is imbedded in the language learned. This is information about the names of things and persons, human relationships, customs, concepts, myths, legends, and history. Some of this information is picked up informally and without any apparent intention to learn it. Much of it comes through more or less formal instruction. In this case there are the teacher and the taught, the giver and the receiver of information. These roles and this relationship are of extreme importance for every human society, since they are involved in the shaping of the mind so that the individual lives in conformity with the established ways of his group.

Many things are taught and learned, but one of the most important is "proper" conduct toward one's fellows. Basically at issue here is conscience, or the superego. Some animals living in close association with human beings and negatively reinforced for "bad conduct" have been known to develop conscience. Professor Köhler in his *Mentality of Apes* tells about a chimpanzee with a bad conscience. The animal had been punished for smearing his face with feces. One day Professor Köhler found the animal hiding behind a box, his smeared face peeking around one edge.[29] Another example of chimpanzee "conscience" is provided by Dr. Leonard Carmichael in *The Making of Modern Mind*. The chimpanzee was Viki, to whom we referred in an earlier

[28] It can be maintained, of course, that information depends upon both the input and the individual's reaction to the input. The problem here is whether or not one *attends* to what is going on (see p. 6).

[29] Wolfgang Köhler, *The Mentality of Apes*, Harcourt, Brace, 1925.

chapter, where her acquisition of a few words was discussed. Dr. and Mrs. Keith Hayes, rearing Viki as a member of the family, had made every effort, through appropriate reinforcement, to inculcate proper human conduct. As Dr. Carmichael says, "A reward of candy was given her for success in toilet training. Later she would herself get the candy out of its jar and go to the toilet. If she did not succeed, with sad reluctance but without prompting she would put the candy back in its jar. Here in a single example we see how subtle and sensitive is the boundary between human and non-human mental life. This act of Viki may make us ask if only man has a conscience."[30] Another possible instance of conscience is cited by Dr. Carmichael. He observed a young chimpanzee looking back at its mother as much as to say "Can I, mother?" as it went to play with a nearby baboon. The mother pulled it back.[31]

Instances of "conscience," whether found in animals or men, are doubtless based on conditioning. In human beings this is facilitated by verbal teachings. Without appropriate reinforcement, conscience would not develop.

Long ago, man learned, for his own best interests, to "go in for ethics" as Professor C. H. Waddington puts it. Ever since that time he has attempted (through reinforcement, precept, and example) to mold his young into "ethicizing" individuals. An important feature of this process, as Professor Waddington points out, is the acceptance of authority by the young. He says:

The essential feature in the role of the taught, of the recipient of information, is to act as though under the authority of something. It may be that some other individual is acted toward as a model to be imitated, or as someone in command, whose signs are to be obeyed, or in the case of man, whose symbolic statements are to be accepted. In sub-human societies so far as we know the authority-bearing entity is always external to the recipient individual. This is no longer the case in man. We find, as an empirical fact, that man

[30] Leonard Carmichael, *The Making of Modern Mind*. Elsevier, 1956, p. 35.

[31] Leonard Carmichael, personal correspondence.

can as it were "internalize" authority. He can with one part of his mental make-up play the role of the taught in relation to some other part which functions as the teacher. Conscience may, as we well know, become a stern internal authority.[32]

Man traditionally supports his own authority by calling upon gods "made in his own image," the spirits of his ancestors, the mythical or legendary great ones of the past, or contemporary authority figures such as the Pope or Chairman Mao. This supporting authority is conveyed through children's stories, songs, myths, legends, "great books," and the sayings of "great men."

Focused upon the child during his most impressionable years, the authority-supported molding process transforms the initially helpless and naive individual into an adult whose conduct is expected to conform to the accepted ways, particularly with respect to prescribed customs, sexual morality, and social obligations. In primitive societies the conformity demanded is more or less absolute. There are prescribed ways for doing almost everything of importance to the tribe. In early civilization, also, shaping was such as to allow very little freedom of thought or action. With the coming of Greek civilization, however, there began a more or less insidious assault upon human conformity. As the noted historian James Harvey Robinson asserted, "The chief strength of the Greeks lay in their freedom from hampering intellectual tradition."[33] He continues:

They discovered skepticism in the higher and proper significance of the word, and this was their supreme contribution to human thought. . . . One of the finest examples . . . was the discovery of Xenophanes that man created the gods in his own image. He looked about him, observed the current conceptions of the gods, compared those of different peoples, and reached the conclusion that the way in which a tribe pictured its gods was not the outcome of any knowledge of how they really looked and whether they had black

[32] C. H. Waddington, *The Ethical Animal,* University of Chicago Press, 1960, pp. 150–151.

[33] James Harvey Robinson, *The Mind in the Making,* Harper, 1921, p. 99.

eyes or blue, but a reflection of the familiarly human. If lions had gods they would have the shape of their worshippers.[34]

Such skepticism was, of course, short-lived. The coming of the Christian era in the Western world backed up the shaping process by reference to divine authority—which prescribed the lines that both conduct and thought should follow—with such symbolic reinforcements as Hell and Eternal Damnation for nonconformity and Heaven and Eternal Bliss for conformity. In other civilizations there were other Gods and Prophets upon whose authority the behavior and thinking of men was prescribed—Gautama Buddha in the Far East, Mohammed in Islam, and the various Gods of India and Japan.

In the Western world, the scientific revolution changed man's concept of the nature of his world and himself, and the theory of evolution added to the growing impression in intellectual circles that man is to a large extent what he makes himself. The new outlook which came with scientific discovery led to a gradual weakening of respect for authority as such. There has been a rebirth of the sort of skepticism which characterized the thinkers of Ancient Greece. Facts are demanded. Authoritative statements unsupported by facts are no longer accepted. There is skepticism, too, concerning the discrepancy between conduct and religious belief, as when the commandment "Thou shalt not kill" fails to restrain Christians from slaughtering their fellows and when good men profess to believe that all men are brothers yet draw a color line.

Young people and adults frequently become alienated from the society that has, up to a point, successfully shaped their minds and conduct. Much that is fostered by "the establishment" is rejected, and a change in the human condition is sought. Of course, man's social evolution is a process of change. Each major change has been considered revolutionary at the time, and "the establishment" has castigated those who fostered it.

[34] Robinson, *The Mind in the Making*, p. 101.

In some civilized societies the shaping process is limited by permissive child training and an emphasis upon individual freedom, advanced education, and creative thinking. One outcome of this is exposure of the individual to information from many sources. In man's cultural evolution the coming of new information was a catalyst of change, if not progress. And so it is for the individual in his own development. He has been shaped to a degree, and basic outcomes in the form of skills and conscience may well be retained throughout life. Other aspects, such as the beliefs implanted, the attitudes developed, and the concepts formed, are often eroded and modified as information not channeled or censored by society comes to hand and is reflected upon.

FROM SAVAGERY TO CIVILIZATION

It has been said that "the savage is very close to us indeed, both in his physical and mental make-up and in the forms of his social life. Tribal society is virtually delayed civilization, and the savages are a sort of contemporaneous ancestry."[35] This statement by a noted sociologist implies that the essential difference between "savage" or "primitive" peoples and "civilized" ones is cultural rather than physical. It is for this reason that the terms "savage" and "primitive" have today been largely replaced by the term "nonliterate." This emphasizes the absence of writing or a written history. The peoples so designated are culturally backward as judged by "civilized" standards, but they are not necessarily "savage" in the usual sense of this term—i.e., "wild," "untamed," or "barbarian."

It has often been claimed that the mental processes of primitive peoples are different from our own, that they are "prelogical" or "mystical" rather than logical and rational. Professor Lucien Lévy-Bruhl once held this view but was induced by criticism to modify it in certain respects.[36] He

[35] W. I. Thomas, "Standpoint for the Interpretation of Savage Society," *American Journal of Sociology*, 1909, Vol. 15, p. 153.

[36] Lucien Lévy-Bruhl, *How Natives Think.* First published in French in 1910, but reissued in translation by Washington Square Press in 1966.

finally concluded that "there is much 'mystical' thinking in modern societies—beliefs that are arrived at by participation in society and not on the basis of rational thought—beliefs that are accepted, held, and defended emotionally, not reasoned, and that are impervious to rational disproof . . ." but that in "primitive" societies "this type of thinking is more conspicuous and more easily studied."[37]

It is sometimes said that the language of primitive peoples lacks abstract concepts. But every living society has an oral language well fitted to its needs, with a complete inventory, sometimes more detailed than our own, of every plant, animal, phenomenon, and relationship which has meaning in the life of the people. That these languages are "deficient" in abstract concepts is refuted in great detail by Professor Claude Levi-Strauss, who concludes that "richness of abstract words is not a monopoly of civilized languages."[38] This view was supported by such noted linguists as E. Sapir and B. L. Whorf, who believed that the most highly abstract philosophical concepts could be expressed even in such primitive languages as Eskimo, Hottentot, and Hopi.[39]

Ethnologists and others who study the behavior and thought of nonliterate peoples are usually impressed by the complexity of their culture. It is far from simple and childlike. Although the "stone-age" society of the Australian aborigine appears on the surface to be as simple as any in existence, it is so complex that ethnologists have expressed extreme difficulty in comprehending its various ramifications. As Levi-Strauss says:

The greater our knowledge, the more obscure the overall scheme. The dimensions multiply, and the growth of axes of reference beyond a certain point paralyzes intuitive methods: it becomes im-

[37] Ruth L. Bunzel, writing in the introduction to the 1966 reprint edition of *How Natives Think*, p. xv.

[38] Claude Levi-Strauss, *The Savage Mind*, University of Chicago Press, 1966, p. 1.

[39] E. Sapir, "The Grammarian and His Language" in *Selected Writings of E. Sapir*, The University of California Press, 1951. Also see B. L. Whorf, *Language, Thought, and Reality*, Wiley, 1956, pp. 207–219.

possible to visualize a system when its representation requires a continuum of more than three or four dimensions. But the day may come when all of the available documentation of Australian tribes is transferred to punched cards and with the help of a computer their entire techno-economic, social, and religious structures can be shown to be a vast group of transformations.[40]

The individual native of course has no conception of the cultural complexities which so intrigue and puzzle ethnologists. Nor does the civilized individual appreciate the forces which have shaped his own mind and behavior.

Aboriginal culture has undergone possibly 20,000 years of development on the Australian continent. There is no written language, but the myths, legends, and teachings relevant to everyday life are transmitted orally. There are even creation myths: "In the very beginning everything was resting in perpetual darkness: night oppressed all the earth like an impenetrable thicket. The gurra ancestor . . . was lying asleep, in everlasting night, at the very bottom of the soak. . . ." The story continues at length, with many ramifications relating to aspects of everyday aboriginal life. Then something emerges from beneath the sleeper's armpit. "It takes on human shape and grows in one night to a full-grown young man: this is his firstborn son."[41] There is much more to the myth, but these excerpts are sufficient to illustrate its general nature. The myths and legends of a tribe indoctrinate by portraying the accepted ways of life, as well as the dire consequences of failure to conform. Religious writings, and even many fairy stories and fables, have a similar influence in shaping the thought and behavior of civilized peoples. Professor Levi-Strauss says:

Few civilizations seem to equal the Australians in their taste for erudition and speculation and what sometimes looks like intellectual dandyism, odd as this expression may appear when it is applied to people with so rudimentary a level of material life. But

[40] Levi-Strauss, *The Savage Mind,* p. 89.

[41] T. G. H. Strehlow, *Aranda Traditions,* Melbourne University Press, 1947, p. 7. The tale, as told, is translated by Mr. Strehlow, who was himself reared with members of the Aranda tribe and speaks their language.

lest there by any mistake about it: these shaggy and corpulent savages whose physical resemblance to adipose bureaucrats or veterans of the Empire makes their nudity yet more incongruous, these meticulous adepts in practices which seem to us to display an infantile perversity—manipulation and handling of the genitals, tortures, the industrious use of their own blood and their excretions and secretions (like our own more discreet and unreflecting habit of moistening postage stamps with saliva)—were, in various respects, real snobs.[42]

They are categorized thus because T. G. H. Strehlow refers to them as exhibiting "a strong element of snobbery and intolerance." This, he says, "characterizes the Central Australian native in his dealings with strangers, and in his criticisms of the customs and rites and ideas which differ from his own. Dialectal differences and peculiarities of speech, too, are continually being made targets of abuse and biting ridicule."[43]

Many books have been written about the "social fabric" and ways of the various primitive peoples whom ethnologists have studied, but this is not the place for a survey of such information. The Australian aborigines have been referred to here because much is known about their way of life. But all nonliterate societies, and civilized ones as well, are concerned with the same basic problems: satisfying needs, bearing and rearing of the young, communication, carrying on the traditions of the group, dealing with the supernatural, death, and so on. Societies differ not so much, then, in the kinds of problems to be met as in their ways of meeting them. Snobbery and intolerance are ever-present features. Many tribes speak of themselves as "the people"; the others are "outsiders" or "barbarians" or "uninitiated." Civilized peoples are essentially similar in these respects to the peoples they refer to as "savage," "primitive," or "nonliterate," only they use different derogatory terms, such as "radical," "intellectual," "imperialist," or "communist."

[42] Levi-Strauss, *The Savage Mind,* p. 89.

[43] Strehlow, *Aranda Traditions,* pp. 82–83.

There are good reasons for believing that all living peoples have a comparable range of basic mental capacities. They differ culturally, and they exhibit genetically determined variations in color and other racial characteristics, but there is no conclusive evidence that the latter have any significant relation to mental capacity. Differences in skin color, hair texture, and facial anatomy are irrelevant so far as differences in mental capacity are concerned. And even the size of the brain has no relationship to intelligence. It has been shown that "very gifted persons, such as Leon Gambetta, Anatole France, or Franz Joseph Gall, had very small brains, of about 1,100 grams" and that certain "equally gifted persons had very large brains; thus Byron and Dr. Johnson had brains of about 2,000 grams." And we know that some very ordinary persons had equally large brains.[44] With reference to racial groups the picture is similar. Australoids and Negroids have an average brain weight lower than that of Mongoloids and Caucasoids. But the groups with smaller average brain weight cannot be considered inferior mentally, for "on the basis of such reasoning we should have to acknowledge the larger-brained Eskimos as our intellectual superiors and include the Negro Zulie and AmaXhosa along with them. The extinct and primitive Neandertal would also rate as our equal if not our superior."[45]

We know that within every racial, tribal, or other human group that one could name the individual members differ widely in every mental trait that can be measured. And we know that there is much overlapping among groups, even when the average ability of one group appears superior to that of another. We know, also, that differences in test performance which often exist between various racial and national groups reflect the shaping influence of their respective cultures rather than differences in their genes. Motivation is important in mental achievement and also in test

[44] Gerhardt von Bonin, *The Evolution of the Human Brain*, The University of Chicago Press, 1963, pp. 76–77.

[45] E. Adamson Hoebel, *Man in the Primitive World*, McGraw-Hill, 1958, p. 141.

performance. The white American, on whom most of the tests are standardized and whose average performance is taken as a gauge, belongs to an "achieving society" in which the cultural emphasis is upon doing things as quickly and efficiently as possible. The Indian, who has been shaped differently in this respect, takes his time and has no great urge to do things in the most efficient way. In his view, "The white man has the restless sea within his bosom," while the Indian "dreams with the stars and looks on."[46] American Negroes have been subjected to the white man's culture, but usually as inferiors who not infrequently have felt that they cannot get very far regardless of how much they try. The parents are led to feel this way and pass it on to their children. All too often this attitude of inferiority has been maintained by substandard educational and vocational opportunities.[47] Difficulties like these underlie all efforts to assess the mental capacities of peoples other than the one on whom the tests have been standardized. There is actually no such thing as a "culture-free" test which would be equally valid for all peoples.

There is no doubt a lot of hidden talent in the world, in both nonliterate and civilized societies, and all that would be needed to make it manifest is motivation and opportunity. We see this every day in our own society, where members of underprivileged classes, through some fortuitous circumstances, break the shackles of the past and become leaders in various fields, such as the professions, the arts, and politics. The same thing is happening among hitherto "savage" peoples.

Margaret Mead tells of the transformation undergone by the Manus peoples of the Admiralty Islands through cultural contacts and the leadership of a native named Paliau (p. 257),

[46] Quoted from H. W. Hepner, *Psychology Applied to Life and Work,* Prentice-Hall, 1941, p. 394.

[47] A more detailed discussion of these issues, as they involve mental testing, will be found in Norman L. Munn, L. Dodge Fernald, Jr., and Peter S. Fernald, *Introduction to Psychology* (2nd ed.), Houghton Mifflin, 1969, pp. 444–450.

Kapeli   Pomat   Yesa   Kilipak   Loponiu
(Yesa has moved away.)

From savage boyhood to modern maturity.

Stefan Posanget Petrus Pomat   John Kilipak   Johanis Lokus
(Kapeli)   (Loponiu)

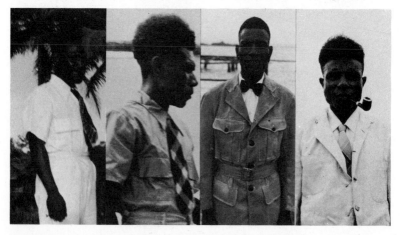

Paliau (right) and a transformed elder in 1953.

who had been initiated into civilized ways. The change occurred between the time of her first visit in 1928 and her return 25 years later. These people had gone from savagery to civilization in this period—Sir Ghost, the spirit of the dead, no longer held sway, the Christian calendar had been adopted, there was formal education, and so on.[48] The details of this transformation need not concern us, for the only point to be made is that nonliterate people *do* have the capacity to be something different, especially when cultural contacts are possible and they have effective leadership. In such instances, they advance culturally, without any change at all in the nature of their genes, that is to say, in their inborn endowment. As Professor C. H. Waddington says:

Human populations have changed ... in periods of time which seem much too short to allow of noteworthy alterations in their

[48] Margaret Mead, *New Lives for Old*, Morrow, 1956. For a report on the former Manus society, see *Growing Up in New Guinea*, Morrow, 1930.

genetic endowment. Such a change is in fact probably proceeding in China at this moment. The change in West and East Africa, from the conditions described a century ago to the present situation of highly sophisticated and technologically competent modern societies, can only have been accomplished by exceedingly small, if any, changes in the general gene pool.[49]

Today there is a closer contact between peoples than ever before and a rapidly increasing exchange of information on every subject of human concern. The effect of this will be to change the lives of individuals and groups immeasurably more than in the past—whether for better or worse remains to be seen.

[49] C. H. Waddington, *The Ethical Animal*, University of Chicago Press, 1967, p. 109.

CHAPTER EIGHT

WHAT OF
THE FUTURE?

There is no more fitting conclusion to a discussion of mental evolution and the shaping of modern minds than some consideration of the future of mankind. But what man is coming to cannot be predicted, for there are many incalculables. Nevertheless, this has not prevented thinkers in various related fields from speculating about his future.

Looking back over the last two million years we see that prehuman and human types underwent profound changes in anatomical structure, culminating in the large-brained *Homo sapiens sapiens*. During the last 30,000 years or more the various races now living were evolved. But will man undergo further biological evolution? We know that if natural selection were to continue as in the past, the answer would be "Yes." But man has evolved a cultural heritage which provides some shelter from the elements involved in natural selection. If this does not prevent his further biological evolution, it must certainly influence the process, either by slowing it or by diverting it from what might be considered its "natural" channels. Through the application of knowledge acquired during his cultural evolution, man has interfered, more or less directly, with biological evolution as it concerns himself. He has done this by curing the sick and protecting the lame and the weak. Now he speaks of directing his evolution by altering the genetic structure, by using artificial insemination, and by rearing test-tube babies. So it is impossible to predict what the future may hold for man as a zoological specimen.

What the future holds for man as a culture-accumulating and culturally molded being is also far from clear. In his remote past he became a thinker. He not only existed, but he knew that he existed. He knew more and more about his world; what is more important, he knew that he knew. But there has always been much that man did not and could not know. He of all animals knew that he, as an individual, would eventually die. But there was much in the future that this forward-looking animal could not predict. In some respects he came to conceive of himself as master of all he surveyed. But there were forces over which he had no control. Perhaps because of his helplessness as a child, his dependence on others who could serve his needs, some of the more thoughtful of his kind conceived of forces, and beings, superior to man who could by various means be induced to help him in his struggles. Different peoples in various places throughout the earth developed concepts of the supernatural which were peculiar to themselves. Western man had *the* God, who created him and *his* world, and who took care of him so long as he behaved. But new information of shattering significance was to become part of the cultural heritage. And with it, man could no longer enjoy

the certitude that he stands at the center of a universe created especially for his sake or the twin certitude that this universe is presided over by a Power which can be implored or propitiated and which cares for man, individually and collectively. Copernicus and Galileo suddenly broke the news that the world does not revolve around man but man, instead, revolves around the world.

And in this world, vast and merciless instead of smug and familiar, man is incidental and almost superfluous.[1]

The concept of evolution was a further shock, because it placed man in the animal kingdom rather than above it and gave him an affinity to the apes which he did not appreciate. This, also, was difficult to reconcile with the belief that God had created man in his own image and was preoccupied with human welfare.

The impact of scientific findings, the concept of evolution, various trends in philosophic thought, and perhaps also the perverseness of human beings in exploiting and killing each other have gradually so undermined the belief in God that some influential members of the clergy are proclaiming that "God is dead," that the future rests with man alone, unaided by supernatural powers. Almost everybody in touch with current events has come to feel that modern man is beset with serious social problems and that mankind's future depends upon his ability to solve them.

Some of these problems require solution if for no other reason than that failure to solve them might be suicidal. It is a case of man's cultural evolution having reached the stage where, for the first time, he has the means of destroying the human race. There have always been prophets of doom. Freud was one. In his *Civilization and Its Discontents* and other writings, he posited the existence in man of a self-destructive urge, or a "death instinct." The final aim of this "is to reduce living things to an inorganic state." Since "living things appeared later than inanimate ones and arose out of them," Freud said, the destructive urge tends toward "a return to an earlier state."[2] Freud's concept of a human self-destructive urge has not been widely accepted by psychologists and psychiatrists. Nevertheless, whether because of his bio-

[1] Theodosius Dobzhansky, *Mankind Evolving,* Yale University Press, 1962, pp. 345–346.

[2] Sigmund Freud, *An Outline of Psychoanalysis,* W. W. Norton, 1949, pp. 20–21; *Civilizations and Its Discontents,* London: Hogarth Press, 1930.

logical nature or his cultural shaping, man does indeed appear to be hell-bent on his own destruction.

As Professor Ernst Mayr says in *Animal Species and Evolution*, "Innumerable administrative rules and laws of the government discriminate inadvertently against the most gifted members of the community."[3] He has reference to excessive taxation of the most gifted; educational opportunities based on ability to pay, rather than on ability and performance; and other features of society which tend to reduce the size of families among the gifted and thus reduce their contribution to the human gene pool. But, he continues, the

progressive loss of valuable genes is not the only danger facing the human species. Indeed, overpopulation is a far more serious problem in the immediate future. I am not speaking of the material aspects such as the exhaustion of mineral and soil resources and the increasing difficulty of food supply for 6, 8, or 10 billion people. Human technology may find answers to all of these difficulties. Yet I cannot see how all the best things in man can prosper—his spiritual life, his enjoyment of the beauty of nature, and whatever else distinguishes him from the animals—if there is "standing" room only, as one writer on the subject has put it. It seems to me that long before that point has been reached man's struggle and preoccupation with social, economic, and engineering problems would become so great, and the undesirable by-products of crowded cities so deleterious, that little opportunity would be left for the cultivation of man's highest and most specifically human attributes. Nor do I see where natural selection could enter the picture to halt this trend. Man may continue to prosper physically under these circumstances, but will he still be anywhere near the ideal man? Let us hope that the biological aspects of man's evolution are duly taken into consideration by those entrusted with the task of planning for the future of mankind.[4]

Loss of valuable genes, the plundering of natural resources, and the threat of overpopulation are not the only dangers

[3] Ernst Mayr, *Animal Species and Evolution*, Harvard University Press, 1966, p. 662.

[4] Ernst Mayr, *Animal Species and Evolution*, p. 662.

to the future of mankind. To these can be added the increasing pollution of air and water, on which something is apparently about to be done.

The "pill" may alleviate the population explosion, but it has its own peculiar dangers. There is the possibility of deleterious side effects from its prolonged use, a possibility not yet fully explored. Apart from this, there is the danger that its more widespread use by the more intelligent than by others would deprive the gene pool of valuable hereditary components—the danger already cited by Professor Mayr as coming from government follies. And we cannot completely overlook another danger—that injudicious use of the pill or other contraceptives on a worldwide scale and resulting birth control might, in the long run, lead to extinction of the human race.

Another threat of vital significance for mankind's future is the existence of atomic weapons. In the cartoon reproduced on p. 264 "homo sap" is pictured as sailing between a modern Scylla and Charybdis, the pill and the bomb. Like the mariner of mythology, he might well overcome the dangers of one, only to be wrecked by the other.

Man's ability to solve his social problems has lagged far behind his technological advance. Some of these problems have always existed, some are products of civilized life. But they have become so grave that the future of mankind may depend upon their solution. Among these are: millions starving in a world of plenty, great wealth beside abject poverty, racial intolerance, and international strife. There is a crying need for social justice. And, as John R. Platt says:

If we survive at all . . . it can only be by working out a new attitude of tolerance and mutual support for each other, between colored and white, between rich and poor, between advanced nations and retarded ones. The unemployed, the underprivileged, the underdeveloped, all the groups neglected or exploited by our present arrangements or condemned to exclusion from our prosperity by the accident of parentage or place of birth, form a seedbed for spokesmen and would-be dictators whose juntas may take over nuclear administration in the name of correcting these wrongs.

Scylla and Charybdis

Our failure to eradicate these evils depresses the standard of living and shortens the probable "half-life" of everyone. We are now realizing this, in Congress as well as in the councils of the world. What is fortunate for us today is that our new understanding of the educational and developmental basis of prosperity has made it possible and profitable to cure these evils just at the instant when our new weapons technology has made it absolutely necessary to do so. . . . The world has now become too dangerous for anything less than Utopia.[5]

Another danger that we all face is the conflict of ideologies represented by the so-called "democratic" and "totalitarian" regimes. The opposing forces are so well equipped with missiles and other atomic weapons that any attempt to resolve the conflict in an all-out war would lead to the extermination of total populations and possibly of all mankind.

[5] John R. Platt, *The Step to Man*, Wiley, 1966, pp. 199–200.

Peaceful co-existence seems to be the only reasonable alternative, and Professor C. H. Waddington speaks for many when he says that one must

welcome in the name of biological wisdom the dawning—if it does dawn—of a period of "co-existence" between the two major cultural forces of the world today, those deriving from what we may loosely call Capitalism on the one side, and Communism on the other. Both these systems are rapidly evolving, as all human affairs must do, and it would be quite inappropriate here to attempt to describe either of them as they stand at present. But any impartial consideration of them must surely suggest that both contain much of value and also much which is to be deplored. The complete obliteration of either would gravely impoverish what one might call the "Idea Pool" of the human species: the store of socially transmittable variations which are available as the raw material for future evolution.[6]

The hope can still be held, despite the failure of the League of Nations and the impotence of the United Nations today, that some peace-keeping structure, guided by international law and supported by an international police force derived from all nations, will evolve in time. Dr. John R. Platt discusses several of the problems involved in developing what he calls a "self-stabilizing" social structure in a disarmed world—a "system of stabilizing feedbacks" or "checks and balances" such as the Federalists conceived. He points out that:

The thirteen independent American states in the 1780's faced a situation curiously parallel to that in the world today. They had just emerged a few years earlier from an exhausting war against a common enemy and they were turning to problems of internal development, but they were divided and confused. They had tried to set up a confederation or union to deal with their common interests, but it had been plagued, as the United Nations is now, by an inability to persuade or coerce the individual states into general

[6] C. H. Waddington, *The Ethical Animal,* University of Chicago Press, 1967, p. 210.

adoption of any of its measures, or into contributing their assessed shares of revenue for paying its debts or the wages of its soldiers.

He regards the calling of a Constitutional Convention under these circumstances "an instructive precedent," and he applauds the "engineering design" which, in the American Constitution that resulted, provides what "may be our greatest text on how social feedback design can be used to achieve social stabilization and effective government, without dictatorship and without limiting the freedom of individuals and groups to differ and to oppose each other and the government and to produce continual changes in the system." And,

Certain characteristics of these early American designers—their insistence on the value of analysis, their beliefs that men could plan rationally a new social design that would really work, their hard-headed realism and avoidance of mere "paper prohibitions," their insistence on mechanisms which were shown to be adequate for dealing with various kinds of stress, but which were nevertheless minimum mechanisms—may be just the characteristics we need in thinking about new design.

After discussing some of the shortcomings of the present world set-up, Dr. Platt says, "When men need to build new buildings, they call in architects. Calling together a conference of architects who can design a better, safer, structure for the world is now our only hope and our most urgent need if we are to survive even another decade without probable catastrophe."[7] But do the nations of the world want a planned international organization, and if and when they do, where are the architects to be found? And if they are found, and an international organization is designed, with however many self-stabilizing feedbacks, will the major powers sufficiently subordinate their own self-interests to make it work? Perhaps when there is clearly no alternative but human extinction, they will.

[7] Platt, *The Step to Man*, pp. 108–109, 131.

In these days of social and intellectual turmoil and fore-bodings about the future or possible extinction of mankind, it is refreshing, if not reassuring, to consider the future as envisioned by Pierre Teilhard de Chardin, a biologist, pale-ontologist, Jesuit father, and prodigious creative thinker whose works are being published posthumously because publication during his lifetime was not permitted by his superiors in the Church. In the *Future of Man,* he speaks of mankind as still possessing a reserve upon which to draw for the future. "We have only to think," he says, "of the immensity of the forces, ideas and human beings that have still to be born or discovered or applied or synthesized. . . . 'Energetically' as well as biologically the human group is still young, still fresh. If we are to judge by what history teaches us about other living groups, it still has, organically speaking, some millions of years in which to live and de-velop."[8] He continues, "Our modern world was created in less than 10,000 years, and in the past 200 years it has changed more than in all the preceding millenia. Have we ever thought of what our planet would be like, psychologically, in a million years' time?"

In the book already quoted, and in his *The Phenomenon of Man,* Teilhard de Chardin[9] sees the future of man as an evolving psychosocial condition, with closer communication and cooperation between all men guided by what he calls the *noosphere,* the sphere of mind or of thought, a "thinking envelope of the earth." The hereditary mechanism of the *noosphere* is "the heredity of example and education"; its cerebral apparatus, its brain, is the "apparatus of social thought." Teilhard de Chardin says:

Between the human brain, with its milliards [billions] of inter-connected nerve-cells, and the apparatus of social thought, with its hundreds of millions of individuals thinking collectively, there is

[8] Pierre Teilhard de Chardin, *The Future of Man,* London: Collins, 1965, p. 71.

[9] Pierre Teilhard de Chardin, *The Phenomenon of Man,* London: Collins, 1955.

an evident kinship which biologists of the stature of Julian Huxley have not hesitated to examine and expand on critical lines. On the one hand we have a single brain, formed of nervous nuclei, and on the other a Brain of brains. It is true that between these two organic complexes a major difference exists. Whereas in the case of the individual brain thought emerges from a system of non-thinking nervous fibers, in the case of the collective brain each separate unit is in itself an autonomous centre of reflection.

With respect to the structure and functioning of this "cerebroid organ of the Noosphere" reference is made to machines:

Thanks to the machine, man has contrived both severally and collectively to prevent the best of himself from being absorbed in purely physiological and functional uses, as has happened to other animals. But in addition to its protective role, how can we fail to see the machine as playing a constructive role in the creation of a truly collective consciousness? It is not merely a matter of the machine which liberates, relieving both individual and collective thought of the trammels which hinder its progress, but also of the machine which creates, helping to assemble, and to concentrate in the form of an ever more deeply penetrating organism, all the reflective elements upon earth.

I am thinking, of course, in the first place of the extraordinary network of radio and television communications which, perhaps anticipating the direct intercommunication of brains through the mysterious power of telepathy, already links us in a sort of "etherised" universal consciousness.

But I am also thinking of the insidious growth of those astonishing electronic computers which, pulsating with signals at the rate of hundreds of thousands a second, not only relieve our brains of tedious and exhausting work but, because they enhance the essential (and too little noted) factor of "speed of thought," are paving the way for a revolution in the sphere of research.[10]

According to Teilhard de Chardin, man's social evolution, in spite of modern problems, is leading inexorably toward peace—"all appearances to the contrary Mankind is not only

[10] Teilhard de Chardin, *The Future of Man*, pp. 166–167.

capable of living in peace but by its very structure *cannot fail eventually to achieve peace.*"[11]

The "Teilhardian synthesis," as Professor Dobzhansky calls it, goes far beyond existing scientific conceptions of the future of man. To him it is a system of metaphysics and a prophecy. He appreciates its "intellectual grandeur" and the theme that "man is not to be a passive witness but a participant in evolution."[12] It is quite clear, of course, that man *has* begun to control his own evolution, and that he could even contrive his own extinction. Much of this has become more evident recently than it was when Teilhard de Chardin was formulating his views.

Several religiously oriented research scientists have treated Teilhard de Chardin's views with little sympathy. In a recent conference on science and religion they referred to "this new gospel" as "pure speculation," "a kind of pantheism," "a humanistic religion without revelation," and "an opiate presented in the name of Science." This "gospel" has been "embraced by so many," because "the world has become so afraid of the atomic bomb that in desperation it grasps eagerly" at the promise "that after all there is an optimistic end for all of us. . . .[13]

Whatever value they may have as metaphysics, prophecy, or a gospel, Teilhard de Chardin's views exhibit the time- and space-piercing features of conceptual thought when it is functioning at its highest level. And what men believe, whether fact or fancy, has a tremendous impact on their lives and perhaps the future of the race.

Early man took the world pretty much as he found it. His conceptual ability led him to the invention of tools and weapons, with resulting control over some of the exigencies of his world. But this was not enough. He went on to change his mode of life from that of a wanderer to that of a cultiva-

[11] Teilhard de Chardin, *The Future of Man*, pp. 151–152.

[12] Theodosius Dobzhansky, *The Biology of Ultimate Concern*, New American Library, 1967, p. 137.

[13] Malcolm Jeeves, *The Scientific Enterprise and Christian Faith*. London: Tyndale Press, 1969, pp. 110, 112–113.

tor of plants and animals. This led, in time, to community living, to cities, to civilizations, to science and specialized technologies. Increasingly, through all their cultural evolutions, human beings have changed their world and themselves.

Man-made change is now exceedingly rapid, and nobody can get a clear picture of what the future may hold. But it is of inestimable significance that we are capable of anticipating dangers and planning improvements in the human condition. And there is no doubt that our conceptions relating to these things will have a tremendous impact. They will remake man's world and himself for good or ill.

ART CREDITS

Page 14, N. L. Munn, L. D. Fernald, Jr., and P. S. Fernald, *Introduction to Psychology* (2nd ed.), Houghton Mifflin Company, 1969, Fig. 5.3. **p. 15** (top) After Herrick. (bottom) After Ranson and Clark. **p. 16** (top) After Zanchetti; in Quarton et al. (Eds.), *The Neurosciences*, Rockefeller University Press, 1967, p. 613. (bottom) After MacLean, in chapter by R. B. Livingston, in *The Neurosciences*, Rockefeller University Press, 1967, p. 506. Original drawing appeared in a paper by Dr. MacLean, "Contrasting functions of limbic and neocortical systems of the brain and their relevance to psychophysiological aspects of medicine," *American Journal of Medicine*, 1958, Vol. 25, p. 615. **p. 17,** From *Biology* (3rd ed.), by Willis H. Johnson, Richard A. Laubengayer, Louis E. Delaney, and Thomas A. Cole. Copyright © 1956, 1961, 1966 by Holt, Rinehart and Winston, Inc. Adapted and reprinted by permission of Holt, Rinehart and Winston, Inc. **p. 18** (top and middle) N. L. Munn, *Psychology* (5th ed.), Houghton Mifflin Company, 1966, Fig. 2.16. (bottom) Munn *Psychology* (4th ed.), 1961, Fig. 3.23. **p. 19** (top) S. H. Bartley, *Vision: A Study of its Basis*, Van Nostrand Reinhold Company, 1941, Chapter IV. (bottom) Munn, *Psychology* (4th ed.), Fig. 20.5 **p. 45** (top) N. L. Munn, *The Evolution and Growth of Human Behavior* (2nd ed.), Houghton Mifflin Company, 1965, Fig. 4. (middle) After Tjio. (bottom) D. C. Pease and R. F. Baker, "T-Preliminary Innesticatrons of Chromosomes and Genes with Electron Microscope," *Science*, 1949, Vol. 109, pp. 8–10, and 22. **p. 48,** Adapted from C. C. Dunn, *Heredity and Variation*, Midland Park, N. J., The University Society, 1932, p. 33. **p. 51,** J. D. Watson, *The Double Helix*, Atheneum, 1969, p. 202. Reprinted by permission of Atheneum, and Weidenfeld and Nicolson Limited. **p. 52,** J. D. Watson, *The Molecular Biology of the Gene*, W. A. Benjamin, Inc., 1965. **p. 59,** Photo, courtesy of C. Nash Herndon. **p. 61,** H. B. D. Kettlewell, "Insect Survival and Selection for Pattern," *Science*, Vol. 148, pp. 1290–1296, 4 June 1965. Copyright 1965 by the American Association for the Advancement of Science. **p. 67,** *American Heritage Dictionary*, Houghton Mifflin Company, 1969, p. 551. **p. 71,** From "Tools and Human Evolution," Sherman L. Washburn. Copyright © 1960 by Scientific American, Inc. All rights reserved. **p. 74,** From R. Buchsbaum, *Animals Without Backbones*, University of Chicago Press, 1948; photo by Ralph Buchsbaum. **p. 77,** C. B. Ferster and B. F. Skinner, *Schedules of Reinforcement*, Copyright, 1957, Appleton-Century-Crofts, Educational Division, Meredith Corporation. **p. 78,** From "The Evolution of Intelligence," M. E. Bitterman. Copyright © 1965 by Scientific American, Inc. All rights reserved. **p. 80,** N. L. Munn, "Discrimination-Reversal Learning in Kangaroos," *Australian Journal of Psychology*, 1964, Vol. 16, pp. 1–8. **p. 81,** After Harlow. Courtesy of Wisconsin Regional Primate Research Center. **p. 83** (top) W. F. Pauli, *The World of Life*, Houghton Mifflin Company, 1949, Fig. 249. (upper middle) After Conn. (lower middle) Pauli, Fig. 290. (bottom) Munn, *Psychology* (4th ed.), Fig. 3.3. **p. 87,** After F. W. Jones and S. D. Porteus. **p. 91** (top) After Romer. (bottom) Munn, *Psychology* (4th ed.), Fig. 21.8. **p. 102,** Reprinted with permission of The Macmillan Company from *Evolution Emerging*, by

INDEX